The Ecology of Spirituality

The Ecology of Spirituality

Meanings, Virtues, and Practices
in a Post-Religious Age

Lucy Bregman

BAYLOR UNIVERSITY PRESS

Cover Design by Rebecca Lown
Cover Image: The seal of the wine merchants of Bruges, available in Inventaire des sceaux de la Flandre, recueillis dans les dépôts d'archives, musées et collections particulières du Département du Nord, ouvrage accompagné de trente planches photoglyptiques by Germain Demay (Paris, Imprimerie nationale, 1873).

Library of Congress Cataloging-in-Publication Data

Bregman, Lucy.
  The ecology of spirituality : meanings, virtues, and practices in a post-religious age / Lucy Bregman.
  198 pages cm
  Includes bibliographical references and index.
  ISBN 978-1-60258-967-4 (pbk. : alk. paper)
  1. Spirituality. I. Title.
  BL624.B6358 2014
  204—dc23
                              2013016353

Printed in the United States of America on acid-free paper with a minimum of 30% post-consumer waste recycled content.

Contents

Acknowledgments

My thanks to the following organizations and individuals who contributed to the development of this project. They would not all agree with all the ideas in the book, but they helped and encouraged me in my thinking about the subject. Person, Culture and Religion Group (now Psychology, Culture and Religion Group) of the American Academy of Religion, particularly Kelly Bulkeley. *The Journal of Pastoral Care and Counseling*, in which an early version of some of the material appeared as a guest editorial. Interdisciplinary.net, which organized a conference on "Spirituality in the 21st Century" at which I presented some of the material in chapter 1 in 2011. Temple University, which awarded me a study leave in spring 2011 so I could do the reading and research, especially for chapters 7, 8, and 9. Dennis Klass, who read and carefully commented on an early version of the manuscript. Herman Westerink, whose own interest in the topic has encouraged mine. Carey Newman of Baylor University Press for his editorial guidance. And finally, thanks to those who supported me in nonacademic ways: my loyal sister Emily Rizzo and the Wednesday night prayer group of St. Stephen's Church.

Lucy Bregman

The Making of Contemporary Spirituality

Spirituality: a marvelous word, ubiquitous today and bursting with possibilities. We are disillusioned with both science and religion, with politics and business, and, in a deep way, with who we have become. Spirituality is what our world—and we ourselves—seem to lack. Spirituality is the depth and truth and all-inclusive wholeness of life, our lost and lamented connection to the universe.

But what is spirituality? This is a study of the concept, of what it now means and how it is now used. We look at its origins and what it has displaced in order to occupy the prominent niche it now does in our minds, hearts, and imaginations. As it is used today, however, the word is almost completely disconnected from its historical meanings. This transformation has come very quickly. I can vividly remember how, early in my teaching career, a curriculum committee of the religious studies department reviewed a proposal for a course on Jewish spirituality. The course would use the traditional Jewish prayer book as its primary text and show how this had shaped Jewish practice, beliefs, and worldviews over the centuries. We on the committee loved this class, except for one detail: "You must find a new title," a colleague said. "No student will want to take a course with such a hopelessly pious word as *spirituality* in it!" To all of us at the time, spirituality conjured up elderly aunts singing hymns or perhaps nuns in a convent. Spirituality then signified the practice of the most stodgy and old-fashioned type of devotion. This older meaning is now gone, and today students would be drawn to a course that had *spirituality* in its title.

The word *spirituality* now has many definitions, an overwhelming number, in fact, all of which express that sense of yearning for wholeness that lies within so many of us. For samples, here are three definitions, cited with approval by other writers than those who first proposed them:

> [Spirituality] is simply our basic life orientation and the patterned ways in which we express them. It is the patterning of our thinking, feeling, experiencing and nurturing of whatever we take to be fundamentally important.[1]

> The manner in which humans transcend themselves and reach out to the ultimate possibilities of their existence. As such spirituality entails both an understanding of the deepest meaning of human existence and a commitment to realizing the same.[2]

> The aspect of humanity that refers to the way individuals seek and express meaning and purpose, and the way they experience their connection to the moment, the self, to others, to nature and the significant or sacred.[3]

The third definition is from 2009, while the first is from around 1989—but there is no progression from obscurity into clarity, and indeed the third was offered with an apology that it was "definition by committee" and therefore lacked internal coherence.

Note how all of these omit or avoid some of the common older implications of *spiritual* and *spirit*. No elderly aunts or nuns here. First, there is no reference in any to the third person of the Christian Trinity, the Holy Spirit. Such a specific theological reference would be inimical to the universal scope of all of these definitions. Nor, second, is there any mention of "spirits" in the sense of "spirits of the dead." Spiritualism, a nineteenth-century movement centered on contact with these beings, is entirely separate from today's spirituality. Only because she was completely unfamiliar with the current discussion, could my atheist sister deny that she and her husband could be considered "spiritual" because "We don't believe in spirits." Third, all of the above definitions avoid the traditional opposition between spiritual and material/physical. Today's spirituality helps connect people to the world of nature not to rise above it into a Platonic realm of pure Forms or Ideas. Spirituality is committed to a holistic vision, not a dualism between spirit and matter. Even those much closer to the traditional usages of *spirituality* than the authors of the three definitions above want to avoid the dualist message carried by the history of the term.

But while all three of these connotations and associations are absent, what is present today are the hopes and aura and glow surrounding the term *spirituality*, which is our focus. We note the excitement and enthusiasm packed into current discussions of spirituality in a remarkable number of contexts. Indeed, the term glows so strongly that it is hard to say anything really *bad* about spirituality, which ought to make more of us wonder. Maybe a term with so many definitions is, in the words of one of its advocates, "amorphous," an "umbrella" for a range of disparate elements.

> The persistent interest in the phenomenon of spirituality is all the more remarkable given the fact that there is no clear, unequivocal definition of the concept. . . . In fact, in many circles there is widespread confusion regarding the very meaning of spirituality and its use has become "fluid." It is an umbrella term which covers a myriad of activities ranging from the deeply creative to the distinctly bizarre. . . . The amorphous nature of the term thus contributes to the fact that it is resistant to precise definition.[4]

This is written by someone absolutely convinced that the turn to spirituality is the wave of the future and therefore it really does not matter whether we are uncertain what we are speaking about. Perhaps it is like pornography: we cannot define it, but we know it when we see it. Or so some believe.

As we can learn from this, what we cannot do is offer once and for all a clear, comprehensive, and authoritative definition of spirituality that will be relevant today. It is part of our argument that no such precise entity as spirituality really exists in the same way that, say, seedless watermelons now exist but did not when I was a child. The quest for such a once-and-for-all accurate and unambiguous meaning for spirituality is at one level a fool's errand. The term is deeply and irrevocably ambiguous, and the construction of definitions, and of the whole concept, is a study in how multiple meanings, agendas, and issues are gathered together into one word made to do duty for a whole aggregate of hopes and yearnings. To disentangle these, to see where the definitions come from, to map the intellectual ecology of contemporary spirituality, is our first goal. The second stage of our analysis is to look at how spirituality is introduced into health care, business, and recreation to solve problems endemic to each context.

The importance of doing this unglowing analysis is that we need to know what is at stake in resting so many hopes on a concept so murky and impossible to define. We here means those of us who use the term, whose eyes light up when we hear it or read about it, who are normally very willing to leave things at the "I'll know it when I see it" stage. We may not mean the whole world, but a good proportion of North

Americans now feel comfortable with this blend of hopefulness and confusion. Consequently, a huge amount of effort and energy and professional activity has already been put into spirituality by persons largely clueless about its intellectual antecedents or implications.

For example, early in the previous decade the Canadian Association of Occupational Therapists (CAOT) issued an official statement that claimed "spirituality" lay at the core of their profession, so that it was therefore vitally important to integrate spirituality into the daily work of O.T. But there was also a widespread admission that most practitioners were "confused" about what spirituality was, let alone how to apply it.[5] The definition generated by the CAOT was intended to be helpful but turned out to be just as amorphous, just as much an umbrella term, as all the previous definitions. And one irate practitioner protested at how spirituality seemed to have displaced occupation as the core concept of their profession! In a nutshell, unrestrained enthusiasm for spirituality led to more confusion than illumination and wasted a lot of time.

Given the enormous fascination with spirituality and the heady glow that surrounds the term, we need to know what is going on before more time is swallowed up in generating definitions. We should not put more effort into spirituality and health—or spirituality and anything—when we still are not sure what we are talking about. It is hard to say anything bad about spirituality, but that does not make it worthy of the enormous attention it has recently received. Especially since the assumption that a single *it* exists, long neglected but now attended to, is one of the dubious but plausible-sounding claims of the discussions. We will have to look hard at what gets pushed under the umbrella of spirituality, and why some phenomena get excluded.

Yet we are not telling readers that spirituality is simply an intellectual Ponzi scheme, a fad or a fake. We do not find nothing at the bottom of all the interest in the concept, and we do not see a conspiracy or an "emperor's new clothes" hype ripe for exposé. When twice as many persons as anticipated wished to participate in a conference on Spirituality in the Twenty-first Century, they all must have expected something coherent and worthwhile. There is indeed something positive, something worth discovering, behind all the usages of spirituality today. It is just not the story most of the writings about it tell, it is not even the story I thought I would find when I began this project. It is much more complex and nuanced, a construction project in the making, and a tale of the renegotiation of some important cultural stances regarding religion, science, and society. It is important to get this story told and get it right, so that we become aware of these concerns and aware about ourselves. We are, as we have always been, beings who want to make claims about what is ultimate and meaningful, but we can no longer automatically use older languages to anchor such claims. Religious language has faded, and some of its substitutes, particularly the language of psychology, have lost a lot of their allure and prestige. Spirituality as a concept carries with it stories of disillusion, as well as hope. If we fail to understand these ambivalences, we will not only waste our own time, but we will bequeath to the next generations a legacy of mush and confusion, an unhelpful dead-end approach to solving long-standing problems they too will face.

To make this case, let us tell the most popular, conventional story of spirituality, the one voiced by its advocates. It begins with the idea that spirituality as an essential universal ingredient of our humanity has always been a deep element of our inner nature, just as all three of our initial definitions postulate. We will see this theme embedded in many more of the contemporary definitions that we will examine in the next chapter. But, according to most versions of this story, spirituality has been confused with religion for most of history, while our Western scientific rationalism has ignored and repressed spirituality. Now, at last, spirituality is visible, recoverable, and will return us to our indigenous wholeness and freedom. Now it is a category in and of itself, so that "if William James were writing today, he'd call his book *The Varieties of Spiritual Experiences* and leave out religion altogether." And, to match this, "if Kübler-Ross were working with dying patients today, she'd be doing spirituality, not psychology." Casual remarks such as this provide clues for how pervasive "spirituality" now is. We will examine both of these revealing real-life statements in detail later on, but the idea is that now spirituality can cover the work of these two important thinkers, because it is what they were really getting at when they wrote (in 1902 and 1968, respectively). Now that spirituality stands within a niche of its own, the argument goes on, we can see how it will promote certain key values and virtues very separate from those associated with most religions. It can invigorate and inspire the practice of many professions, just as in the CAOT example, and the entire atmosphere of hospitals and business workplaces will be changed. It can restore "soul" where soullessness and dehumanization reign. Spirituality can also deepen our experiences of recreation, so that as we play or experience the natural world we can open ourselves to connections to whatever is really ultimate and valuable. Spirituality will do this and provide a grounding for world renewal in a postmodern age, when both science and religion badly need replacing by something that will transcend both. We cannot continue doing things as before; we need a new paradigm. The rediscovery of spirituality will bring world peace and alleviate our planet's current ecological crisis. This story has a utopian aura to it, but even in its more moderate tellings it is a tale of liberation and hope.

In this story, religion is part of the "old" divisive and divided paradigm. Science accepted what was rationally demonstrable; religion was its polar opposite. Religion valued hierarchy, obedience, and rules held up with belief and faith in dogmas and institutions. Neither of these domains will remain unchanged; they are already being challenged. But what replaces them, spirituality, will contain what was really valuable in both religion and science. In this account, those persons who still cling to old-style religion are obsolete, for the 14 percent of the population who are "spiritual but not religious" is already the wave of the future. (Exact percentages vary, but when arguments take this form, a minority designated as "the wave of the future" carries disproportionate weight.) Meanwhile, the sign of this transition is that practices once entirely under the domain of religion, such as meditation and yoga and mystical contemplation, are now available apart from their religious origins. They can be better understood as "spiritual techniques" or as "wisdom technologies" that will enhance our spirituality without the cost of our freedom and individuality. To those who read the story of spirituality in this way, the whole drama is a recent development, within the time of the Baby Boomer generation (roughly the late 1960s). It is not a story about the German romantic movement or the mid-nineteenth-century transcendentalists or the struggle in the twentieth century against totalitarian politics. These will all play some role, however, in *our* version of spirituality's history and its emergence as a concept today. As we will show, the entire pattern of argument predates Baby Boomers by a long, long time.

The alternative conventional story of spirituality, one that will play a very small role here, is of a conspiracy of New Age gurus and other religious charlatans to undermine authentic Christian faith (or Judaism or Buddhism, etc.) in the name of narcissistic individualism run wild. Spirituality makes space for the "distinctly bizarre" because it is by its nature committed to an "anything goes" relativism that masquerades as tolerance. This spirituality conspiracy story sees real religion as threatened by a clearly identified alternative that offers an easy compromise with the world and consumer culture. We first find this plotline even before spirituality as a separate concept emerged, so that charges of "narcissism" and "self-worship" abounded in the 1980s. What counts as "authentic" rather than false religion here is not just or even primarily its organizational structure. It is its prophetic critique of contemporary life. Real religion values the common good, intergenerational bonds among persons and community. Real religion has ethical depth to it, while spirituality is "religion lite." Those who tell this story admit that lots of "real," that is, visible and traditional, religion today is also "lite," filled with shallow glitziness and complacency. But spirituality, according to this critique, is nothing but religion "sold out" into self-help, feel-good self-worship. This version of the story, we find, is not very interesting or illuminating. Perhaps the problem is that we have all heard it before. It can be expressed by Evangelical Christians or Marxists or Freudians, but the critique hardly differs.

Our approach tries to get past these two conventional stories, to find whatever it is that makes spirituality so appealing. We may not learn to love it, but at least we will learn to understand what the concept and those who work with it try to accomplish. It is not a story focused on human heroes and villains but on ideas and their interactions, adventures, and rivalries. Were the concept, our central protagonist, a human, he or she would be the flawed, vulnerable figure whose hope and energy is increasingly hampered by basic ignorance and lack of self-awareness. The one for whom things will never turn out right not because of evil intentions but because of inner screw-ups in a recalcitrant and equally unaware environment. In such a story, there is an ending where the protagonist looks back and realizes for the first time that he or she was doomed from the start, sometimes with bitterness and guilt. Or, in the trickster tales, the protagonist learns his limitations and, for the first time, how to laugh at himself and thereby teaches us to laugh too. Neither of the conventional stories for spirituality end this way, and perhaps it will be in our retelling that such endings as these will become the most plausible outcomes.

CHAPTER ONE

Definitions of Spirituality

Ninety-Two and Still Counting

Tracing the History

Spirituality today has become newsworthy and glamorous, and yet it remains confusing and mysterious. In our introduction, we focused on this and noted how the many definitions of this term go along with an overall sense that spirituality is resistant to clear definition. That has not stopped people from trying, however. So this chapter includes both a brief history and a survey of the available definitions, already in print, that came directly out of a professional organization's enthusiasm for the whole topic. What is remarkable is the discontinuity between past and present and the manner in which a concept once upon a time clearly and narrowly defined is now so open to any and all meanings originating from such a diverse assortment of people and professions. In tracing the history, it is impossible, therefore, to consider this a straightforward story of progress from less to more sophisticated or from more abstract to more operational definitions. Moreover, there are some key transitions in this history, from one context for use to many and from one style of definition to another. But it is hard to say that the acorn grew into an oak or that the original earlier meanings naturally birthed the more contemporary ones.

Here, to start, is a time line for shifts in definitions of spirituality over the last forty years.

Catholic	Principe (1983)	"Secular	Morgan (1993)	92 definitions
Religious	3 levels, two-poled	spiritualities"	one-poled	(2002) Versnel
Orders		Van Ness		Kerr, Unruh

This line traces the precontemporary definitions of spirituality on the left to the present on the right. It is not a line of progress or development because, in a real way, the stages toward the left are clearer and more directly useful, albeit for a smaller number of persons, than those toward the right. But, as in many construction projects, the more recent stages are more expansive, cover far more ground. Or, to use the image provided by Kourie in our introduction, the umbrella has stretched and become far more inviting and inclusive by the time we reach Anita Unruh, Joan Versnel, and Natasha Kerr.

Principe's Retrospect and Suggestions

Going back several decades, to an earlier phase of this story, we already find this stretching out of the word and an optimistic vision of its potentials. In 1983 Walter Principe wrote an erudite review of the history of the term *spirituality*, including its premodern, distinctively narrow, religious usage. Principe's essay was titled "Toward Defining Spirituality," which is ironic, given what we now know of how spirituality definitions have moved away from rather than toward clarity and unanimity. Principe was a professor in the Pontifical Institute of Medieval Studies at the University of Toronto, which would have been just about the only professional location from which anyone in 1983 could have studied or written about spirituality. Principe documented how rare this term as a substantive once was in both English and French writings. French is important not just because Principe wrote in Canada but because *spirituality* was a thoroughly Roman Catholic term, actually restricted to writings by and for members of religious orders. Recall that in the early 1970s, the term was "too pious" for undergraduates at a midwestern state university. Principe's citations are all hopelessly "pious." He mentions titles like Saudreau's 1916 *Manuel de spiritualité*. By 1932 there was a *Dictionnaire de spiritualité ascétique*, and in 1943 the Institut Catholique de Paris established a chair in Histoire de la Spiritualité.[1] What did these ultra-Catholic uses of the term signify? According to Principe, *spirituality* here referred to the systematic practice of the "spiritual life," explicitly separated from the "worldly life." Platonic dualism and a very traditional split between the religious and the laity were intrinsic to this setting and the writings it promoted.[2] Monks and nuns possessed a spiritual life and needed manuals for it; ordinary persons living in the world did not.

By the time Principe wrote, he and many others had traveled away from this beginning. The term already generated a certain amount of confusion, and so he proposed a three-level definition that would clarify both the substance of spirituality and the stance of those who practice or study it. First-level spirituality is "the real or existential level. This is the quality . . . of a person. It is the way some person understood and lived, within his or her historical context, a chosen religious ideal in sensitivity to the realm of the spirit or the transcendent."[3] This is the foundational level. The second level Principe describes is "the formulation of a teaching about the lived reality."[4] This is where training manuals and living teachers and guides are found, for example, the above-mentioned Saudreau or St. Teresa of Avila's classic *The Interior Castle*, written for her nuns as a guidebook. A third level is "the study by scholars of the first and especially of the second levels of spirituality. Here spirituality has become a discipline using the methods and resources of several other branches of knowledge."[5] This proposed three-tiered definition is an elegant example of a theory-based exposition, and it is well grounded in Principe's own theological anthropology and historical outlook.

Immediately after proposing this three-level definition, Principe raises the question of whether there is only one "Christian spirituality" or whether one may speak of "spiritualities" in the plural. And, by extension, other religious traditions have their own spiritualities as well, since they would include their own chosen religious ideals. Perhaps one could speak of "comparative spiritualities," both within and beyond Christianity. Principe does not seem to have a problem with this.[6] Even when the chosen religious ideal remains jointly Christian, it makes sense to speak of Benedictine spirituality in contrast to Franciscan spirituality, for the actual models of the religious ideal and the ways that it is expressed in history are different. For Benedictines, the balance of prayer, work, and study is intrinsic to the chosen ideal, while for Franciscans, poverty plays a major role in their living out of their Christian faith. What Principe emphasizes is that, in all cases, the full historical, cultural, social, and psychological context should be studied by those engaged in level three. Spirituality is part of tradition, of cultural history; it is shaped by theology and doctrine, but its study is not the same as the study of theology. In short, spirituality for Principe "points to those aspects of a person's living a faith or commitment that concern his or her striving to attain the highest ideal or goal. For a Christian this would mean his or her striving for an ever more intense union with the Father through Jesus Christ by living in the Spirit."[7]

Our exposition here reveals the full paradox of how a term so carefully defined for such narrow purposes in 1983 could have become the enormous umbrella-like category believed by many to be intrinsically resistant to definition. While he may have considered himself adventurous, retrospectively, Principe's definition appears stodgy and restrictive. Far from moving toward a definition, as Principe hoped, it appears most of us moved far away from one clearly located within the confines of academic study of religion. Once again, Principe's discussion took place among a relatively narrowly drawn circle. He never imagined much academic study of spirituality beyond the halls of the Pontifical Institute or other religiously sponsored institutions of higher learning. He certainly did not imagine that twenty years later occupational therapists would be weighing in with their own definition and judge it to be central to their own profession. Principe knew what those who study spirituality (those at level three of his model) ought to look for; he knew what they needed to learn in order to look intelligently. The materials of level-two spirituality, including the 1916 *Manual*, would be the subject matter. But level two points back to level one, which is individuals pursuing their highest religious ideal. Living a faith or a commitment requires long-term dedication over time, a set of beliefs about that commitment, and a community and tradition that supports individuals in their aims. All of this occurs in an historical setting that cannot be ignored or severed from the life of faith. An occupational therapist could certainly pursue spirituality by this definition—but by virtue of being a devout Christian not by virtue of being a professional occupational therapist.

Yet on one issue Principe's discussion opens the door to an expansion away from the audience and readership of the traditional writings on spirituality. Principe here is well aware of the dichotomy between religious and worldly lives and concerns, a view embedded in the older Catholic literature he surveyed. Today, he believes we know better: we know that this kind of dualism impedes the practice of committed faith and so of a true quest to attain "the highest goal or ideal." The dichotomy between the religious who possessed and exercised spirituality versus the laypeople stuck in the world who did not was repugnant to Principe. It is based on an erroneous view of transcendence, indebted more to Plato than to the Bible. The study of spirituality must not replicate such a dichotomy. It should take into account all the range of influencing factors and the disciplines that study them. Scholars should not turn up their noses at sociology or psychology, for instance, just because these disciplines are too "worldly" and insufficiently "spiritual." That would be a sign of the legacy of the church's unfortunate and mistaken dualism.

Principe assumed we knew better in 1983. The spiritual life—level one—is to be lived within an historical context, in the world of culture, language, and institutions. Principe was already in tune with the turn, in humanities study generally, to contextualize concepts and philosophies, to attend to their settings, and to be suspicious of all claims that treat ideas as timeless essences floating above social structures. He might have said he was also part of a rediscovery of the very incarnational dimension of the life of faith as actually lived out. Indeed, this theme shines through his presentation and his hope that, as we move toward defining spirituality, we will locate and ground it in the world of lived experience.

But, if we briefly return to the three definitions given in the introduction—using phrases such as *patterns of experiencing* and *meaning and purpose*—we see no explicit linkage to anything that locates an individual within time, space, and traditions. "Connectedness" to plants, animals, nature, people, and the sacred is a quality of spirituality, but it is not the same as the historical contexts Principe wants to include even at level one. Connectedness remains a sense of inner affinities to these as experienced by an individual. Although the intent of the definitions' authors is to be inclusive, the result is that the individual feeling "connected" to plants and nature and the sacred will not, *in his or her spirituality*, be immersed in history, culture, and institutions. And, as we will see, eventually the proliferation of contemporary definitions also avoids the kind of cultural and historical connectedness Principe valued. Indeed, the dualism between spiritual and worldly criticized by Principe back in 1983 appears curiously to have endured in many of the more supposedly secular of today's definitions. Ironically, Principe of the Pontifical Institute of Medieval Studies was more worldly and less dualistic in his definition than those at work in health care or business.

Spirituality Moves outside Religion

"Ah," one might say to this, "But Principe's definition is still explicitly, narrowly 'religious.' He cannot really imagine spirituality freed from a religious framework, and that is why we need to move spirituality toward something beyond this 1983 proposal. Newer definitions should be broader, less tied to theologies and doctrines. They will work for those who aren't conventionally religious." As one of the advocates for spirituality quoted in our introduction represents this popular point of view, spirituality concerns "ultimate values" "whether or not they are religious or non-religious."[8] Broader is clearly better, less restrictive, and more liberating. Principe might have accepted the course on Jewish spirituality as an example of level-three study about spirituality. He would have agreed that its proposed text, the Jewish prayer book, serves as a repository of level-two wisdom, training, and guidance for how to live as a Jewish person, just as *Manuel de spiritualité* served for monks. He might have been willing to accept borderline cases from well outside Western religions, especially from countries and traditions where religion itself was never a sharply differentiated category, as, for example, with "the spirituality of Japanese tea ceremony." Or his definition could be stretched into nontraditional expressions such as those studied by Leigh Schmidt and Courtney Bender and other historians of "Emersonian spirituality."[9] Viewed through a Principian lens, these constitute an alternative, relatively long-lasting, tradition in America, and there are level-one and level-two materials for those scholars who study it as part of the history of American religious pluralism. Transcendentalists were located historically and geographically in places such as Cambridge, Massachusetts. They taught and wrote for particular audiences. They became participants in a tradition as surely as did St. Teresa of Avila. Therefore, they are to be studied using the same tools and methods as any other figures within the domain of Principian spirituality. (This is exactly what Schmidt's book *Restless Souls* does.) This approach does not exclude the existential level, but it refuses to isolate it from all the rest. From Principe's standpoint, the study of a figure like Emerson does not move us "beyond religion"; it moves us into the history of religions in the plural and away from traditional dogmatic theology studies.

Move one step further from this place along our time line to ask whether there could be an entirely "secular spirituality." This would be a spirituality that is present whenever an individual pursues a highest ideal that somehow links to a transcendent reality but is never explicitly tied to anything religious (mainstream or alternative). This is exactly the project of Peter Van Ness' *Spirituality and the Secular Quest*, an anthology in the Crossroad's World Spirituality series. It was published in 1996, but the definition of spirituality used by all the Van Ness contributors is actually very Principian:

> Facing outward, human existence is spiritual insofar as one engages reality
> as a maximally inclusive whole, and makes the cosmos an intentional object
> of thought and feeling. Facing inward, life has a spiritual dimension to the
> extent that it is apprehended as a project of people's most enduring and vital
> selves and is structured by experiences of sudden self-transformation and
> subsequent gradual development.[10]

This is much more similar to Principe than we might have expected, given the purpose of the anthology. The issue here is not the secular versus the religious contents of any spirituality; the issue lies in the definition's fundamental structure. Like Principe's level one, Van Ness' definition includes the individual and an external object of apprehension and aspiration. It is two-poled, in other words: it has an "outward" or objective pole and an "inward" or subjective pole. As we will see, the majority of the more contemporary definitions lack this; they are one-poled in their basic structure. This is evident in the language Van Ness uses to portray the "objective" pole: reality as a "maximally inclusive whole," the cosmos as an intentional object. Note that this definition was designed explicitly for secular spiritualities, but it captures the sense of intention, of directing one's life and goals toward a fuller apprehension of the "what" that is the objective pole for spirituality. This is quite different from the sense of connection to anything and everything mentioned in many contemporary definitions, a connectedness experienced momentarily perhaps as a quality of an individual. But it does not require any "maximally inclusive whole" to be its *object* of connection. Because of the language of intentions, Van Ness can speak also of "gradual development," as persons aim to move toward their awareness of and harmony with that cosmos that is the objective pole of their spiritual quest. Whether through "sudden self-transformation" or "subsequent gradual development" or a combination of both, persons can become more spiritual, reaching out in hope toward a goal. Van Ness' book is about people who pursue spirituality and who must learn to become spiritual. They are not just born that way.

Somewhat ironically, this puts all these "secular questers" in the same league as those Roman Catholic religious who studied the 1916 *Manual de spiritualité*. They work at their chosen ideal and spend large amounts of time, energy, and money on this quest. In writing the chapter in Van Ness on psychotherapies, I found that the best autobiographies by therapy patients stress this.[11] Lucy Freeman's 1951 bestseller, *Fight against Fears*, covers her very Freudian psychoanalysis, and yet what emerges is not just her harrowing struggles with herself but her increasing awareness of the cosmos as a whole, in which she gains a sense of vitality and transformation. I picked this example deliberately because it was so unlikely to have been viewed as a spiritual or religious autobiography by anyone when it was written. It is a tale of striving, failures, and recoveries of someone painfully moving toward the kind of life goal and awareness that Van Ness' definition fits. St. Teresa could have given Lucy Freeman lots of good advice, or the two could have compared notes about temptations and consolations, even when their beliefs about the cosmos as a whole remain a million miles apart.

Therefore, rather than dwell on the differences between "religious" versus "secular" spiritualities, we stress the two-poled structure of some definitions. Van Ness followed Principe by more than ten years, but he was primarily interested in including a wide range of spiritualities into level two, to be studied as level three, "the academic study" of the materials found within level two. Training in the humanities or traditional theological study was the assumed preparation for this research. For that task, it must be clear where one would look, what kinds of texts or other documents or persons to interview would be relevant to a portrait of a particular spirituality. The choices must be justified by referring back to the definition. (Van Ness the editor made sure of this for his anthology.) Autobiographies of therapy clients fit the method; the definition would work for them. Other kinds of information would be irrelevant for this purpose. But, by contrast, where to look for spirituality is never clear in many of the more recent definitions. We cannot guess who could be chosen to represent spirituality. If spirituality characterizes everyone, then there are no obvious exemplars nor any preferred place to find it.

Spirituality as Universal Human Core: One-Poled Definitions

The next step in our journey to the right-hand end of the time line is to look at those definitions that make explicit the idea that spirituality is an innate potential or capacity or attribute at the center of all persons. Spirituality is neither an achievement nor something a few consciously adopt and practice. It becomes instead a concept that covers a basic human core, signifying our universal freedom and need for existential meaning. Principe's level one included some dimension of this but linked to an objective pole of the chosen religious ideal. The definitions we now examine are one-poled in that they remain focused on the inner-depth dimensions of human nature but omit explicit references to the cosmos as a whole or anything beyond or outside ourselves. John Morgan, as editor of a volume on *Death and Spirituality* in the Death and Meaning series, uses this approach to definition. Morgan was a sophisticated, philosophically trained pioneer in the death awareness movement, and his writings and the conferences he organized brought together many persons from different professions. He worked to promote death studies as a truly interdisciplinary field, a concern very far from that of Principe. For Morgan, the language of philosophical existentialism suited his aims and became a foundation for his thinking on spirituality.

This is apparent in the introduction he wrote as editor, an effort parallel to that of Van Ness. First Morgan wrote of "the uniqueness of the person," then of our need to find meaning. "Human spirituality is to seek an answer to the question 'How can you make sense out of a world which does not seem to be intrinsically reasonable?' "[12] And so, "this ability of persons to self-determine his or her life, is perhaps the most fundamental example of the spiritual nature of the person."[13] Because spirituality is so much the core of our nature, "we cannot escape from our spirituality."[14] Here he follows Viktor Frankl in *Man's Search for Meaning.* Both Morgan and Frankl posit a "will to meaning" that requires conscious choice and decisions. Yet Morgan makes spirituality into a core essence of all persons, in and of itself. It is inescapable, almost closer to an instinct than what Frankl was willing to claim for the "will to meaning." We will see this tension alive in the many definitions of spirituality now available and in the difficulty so many have with the question "How do I learn to be spiritual?" We will address the question of practice in the next chapter, but anything that is said to be inescapable will hardly be fit for learning or choosing at all. Although Morgan's definition predates Van Ness' by a few years, it is a harbinger of things to come.

A one-poled definition such as Morgan's has several appealing advantages that eventually made it the norm for spirituality's meaning. Most obviously, Morgan's inner human core of existential freedom is less religious than Principe's and even Van Ness'. For many of the health-care professionals who attended Morgan's conferences at the Centre for Education about Death and Bereavement in London, Ontario, this was an advantage and a reassurance. They and their clients and patients who may be nonreligious will not be turned off when it is clear that *spirituality* means an inner inescapable human essence rather than religious affiliation. Moreover, to make spirituality a universal human core means that by definition, everyone is spiritual, inescapably so (even my sister, who does not believe in "spirits," would be "spiritual"—as I informed her much to her chagrin). No more division between the elite "spirituals" versus the grungy "worldlies," as the much older literature surveyed by Principe assumed. All people, by virtue of their humanity, have spirituality. Although no one had explicitly suggested that we reinstate the Catholic dualism of lay and religious, the logic of the older literature and even of Principe could have led to this kind of bifurcation.

To affirm spirituality as a universal human quality is to take a stance against elitism, a theme with strong echoes in psychology and in the literature on spirituality in health care that we will examine. Yet it goes even further than this. The move to a one-poled definition of spirituality upholds a crucial kind of dignity for all persons. Here is where Morgan's debt to Viktor Frankl shines through; Frankl came to his psychology of the "will to meaning" by enduring a concentration camp existence. There, the worst deprivation seems to have been denial of even minimal basic human dignity: stripped naked, down to the bare bodies of their existence, the prisoners no longer counted as human. They were vermin, filthy and degraded, in the eyes of the camp authorities. Out of this extreme situation, Frankl came to believe that meaning in one's life is the ultimate need and those who have found it can endure almost any physical conditions at all.[15]

With a bit of imagination, we can see how this theme of intrinsic inner dignity can appeal to so many in the helping professions. Hospitals and social welfare agencies have been accused of dehumanizing patients, as we will see. But no one intends for that to be, no one should further such an aim. Professional staff should guard against everything that furthers dehumanization. This was the context Morgan may have addressed in his introductory essay to the volume on *Death and Spirituality*. To stress spirituality as an innate human core is a protest against this dehumanization, to protect the human dignity of patients and staff alike. This theme resonated with those attending Morgan's conferences or similar gatherings. We will spend time examining this situation and the adequacy of spirituality as the answer to medicalized dehumanization in a later chapter devoted explicitly to health care. For now, the definitions that do what Morgan's does, that explicitly label spirituality as a universal human core, can be seen as protection against both elitism and dehumanization.

But Morgan's philosophical depth did not carry as much weight as his inclusiveness and universalism. The plethora of definitions, most of them one-poled, continued on, and by 2002 three occupational therapists reviewing them collected a total of ninety-two. To their very detailed and conscientious survey we will now turn, for although it is more than ten years old, it represents the situation as of today.[16] As we look at the work of Unruh, Versnel, and Kerr, we also see the emergent context, hinted at by Morgan, in which spirituality becomes a central topic for those with no interest in the religious studies background or discipline of Principe. When spirituality is both universal and inescapable, then everyone has a say in what it means and why it is important.

A Plethora of Definitions
Unruh, Versnel, and Kerr "Unplug" Spirituality

There was no guarantee that Morgan's constructive effort to provide an existentialist definition of spirituality would lead to the enormous proliferation of contemporary definitions. Indeed, one could have argued that by the 1990s existentialism as a philosophy was somewhat passé. But although existentialism's influence faded, nothing could stop the rise of spirituality as a topic and debates over its meanings. By 2000, this had become the state of things and it continues today. Facing this situation, in February 2002, three Canadian occupational therapists published a wonderful survey article titled "Spirituality Unplugged: A Review of Commonalities and Contentions, and a Resolution." Unlike Morgan's work, this study was in direct response to an official statement by the CAOT. That body had become caught up in the enthusiasm for spirituality and claimed that this concept was central and foundational to the field of occupational therapy. The organization stated that many O.T. workers believed spirituality to be neglected yet very important. They were unsure of what it involved and felt unprepared to include or honor it in their work. So the CAOT offered its own definition: "A pervasive life force, manifestation of a higher self, source of will and self-determination, and a sense of meaning, purpose and connected-ness that people experience in the context of their environment."[17] This particular definition and the surrounding claims at which their organization arrived were almost immediately challenged by some O.T. professionals. One wrote to the professional journal, "I do not understand how one can possibly suggest that spirituality is at the centre of our profession. . . . The profession of occupational therapy has always had occupation as its core."[18] What mattered to Unruh, Versnel, and Kerr was not the specifics and adequacy of the CAOT definition but the fact that it was created anew, accompanied by the controversial claim that this "spirituality" lay at the core of their whole profession.

So the three O.T. researchers investigated and found ninety-two different definitions of this same term. They sorted these ninety-two into seven categories but admitted that some definitions were so obscure they were hard to classify at all. (And in the ten years since the article's publication, of course, there are plentiful additional definitions to add to their collection.) The authors wondered why spirituality should have supplanted the core goals and defining center of their field, especially when so many O.T. professionals considered themselves ill informed about it. It seemed bizarre to them that someone had to protect the central role of *occupation* in occupational therapy to prevent spirituality from recentering the entire field. If nothing else, this piece illustrates the pitfall of runaway enthusiasm for the concept of spirituality and an excellent strategy for correcting it.

But it does a lot more than this. The essay also illustrates the do-it-yourself quality of so many definitions of spirituality. It is as if the definers held up a large umbrella and invited anyone or anything they liked to shelter under it. This image reveals a peculiar feature of the entire enterprise. Normal academic or professional definitions of new terms are theory based. For example, Abraham Maslow's hierarchy of needs is based on a personality theory about human development and motivations, a theory intended to challenge Freudian ideas about growth and human nature. Morgan's definition of spirituality is based on Frankl and existential thought. But expressions such as "life force" and "higher self" (to take the words from the CAOT's own definition) do not seem to derive from a specific theory. There is no *one* clear source for terms like these in the multitude of definitions of spirituality but a multitude of sources, some of which do not cohere with one another. This is the major critique of the whole concept offered sarcastically by Pär Salander in a recent essay titled "The Emperor's New Clothes. Spirituality: A Concept Based on Questionable Ontology and Circular Findings."[19] Maybe the term *life force* owes its origin to nineteenth-century biology, when it was still a legitimate scientific concept, while *higher self* could be a legacy of romanticism or the New England transcendentalists. However, it is unlikely that the CAOT cared about the histories of these concepts or would want to adopt particular theories held by those who generated the terms. It must have just seemed as if words such as *life force* and *higher self* were "spiritual" yet less "religious" than conventional religious vocabulary, such as *soul*. These words nevertheless suggest realities important and ultimate. This reluctance to get "too religious" runs through almost all contemporary discussion of definitions for spirituality, but the result here is that the CAOT definition obscures the origins of its terms in specific philosophies, movements, and communities. Once upon a time, life force was just as theory driven as Maslow's hierarchy of needs, but this connection is no longer visible. Only its inner essentialism and romantic aura remain.

This is why a look at what stands under the umbrella of spirituality as a constructed category is worthwhile. It reveals the debris and leftovers of many theories, intellectual movements, and (obsolete) ideologies, all of whose languages carry implications and connotations of their own. Sometimes these are traceable to specific individual theorists, sometimes not. But we can see why spirituality is not truly resistant to definition: it is a clutter of fragmented bits of lost theories and ideologies whose terms were once adequately defined for their contexts and uses. The level of analysis here may be picky and detailed, but it is exactly what needs to be done for spirituality as Unruh, Versnel, Kerr, and so many others now find it.

The seven categories for definitions established by Unruh, Versnel, and Kerr are based, once again, on a huge number of definitions found in the literature on spirituality as it existed by 2002.

The first category is relationship to God, a spiritual being, a higher power, or a reality greater than the self. This is obviously the most "religious" category and was therefore the most controversial.[20] It is also the most obvious in its indebtedness. "Higher power" derives from 12-step programs, a genealogy much more visible and familiar than that of transcendentalism. The "religious" and indeed specifically "Christian" character of the 12-step model has been endlessly debated, but at least all debaters can point to the same texts. This makes it resemble Principe's style of definition, however different the context. Although there may be bizarre examples of idiosyncratic "higher powers" as chosen by individual 12-steppers, in general "God" is the model for this. (How idiosyncratic? A Japanese shrine to the deified spirit of the first Tokugawa shogun included a wooden prayer plaque, written in English, giving thanks for a year of sobriety. The sixteenth-century military dictator became, temporarily, and no doubt unwittingly, this pray-er's "higher power.")

The second category includes definitions not of the self, pointing to "a sense of something outside of the self," but whether this is "spirit," "higher consciousness," or some other reality, the three O.T. authors could not be sure.[21]

Third is transcendence or connectedness unrelated to a belief in a higher being. "Transcendence is used to convey something about the capacity to stand apart from day to day material existence" but occasionally was used as a noun, as in "concerned with the transcendent."[22] Connectedness implies an experience that is "separate from day-to-day realities, but . . . typically refers to perceptions and experiences of bonds with people, living or dead, across time and space. Connectedness may include a perception of union with other living things such as animals, plants, and nature."[23]

We will find these terms repeated in most contemporary definitions, with *connectedness* or *connection* used as a substantive, a quality in and of itself. Although none of the associations of these words are as explicit as the 12-step link, they are not without some histories. "Apart from day to day material existence" suggests a world or realm separate from that of time and history, while "union with other living things" evokes the pantheism of American "metaphysical" nature-focused alternative religiousness. The latter is alive and well, as we will see in the chapter devoted to spirituality and recreation, but here that legacy is written into the very definition of spirituality itself.

The fourth category is the existential, not of the material world. Does this mean "beyond everyday life," or does it imply a dualist metaphysics, such as the metaphysics Plato espoused? Probably not, since the philosophy hinted at does not seem especially Platonic. One definition under this category cited by the three authors is "the existential awareness of nonbeing."[24] Although there is no sign Unruh, Versnel, and Kerr recognized it, this reference to nonbeing is a clue that the philosophical sources for this type of definition are very different from transcendentalism or 12-step programs. It echoes the thought of theologian Paul Tillich (of whom more in a later chapter), who used the term *nonbeing* in the context of a coherent and fully articulated philosophical anthropology (theory of human nature). For Tillich, primordial human capacities centered on our encounter with nonbeing and the resultant anxiety that became inevitably and sometimes tragically part of who we are. This is another strand of existentialist philosophy, but it is just as uninterested in life force or any biological images as were the philosophies of Frankl and Morgan. Even when nothing as directly Tillichian as this reference to nonbeing can be found, the existentialist vocabulary contributes a different set of concerns and connotations to the umbrella mix of spirituality's meanings.

The fifth focuses on meaning and purpose in life and is related to "individual needs and life philosophies," often using language such as "the quest for meaning." Unruh, Versnel, and Kerr never question or pursue this idea, since the language does seem so obvious and everyday. Here, as in Morgan's definition, the direct source of this is Frankl's *Man's Search for Meaning*.[25] In this book's second section (the first and most famous is his autobiographical narrative of his concentration camp life, to which we have already referred), Frankl provides the outline of a psychological theory in which the "will to meaning" is more central than the pleasure principle and other instincts. "Man's search for meaning is a primary force in his life and not a 'secondary rationalization' of instinctual drives."[26] However personal and individual his concentration camp experiences were, Frankl grounds his ideas on meaning within the framework of a general theory of personality, intended to counter Freud's view of human nature. Here, in Frankl's theory, meaning is closely tied to the ability to construct a narrative about one's self and the world that has internal coherence and that promotes a sense of connection to the past and hope for a future. Frankl explicitly does not use language of "self-actualization," nor does he want meaning to appear as a kind of "instinct," for it requires conscious choices on the part of the one who searches for it.[27] "Will" and "freedom" are terms preferred by Frankl. We see here that *meaning* is a theory-based term, which in Frankl's book forms a pillar of his therapy. The merits of his theory or therapeutic methods are not under debate here, but he proposes a psychological theory of personality to be measured against competing views, especially Freud's. While Frankl is considerably more optimistic than Tillich, both set themselves against theories of human nature that depend on natural growth and organic functioning as adequate for understanding human beings.

The sixth category addresses the life force of the person. "Spirituality is also defined in many secular definitions as the life force of the person that unites or integrates the person as a unique summative whole."[28] But note how this term, located back in early modern biology, goes against the existentialist rejection of biology as an adequate clue to human distinctiveness. Unruh, Versnel, and Kerr, ignoring this internal contradiction, focus on life force as what is perceived as "private and potentially inaccessible to others because of its subjective nature."[29] The language of wholeness here, while only vaguely related to any particular psychological theory of personality or development, also goes against the thrust of Tillich's kind of existentialism, where awareness of non-being always intrudes upon our fantasies for wholeness and complete fulfillment. In spite of the fact that these definitions appear to be more secular and avoid any references to higher powers, they are not without hidden, unnoticed controversies embedded in their multiple sources.

The seventh and final category of definitions, summative, combines multiple features of the above dimensions. The definition from 2009 cited in our introduction would be of this type; it was described as "definition by committee," just as the definition created by the CAOT probably was.

Even without the action of a committee, we can look over these seven categories and find that they contain legacies and agendas that are, to say the least, unexplored and potentially confusing. Neither the CAOT nor most of the authors of these definitions were aware of, or interested in, tracking down these histories. Therefore, incompatibilities and internal contradictions among these and other possible sources go unnoticed and unexplored, by contrast with Frankl's careful selection among terms that could support his theory's anti-instinctual critique of Freud or Principe's concern to lay out a method for studying spirituality using all available disciplines' resources. Moreover, there is no particular reason why some new ingredients could not be added to these definitions, drawing on ideas from other sources, indirectly and without awareness.

This is essentially the same conclusion reached by D. Hufford in a very thorough review of the literature on religion, spirituality, and health written for the Metanexus Institute in 2006. Hufford makes the same point by saying that the terms used in that body of research have "no scholarly infrastructure";[30] they are used without clear grounding in the normative intellectual discourse of any particular field. While this sounds like an arcane criticism, it is really what we have just discovered: too many fragments of different and incompatible theories are at work within the very definitions of spirituality. Ninety-two different persons crowded under that one umbrella, in other words.

A final point about the *unplugged* in Unruh, Versnel, and Kerr's title: at the end of their survey, the three occupational therapists find that all of these definitions are too distant from the world of work to which their field is committed. "Occupational identity" fits better than spirituality to mark the true core of their profession.[31] While this conclusion is not surprising, it reveals something significant in the turn spirituality definitions have taken since Principe. Remember that he protested the traditional dichotomy between spiritual and worldly, religious and laity, that had clung to all the premodern uses of the term. He wanted an understanding of spirituality that emphasized the spiritual person's connection with the world of history, culture, and community. Like Unruh, Versnel, and Kerr, he would have been dismayed to see so many persons entranced by the thought of a universal human core disconnected, unplugged from that shared and social realm. As spirituality's definitions flourished, so more and more of them seemed to buy in to the motif of a realm beyond the material, beyond actual connections to society, in favor of a disembodied inner sense of connectedness. So the three O.T. authors "unplug" spirituality from their field's core, because it has become loaded with meanings and implicit ideas that unplug it from the world we actually share and within which work is done.

True Self, Biological Imagery, and Some Unresolved Issues

The mishmash of theories and philosophies that now crowd under the umbrella of spirituality bring with them the baggage of intrinsic assumptions and limits. While crowding itself may be a problem, the deep incompatibilities of these once-separate sources convey some particular unresolved issues that will surface again and again as the concept of spirituality is applied in different fields to solve a myriad of problems. As we discussed above, Frankl's "will to meaning" intentionally and explicitly rejects Freud's biological imagery of instincts. Tillich as well wrote against Freud, whom he believed to be a kind of biological reductionist. Therefore, this strand of existentialist thought, whether from psychology, philosophy, or theology, is intensely suspicious of views of human nature that depend on organic growth models to build a vision of the innately human. Yet the language of the true self that appears in several of the clusters identified by Unruh, Versnel, and Kerr is derived from theories that depend heavily on such imagery.

The language of true self takes us away from Frankl and toward a different kind of psychological theory, that of humanistic or "third force" psychology. This was Maslow's term; the other two forces were Freudianism and behaviorism.[32] While some personality theories center on intrapsychic conflict (Freud's pleasure principle vs. reality principle, for instance), Maslow relied on the imagery of natural unfolding and growth. We all begin filled with "potentials," and then these are actualized through our lives. The self of Maslow's self-actualization was there at the beginning; it is our human core. Conflicts, in this view of personality, come from outside obstacles that block the natural unfolding of the self. Some of these outside obstacles may effectively confuse an individual, who will then consciously identity with a false self, but the true self abides within, permanently. Proponents of this view use extensive growth imagery. A seed will grow into a new plant. This will happen naturally, provided there is a minimally supportive environment. Here the personality theories within psychology merge into that life force language that also permeated some of the recent spirituality definitions. Growth depends on the innate potential, and not on conscious decisions on the part of the plant or on our cheerleading.

But two problems plague this legacy, relevant here as spirituality is now moved into the central core of the human, as in newer, one-poled definitions. Because self-actualization happens naturally and spontaneously, it is not clear whether it is something we can or should "pursue" and, if so, how and where do we start? A practice, whether individual or group led, dedicated to self-actualization or growth is a bit like yelling, "Grow, plant, grow," over a flowerbed. Peggy Rosenthal's discussion of *self-actualization* as a "glow word" focuses exactly on this ambiguity. The language of potentials and actualization is used confusedly here, especially when the true self is depicted as containing "infinite potentials." In Rosenthal's judgment, Maslow's growth and actualization language "comes to act as a floating halo, coming to rest glowingly on whatever in human life we already value."[33] For if potential and growth are more like natural events than like goal-directed behavior, then we should not worry over choices and commitments. Compare this with the definition of spirituality's foundational level one by Principe, where a chosen ideal and a life lived intentionally to reach it were the essence of what spirituality really meant. Even Morgan, whose one-poled definition led the way for so many others, focused on human will and freedom, not on natural unfolding. No one could claim that spirituality as a topic began this problem; it was there all along in the tension between Frankl and Maslow and was imported unwittingly into the contemporary definitions.

The second problem with the language of growth and inner potentials that haunts spirituality when it is defined as the universal human core was uncovered and brilliantly analyzed by Don Browning in his

Religious Thought and the Modern Psychologies.[34] Browning looked for implied religious imagery in a wide range of psychologies and also for their ethical dimensions. All of these theories, he discovered, have built-in values and ethics, even if they claim to be "value free" and scientifically objective. Maslow's theory is no exception to this, according to Browning. Maslow's vision of an innate core of potentials to be self-actualized by each individual seems to assume an isolated individual carrying out his or her own actualization. Or, if we update this to our context, we each express our own unique but inescapable spirituality. But what do I do when my self-actualization conflicts with yours? There may be times when my unfolding potentials or sense of life force or meaning impede your equally unfolding and innate growth. Both yours and mine may be equally the flowering of our true selves and express our inner life forces, spirituality, or quest for meaning. It is important to determine who has priority and who should give way.

Ordinarily, there are two possible answers to this. First, the more mature and self-actualized person should give way to the less "grown" one, so the latter may have the opportunity to advance. This antielitist ethic stresses the dignity and potential of all. Alternatively, the process of self-actualization itself requires that the more "grown" achieve fuller growth, even if this slows down the relatively stunted. This is in nature the normal pattern for two adjacent plants when the more vigorous eventually overshadows the other. In that sense, it is more biologically "natural." But the first answer appears more altruistic, echoing the pathway recommended by St. Paul in his advice about the consciences of the strong and the weak (1 Cor 14). No amount of growth alone can help us answer this question, without commitment to some outside, additional ethic.

But the actual response of self-actualization psychology, Browning shows, is to deny that this is a real dilemma. Maslow and those who use his language

> assume a kind of pre-established harmony in the world that functions in such a way as to assure that "what is to one person's advantage coincides with what is to that of all the others." This view postulates that the actualization of all potentialities is basically complementary . . . and that for this reason, all people can pursue their own interests without fear that they will conflict with . . . the interests of other people.[35]

Behind this lies a faith in "a hidden pre-established harmony." Every individual should grow, and when that happens, all our growths will harmonize. Automatic harmonization therefore makes ethical reasoning unnecessary: there will never be true unresolvable conflicts at all. It will all work out well for everyone in the end. Browning believes this "harmony assumption" characterizes the ethics, or lack thereof, of much psychological theory. Once he has helped us spot this idea in one psychological theorist, we will, I am afraid, discover it scattered widely in writings that now define and promote spirituality. There was nothing of this harmony assumption in Frankl's theory, any more than in Principe's. Both avoided the imagery of natural growth that seems to pair with it.

We have not wandered off the track of spirituality definitions but have discovered how some issues trailing Maslowian imagery and ideas continue on from psychology into the contemporary definitions of spirituality and its benefits. To the extent that they relocate spirituality as an innate, universal human core that is best construed as a natural potential in all of us, the definitions carry with them two problems. First, while Principe's and Van Ness' two-poled definitions made it clear that intentions and commitments to an ideal were intrinsic to the structure of spirituality, these drop out of the more recent definitions. Everyone by virtue of humanity has spirituality; it is inescapable. What if anything we ought to do to develop it is not clear. Second, the automatic harmony assumption unplugs spirituality from the kind of ethical reasoning that most "highest ideals" support (to use Principe's language).

The narrow focus of this chapter on the exact language and structure of an amazing number of definitions may seem excessively picky and focused on tracing obscure connections. But even if spirituality is a new category needing new definitions, it is also itself a legacy of other areas and activities and theories about human nature. Those who offer seemingly fresh and original definitions of spirituality do not appear to have pondered the strengths and weaknesses of this ancestry. The belief that spirituality is intrinsically resistant to definition seems to justify this neglect. Hence, Frankl, Maslow, Tillich, Emerson, and Alcoholics Anonymous (AA) rub shoulders under the umbrella. Meanwhile, the transitions from Principe through Van Ness to Morgan and all the ninety-two definitions are a tiny but visible piece of an important and complex intellectual shift. To learn how spirituality became a new and expanding category, we need to look at its relation to other categories, its intellectual ecology, and then at its treatment of values and virtues. That is the story we need to discover, and the story that all of the ninety-two definitions combined cannot by themselves yield. Ninety-two and still counting.[36]

CHAPTER TWO

How Do I Become Spiritual?

Practice as a Category

A Traditional Model of Spiritual Practice and Learning

Contemporary definitions of spirituality are, as we have seen, very abstract and generic. It is one of the paradoxes of the concept of spirituality today that almost all of its advocates follow up their definitions with examples of specific practices such as meditation or yoga. These, it is assumed, demonstrate spirituality. They are separable from religion, whatever their religious origins. The turn to spirituality is a turn away from just believing things toward doing something. Several anthologies on spirituality are mostly samplers of various practices, and a textbook on spirituality in nursing includes sections not only on meditation but on Chinese geomancy. The goal is to be as eclectic and inclusive as possible, at least in theory.

But the relation between these practices, sometimes called "wisdom technologies" after Ken Wilbur (in order to free them from association with religion), and the spirituality definitions focused on meaning and connection is obscure. Our argument will be that, so long as traditional two-poled definitions such as Principe's were the guide, the link to practices made perfect sense. When one-poled definitions triumphed, making spirituality universal and inescapable, this link became problematic conceptually. Or, to begin from Principe's phrasing, when spirituality included by definition a pursuit of a "chosen religious ideal," it made sense to provide set answers to the question "How do I become spiritual?" That is what all the traditional practices aimed to do. When spirituality's meaning loses its tie to a chosen ideal or to an intentional pursuit of something beyond the self, the link is hard to determine. That is why in the more recent literature, it is rare to find someone ask directly, "How do I become spiritual?" The answer is: you do not need to become; you already *are*. But the inclusion of practices is important, even for those who would answer this way. Practices matter, whether traditional or modified practices. Spirituality is more about doing than about believing. Why and how may be hard to determine. Once again, there is no necessary connection between definitions focused on meaning and connection and the particular activities, such as yoga, recommended to those interested in spirituality.

So to investigate this question is not to turn away from definitions but to view them from another angle and to discover a more useful and better-defined category than spirituality. The concept of practice will supplement, balance, and in the end contrast with that of spirituality. It will also help us toward clarifying the values and virtues attributed to spirituality, a concern of great importance and even greater confusion. Once again, close focus on this topic serves as a window, giving us a glimpse into wider cultural shifts that lie behind the rise of spirituality and the felt need for such a category.

When Principe looked back at the traditional meaning of the term *spirituality*, he found it lodged in the devout lives and activities of Roman Catholic religious. It had no other positive use beyond this context, he discovered. Even when he expanded the meaning of the term to correspond to 1983 sensibilities, he kept some key features of the original. For, even with the more contemporary usage, Principe assumed that we were speaking of individuals whose lives centered upon a "chosen religious ideal." All three words were necessary and important. It was chosen, not passively absorbed. It was religious, although as we have seen, this could be eventually expanded to include all the Van Ness "secular quest" possibilities. And it was an ideal, something to strive to meet. Those who pursue spirituality in Principe's definition need no longer be members of religious orders, but their existential level-one spirituality is likely guided by the traditional teachings and doctrines of level-two spirituality. The spirituality of the devout occupational therapist, for example, would be centered on his or her faith and life goals as a Christian, not (for Principe) by his or her membership in the CAOT. His or her way to live out a chosen religious ideal might lead to this career, but his or her spirituality drew its source material from Christian tradition.

When this was what spirituality meant, there was little need to ask what values and virtues went along with it. The ethical content for the spiritual life was derived from the teachings of the church, as mediated by the religious community and its leaders. The elaborate initiation and training programs of such communities presupposed a "higher" ethical standard than that which all Christians were to follow. A monastic lifestyle included the intentional cultivation of certain virtues and certain specialized techniques and activities through which beginners could learn how to become spiritual. For Principe's traditional model, even with his revisions, assumes that spirituality is something that one must learn.

Yes, learn. Spirituality may draw upon universal human capacities, but it is formed, guided, studied, and practiced. It is a kind of specialized education, closer to craft learning than to today's classrooms, but definitely structured learning. The whole point of what Principe called level two is to instruct both budding practitioners and those who train them. No one is born a spiritual person; one becomes a spiritual person, living out a life aimed at fulfilling a chosen religious ideal. Generations of wise persons have come to understand how to prepare and train, encourage and correct those on this path. Not only does it make sense to ask, "How do I become spiritual?" but if I *fail* to ask this, I am wasting my time in the monastery (and the time of those trying to train me). Principe's level two, then, is not just "doctrines"; it is vital information of a very practical sort, written as an instruction manual for the soul. Along with this written instruction, there are of course other even more basic resources for becoming spiritual: the worship routine (including sacramental participation), study of Scriptures (or listening to them read at meals), and personal guidance from a director or confessor. Each is going to help the properly prepared beginner become spiritual. Some may never make it, but not even God can bring a two-year-old instantly to mature full spirituality. (Even the boy Jesus grew daily in wisdom, according to Luke 2:52.)

At this point, the deep contrast between these ideas and the contemporary meanings of spirituality should be apparent. Advocates of the latter wish to separate spirituality from structured, organized religion so that spirituality is an innate, inescapable human capacity, not a field for achievement. And to think of training in spirituality as the cultivation of certain virtues is also odd, although some virtues and values are repeatedly mentioned as intrinsically spiritual. In all the more recent writings, I have found only one essay that deals explicitly with the question: "How Does One Learn to Be Spiritual? The Neglected Role of Spiritual Modeling in Health," by Doug Oman and Carl Thoresen.[1] Ironically, in this one example "spiritual modeling" turns out to be "social modeling" or "role modeling," neither more nor less. The learning involves the four basic processes of

> attention to a model's actions, retention in memory of what was observed, and attempts at reproduction in behavior. Finally, unless adequate motivation is present, a learned behavior may never be practiced or implemented. The same four processes are involved in learning from contemporary models, as well as from historical models that may be encountered through reading, storytelling or other media.[2]

One learns to be spiritual along the same principles that one learns from role models generally, and spiritual learning follows the rules of cognitive social learning found in every setting. The use of live models or guidebooks is not a key differentiation, but neither is the spiritual dimension of what is learned and how. Perhaps the reason for this skimpy and unimaginative treatment is that in so much contemporary usage spirituality is innate. To learn to be what we already and inevitably are is a false task. If there is a more prevalent responses to the question "How do I learn to be spiritual?" it is likely to be "Listen to your own deepest wisdom" or "Follow your inner spirit," along with "Do not put yourself in the hands of an external authority." Principe and his traditional sources would say that these answers are radically insufficient for beginners. To begin from Principe's older definition and context is useful not because we are nostalgic for the good old days of traditional monastic piety but because the older ideals and lifestyle had internal coherence and answered questions that more recent advocates of spirituality have difficulty even articulating well.

To give readers a better sense of traditional level-two spirituality, as an answer to the question "How do I learn to be spiritual?" let me use a famous guide to the soul. Saint Teresa of Avila wrote *The Interior Castle* in the late sixteenth century, as a guide for her nuns in the practice of prayer and the mystical life. She wrote under obedience, meaning she was required to do so as a religious obligation from her superior. She wrote with frequent interruptions from illness and travel. And she wrote with the Inquisition breathing down her neck (they had impounded the manuscript of her early book, her life story). So much for the peace and quiet of the spiritual life! But she wrote to explain in detail how the soul moves from the outer walls of its castle into a series of rooms or "dwelling places," eventually reaching the center throne room where His Majesty awaits her. The soul is a wonderful, mysterious realm of which most of us are ignorant. And in its deepest heart is God, the beloved spouse of the eventual union or marriage. When she gets onto this topic, Teresa forgets all her distractions and woes and just sparkles.

The "rooms" or divisions are seven. They are sequential; everyone starts at the starting place. The first four she thinks of as "natural," resting as they do on the inborn capacities of the soul now aided by divine grace. In this model, by the way, nothing is natural apart from grace, for we always receive God's blessing and help and empowerment, even from the beginning. Because she writes for nuns, she assumes they have all made the decision to enter the castle, which corresponds to Oman and Thoresen's motivation, among their four learning processes. Yet in the second dwelling place of Teresa's castle, there are vile animals (serpents and reptiles) that represent the stupid, sleazy, worldly impulses and habits left over from their lives and identities prior to entering the monastic life. Motivation is complex and conflicted, although the psychological model of processes glosses over its ambivalences.

Let us stop here briefly to provide a bit of background. I may imagine sixteenth-century Spain as a paradigm of fanatical piety, but apparently a large number of women ended up as nuns because there was no other choice for them. Their brothers sailed off to become conquistadors around the world, and so the girls got dumped into the only available option for single women. Once in the convent, they received very little instruction. They could spend their days in needlework, gossip, and boredom. Teresa herself may never have been like that, but she knew that simply to move the girl to the convent did nothing much for her soul. Hence the encouraging and enthusiastic tone of *The Interior Castle* is aimed not just at those who embraced a chosen religious ideal as a personal existential commitment but at those who had to recognize this as the life chosen (by God and their families) for them.

Those serpents and reptiles lurking around the outer walls can still strike and bite the beginner. The novice may complain to herself about the life of a nun and wallow in self-pity and petty resentment. Teresa tells us how to spot and check this flow of unhappy, sinful ruminations and how to become aware of the ways our habits bind us to our own unhealth. She is here, as throughout the book, always able to admit how silly, selfish, short-sighted, and timid she herself has been. Everything she writes about she knows from her personal experience.

This is where one feature of *The Interior Castle* bothers many contemporary readers (especially women). Teresa constantly belittles herself. She is weak minded, she hates to write, she knows she is a scatterbrain, she has hardly ever done anything perfectly, and so on. She seems intent on beating up on herself. This may have been deliberate, to defuse the Inquisition's readers by making herself seem too puny a target for them. But it also plays into her role as "the guide who's been there herself" and invites the readers to identify with her and attend to her message. "Look, sisters, if I can do this, so can all of you!" Contemporary self-help authors know this strategy well. "If someone as hopelessly neurotic as I am can overcome this problem, then you, readers, have no excuse at all!"

The material in the book's second half, the final three rooms, is qualitatively different from what came earlier. Teresa's own famous image is the contrast between water drawn from an aqueduct and water bubbling up from a spring.[3] The effort of the first shows that it is a work of our will, guided by God. Consolations obtained here are "through thoughts, assisting ourselves, using creatures to help our meditation, and tiring the intellect."[4] All the psychological processes of normal social learning could be involved. But the second set of processes happens because God acts directly in the soul. "He produces this delight with the greatest peace and quiet and sweetness in the very interior part of ourselves." Our job is to let God work. In another striking image, the soul is a little silkworm that spins its cocoon and dies to itself.[5] The soul is not entirely passive, for the language of passive versus active is much too gross to capture what she tries to describe. The many detailed depictions of different consolations, states, and "raptures," of visions imaginative and intellectual, show how much work is required to differentiate and provide accurate advice and guidance in such matters.

All this labeling and classifying and evaluating are not externally imposed restrictive rules from outside. They are spontaneous efforts to make sense of what even Teresa has found very alarming and mysterious at times. She knows that just because something happens that feels unusual and overwhelming does not guarantee that it is from God. Nor does it guarantee that it is dangerous and from the devil. She worked in a climate where religious fears about demonic activity were real and pernicious, but Teresa challenged this in her text. God, not the devil, should be our concern, and persons too timid to venture to explore the first to seventh rooms of the castle are dishonoring God as well as shortchanging themselves. Here she has bitter things to say about "timid confessors," spiritual directors who are just too nervous to be good guides. "He fears everything, and finds in everything something to doubt because he sees these unusual experiences."[6] Yes, there are dangers, says Teresa, but there is no point in exaggerating them. Moreover, if the fruits of these raptures and so on are an increase of love for Christ and for one's fellow religious and a great increase in the desire to please His Majesty, then we may know that the devil could not be behind the whole sequence. These results, or fruits, are too inimical to his basic purpose.[7] So Teresa is anything but naïve; her labeling and careful distinctions are aimed at helping others to figure out "Where are we going with all these unusual states?" "How do I see what His Majesty is doing though these experiences?" This is what is traditionally called "discernment," and it is a vital part of learning to be spiritual.

To make this work, Teresa insists, one needs continuous humility. Do not stand on your own accomplishments; do not assume you know what something means because it feels a certain way at first glance. Do not assume having unusual experiences makes you somehow special in the eyes of God or more worthy than someone who never went into mystical raptures. Humility is really a central virtue for Teresa.

> Let's leave aside the times when the Lord is pleased to grant it because he wants to, and for no other reason. He knows why; we don't have to meddle in this. After you have done what should be done by those in the previous dwelling places: humility! humility! By this means the Lord allows himself to be conquered with regard to anything we want from Him. The first sign for seeing whether or not you have humility is that you do not think you deserve these favors and spiritual delights from the Lord or that you will receive them in your lifetime.[8]

To remember the image of the aqueduct and the spring, the water itself comes from the Living God. We may or may not be active in drawing up, but God is the true and ultimate Source. Humility! Humility! Humility for Teresa means that we are to be continuously open to accurate, realistic reassessment of our situations, our failures and successes, our flaws and strengths. It is honesty about ourselves. It is the opposite of the kind of self-obsessive "I'm just little me the perpetual victim" rumination with which it has become for us so disastrously confused. Humility in Teresa's sense is not just one of many virtues; it is a kind of prerequisite for making any progress at all.

Another virtue about which she writes is courage. "Timid confessors" are so pernicious because they play into our own socially learned fears. Remember that sixteenth-century Spanish women had brothers who went off to conquer Mexico and Peru (and the Philippines and Puerto Rico, etc.); these young women Carmelites may have dreamed of exciting adventures too. But the role models they were normally given took few risks and were preoccupied with protecting their own honor. So Teresa has to strike against this, with calls for determined behavior, for perseverance in the face of discouragement and temptations in the form of "I am not worthy" or "I am not ready for this." Self-doubt and feelings of incompetence are not to be confused with humility, and there are times when the best one can do is hold on and wait for the mercy of God.[9] But this too takes courage. Courage is present in exploration of the castle, in accepting what the King himself desires for them. Courage allows them to let go of limited expectations about themselves or to find new confessors when theirs are too timid or ignorant of the interior life. Without courage, she insists, there is no progress through the mysterious castle.

Progress is part of her architectural image and her basic portrayal of the spiritual life. One moves, eventually, from betrothal to marriage, or union. The soul in her journey seeks this union with the King at the center of the castle. There is no possibility in Teresa's imagery for a life of perpetual seeking, because that assumes no destination and no arrival. Instead, Teresa and those who share her ideal believe they travel toward what God has promised them. Whether everyone "arrives" at mystical union, or whether even Teresa herself did, she could not have written a guide to an interior castle where one simply goes from room to room to room, as in a real estate agent's house tour. The journey into God, into deeper union, is never ending, completed in the life beyond this one. But it is as goal directed and structured as a journey from Avila to Madrid.

This look into a classic of spirituality in its traditional meaning—an instance of Principe's level two—sets the groundwork for an examination of how much of today's definition of spirituality can include features intrinsic to Teresa's guide: intention, ideal, progress, particular practices and experiences, and virtues such as humility and courage. We must ask whether any of these apply at all. By themselves, these are not categories dependent on Roman Catholic Christianity, and we could have picked an example from Buddhist monastic practice, where they can certainly be found as well. Indeed, they are not exclusively monastic, either. What they depend upon is a chosen religious ideal and a path to guide the spiritual practitioner toward that goal.

The Built-In Virtues of Any Practice

Up until now, we have used the terms *practice* and *practitioner* as if it were obvious what they mean. Teresa's method of prayer—and indeed her whole plan for the journey toward the King and Spouse at the center of the interior castle—is a guidebook for doing and living, for experiencing and understanding one's experiences. The category of practice works out much more precisely than this, and yet it will fit a wider range of activities than even the most eclectic anthology of spiritual practices includes. We draw here on Alasdair MacIntyre's *After Virtue*, which examines the Aristotelian concept of a practice of virtue. Following Aristotle, MacIntyre conceives of the general category of practice and takes note of how certain values or virtues seem absolutely intrinsic to it: "A practice involves standards of excellence and obedience to rules as well as the achievement of goods. To enter into a practice is to accept the authority of those standards. . . . It is to subject my own attitudes, choices, preferences and tastes to the standards which . . . define the practice."[10] This offers MacIntyre a way out of a post-Kantian dilemma about ethics and knowledge. But for us it is a way to link traditional spirituality level two with contemporary meanings and implications of spirituality as something that may or may not be learnable. It will help us by distilling some key features behind teachings such as Teresa's and their very recent adaptations that often accompany concern with spirituality.

Beyond the above definition, a practice is an activity done intentionally and with effort over time. A practice could be as elaborate and esoteric as what we have just examined from *The Interior Castle*. Another example would be Japanese traditional crafts (calligraphy, say). It involves head, heart, hands. And it can be fun: white-water kayaking or long-distance running or playing baseball. Each shares certain features. To do them at all, one begins as a beginner, learns the basics, then step-by-step masters the more difficult moves or skills. Natural talent may count for something, but every practice includes a specialized knowledge that no one is born with. Traditional Japanese paper and inks and brushes have qualities that the novice must learn about, and for the kayaker there is knowledge about how to "read the river." Step one in all practices, then, is admitting your ignorance and being willing to overcome it. Step two is getting started. And making a mess of it, and doing it again and again and again. Reproduction of the actions of the model is sometimes excruciatingly difficult ("But he made it look so easy!" says the discouraged beginner of his or her instructor). In other words, we have built into the idea of a practice the courage to try, the willingness to fail and be seen to fail, and the honesty to admit that we failed. One may say that part of learning a practice is willingness to look like an idiot and learning to laugh at oneself in doing so. Humility! Humility!

A really pointed discussion of this kind of humility in relation to competitive team sports is Michael Novak's snide discussion of macho behavior and attitudes in *The Joy of Sports*. Machismo is usually thought of as part of a successful athlete's ostentatious display of manliness. Not so, says Novak. According to him, machismo is the absolute opposite of the true athlete's personal orientation. A guy who is macho is so caught up in his own self-image that he can never risk looking like a failure, looking clumsy or uncoordinated. He is too worried about how imposing he must always appear. He avoids sports, because sports include, necessarily, the willingness to fail and flop at least some of the time. So he scorns sports or claims athletics are silly. But the real reason is cowardice and insecurity.[11] Novak's account is set up for men, but Novak, writing in the 1970s, wanted his daughters to develop the character strengths associated with the skills provided by the practice of sports.

These macho persons of any gender lack courage and also lack the basic humility of which Teresa spoke. But there are other virtues built into the very concept of a practice. A practice has a goal and accomplishes something. Whether growing orchids or paddling down a river with class 4 rapids, it is not primarily competition against others; it is striving to meet an ideal of excellence. Because the goal is so public, measures of success and failure are clearly visible, universal, and meant to apply to all. Therefore, everyone must be judged by the same standards intrinsic to the goal, as in MacIntyre's definition. No one gets promoted or judged successful on the basis of criteria extraneous to the practice itself. One may be the coach's son, have a rich family who donated money for the stadium, or be the heir to the head of the local mafia. Considering any of these relevant for making the team is a disaster for all the practitioners. This is not just true for competitive situations. I, as a kayaker, paddle the same river as everyone else. If my boat cost twice or twenty times as much as theirs, I still face the same river with the same rocks as everyone else. Thus, justice, in this sense of fairness in application of internally relevant standards, is one of the built-in virtues of a practice.

Although Teresa speaks of humility, MacIntyre focuses on honesty, to similar effect. These little examples already show why this is built in as a virtue. If we do not know how to do something, we must admit it. We cannot cheat ourselves or our instructor. We had better learn to ask for information we lack, which implies an ability to assess where we are lacking. If we are taking a class, the instructor's duty is to tell us where we lack and also to call us on our lies or denials. Instructors who give flattery instead of accurate evaluation are frauds, whatever their motivation. And we ourselves need to be open to hearing and discerning unpleasant news. Humility! Humility!

Finally, MacIntyre's category seems to require another virtue. Perseverance is the motivation to persist. "If at first you don't succeed . . ." The water that comes through the aqueduct requires pumping, and we must learn to keep at it.

The problem, however, is pointless, stubborn perseverance at an ill-chosen goal. There really are cases where no amount of effort is going to pay off. Frankly, perseverance must go together with honesty. A student who perseveres as a pre-med major after a series of Bs and Cs in chemistry is being dishonest, not dedicated.

Teresa did not have to deal with this particular problem. She assumed that God wants for us the best that is possible for us. Not the best possible for universal everyone in an ideal universe but the best of what God, His Majesty, can give of himself to us as particular persons. Perseverance in our reception of this best is always going to pay off. We sell God short if we doubt this. Yet tied to this special character of God is another feature of Teresa's example of practice, which distinguishes it greatly from calligraphy or kayaking: its relative invisibility of measures of success or failure. The ultimate instructor and guide for the life of prayer is also God, of course. The confessor or director is to know us as well as any human can know another, but it is finally God who will measure, judge, and approve us. Throughout this life, we know ourselves imperfectly, and, even at the end of it, we may not be in a position to assess ourselves absolutely accurately. God alone has perfect knowledge. Teresa is intensely sensitive to just this area of concern. Yet this does not mean that all models of learning and success be thrown away, only that the practice of the spiritual life is more subtle than psychological theories of normal social modeling can encompass.

Modern Adaptations of Traditional Practices

We now have a clear idea of one type of answer to the question "How do I learn to be spiritual?" It fits perfectly the two-poled, traditional definition of spirituality that includes practices to achieve the chosen ideal. In this context, we learn not just through generic social learning or following role models but through the kind of intense guided instruction that is intrinsic to a practice. And, using the image of water from a spring, we might add that certain advanced forms of learning really require a different model, for which God or some ultimate power is the true source. This answer fits the original meaning of spirituality, which even by 1983 was obsolete. How we learn to be spiritual when the definitions used by contemporary authors, researchers, and clinicians vary so greatly is another story. And, since most of these definitions now make spirituality a universal human core quality, it is still unclear whether "How do we learn?" fits as a question at all. Without some idea of pursuing an intentionally chosen ideal or path, we just do not have the basic building blocks for a practice. Although the "higher power" language of some definitions derives from the 12 steps of recovery programs, which are clearly a type of practice as we have just discussed it, the recent definitions of spirituality are not linked to AA, except in the borrowing of this one phrase, *higher power.*

Take connectedness, a quality intrinsic to many of the definitions. We might ask whether we can learn to cultivate it so as to become more spiritual. In the spirituality literature, sense of connection is not dealt with as a skill or learned behavior. We may say we feel connected to the moment or to the universe, but when we avoid connectedness *to* a particular object or ideal in favor of a generic sense of connectedness, we no longer know where to begin in practicing. To put this bluntly, if I were to seek connectedness to water, I would head to a river or lake. To trees, I would head to a forest. If I wish to strengthen my sense of connectedness per se, I am not sure I would head anywhere or know what comes next.

There is, however, more to it than this. Here is where one of the most intriguing and confounding features of contemporary spirituality resides. No, spirituality cannot or need not be learned, for we all are innately spiritual. The terms used in the definitions do not point toward learning at all. But push even a little bit further, and a lot of suggestions emerge as to how to potentially cultivate awareness or attention to the moment or a receptive connectedness to something. The spirituality materials are filled with allusions to this level of advice and technique, even if the general question of learning to be spiritual is neglected. The techniques and methods and training sessions range from meditation to cognitive retraining to mantrum and mind/body exercises. The populations for which these are intended include therapy patients, employees, volunteers at spiritual centers, and special professional groups. Some presentations feature controlled research studies measuring effectiveness in dealing with specific problems (e.g., anxiety), while other accounts appear to be advertisements for the authors' workshops. But they all are modern, derivative adaptations of the traditional spiritual disciplines such as those Teresa taught and expected her readers to practice. The difference is that, in their original settings, these practices were all explicit and clear about connection to something specific and pursuit of a chosen goal. In the current adaptations, the outer or objective pole is missing or considered dispensable.

Let me repeat this. All the practical pieces on "enhancing our spirituality" promoted today tout techniques that derive from and depend upon ancient disciplines such as yoga, meditation, contemplative prayer practices, and so on. These may be adapted or "secularized" into new wineskins, but they are practices in MacIntyre's sense. They were once and sometimes still are traditional, religiously based disciplines of the spiritual life. They were developed within sacred frameworks, even if one labels them wisdom technologies. Today, they may be streamlined or dumbed down or taught as physical fitness techniques. They may for legal purposes today have nothing to do with religion. But they do not, repeat, do not grow directly from the definitions of spirituality as "the search for meaning" or "sense of connection." You could stare at those definitions forever and not, from them alone, deduce or postulate or extrapolate yoga or concentrative meditation techniques. There is no conceptual continuity between the contemporary definitions of spirituality (one-poled, dependent on the inner self) and the practices that now fascinate many of spirituality's advocates, along with many of the more traditionally religious.

Take, for example, the unusually good discussion of several such modernized techniques found in *Spirit, Science and Health*, edited by Thomas Plante and Carl Thoresen, the same volume that contains the essay, "How Does One Learn to Be Spiritual?" This volume, like Joan Marques, Satinder Dhiman, and Richard King's edited anthology, *The Workplace and Spirituality*, showcases methods and techniques to "enhance spirituality" in various settings and diverse populations. The Plante and Thoresen anthology includes an essay entitled "The Eight-Point Program of Passage Meditation," which explains a method to concentrate and focus attention, with certain health benefits promised. The passages are taken from sacred texts culled from a wide range of religious sources (the authors see this as "nonsectarian").[12] They include some very familiar ("The Lord is my shepherd") and others much less so to Westerners ("May all beings be filled with joy and peace"). Subjects are instructed to learn the passage and recite it to themselves whenever stressed or bored or caught up in an emotion-laden situation. The authors present data about how well the experimental and control groups did immediately after, at eight weeks, and at nineteen weeks in coping with stress.[13] The choice of passages is very explicit; these particular texts have a successful track record and bring "a person into direct daily contact with the words of the world's great wisdom traditions."[14] The psychological mechanism by which these work—that is, refocusing of attention—is discussed in the final part of the essay Here the authors invoke Albert Bandura's social cognitive theory and its focus on the enhancement of "self-efficacy."[15] This is a perfectly normal explanation, whether accurate or not. It does not require any specific religious or spiritual elements, such as the grace of the Holy Spirit or the blessing of Amida, the Buddhist divinity. The whole contribution is also noteworthy for the modesty of its claims. The authors do not promise that a new, postmodern utopian age will arrive when the rest of us take up this practice.

What remains unclear, however, is the connection between recitation and repetition of the opening verses of Psalm 23 and spirituality itself. I may learn and practice the passage meditation technique, and indeed I may reduce or cope better with stress in my life, but it is very hard to determine whether this means I have learned to be spiritual. Recall that meaning and sense of connection were two of the elements of many definitions, and the Twenty-third Psalm is definitely about connection. "He leads me beside green pastures," and we remain connected even in the valley of the shadow of death. But it is very explicitly connection to God; it is not just connectedness in general. Some of the other sample passages do not seem focused on this at all.

Moreover, and here is Principe back in the picture, the recitation of psalms is part of a "chosen religious ideal," and indeed recitation of these texts is the major prayer activity of those who follow the monastic rules of life. Humility, justice, honesty, courage, and perseverance are all part of that way of life, but it is not clear to what extent the recitation to oneself of one part of one psalm carries with it all those values and virtues. As for self-efficacy, it is a good thing, but it is not on the list of practice virtues, because it is at best a kind of side effect rather than a primary goal in the original settings for monastic practice of psalm recitation. Monks aimed for humility; self-efficacy may have resulted unintentionally. This seems like a good instance of what we will call "residual religion," in which a fragment of what was originally a comprehensive and well-planned program of practices aimed at a chosen ideal is now preserved with the implicit hope that it will carry within it the benefits once attributed to the whole.

By now, some of the difficulties we face in sorting through how to interpret such contemporary techniques as passage meditation are familiar—or should sound familiar. At issue is more than what counts legally as religion, although this was the explicit focus of early debates over Transcendental Meditation (TM). Transcendental Meditation was first marketed in the 1960s and 1970s as a technique to relieve stress and produce various health benefits. During the 1970s, when TM was proposed as an addition to the public school curriculum, it was promoted as a technique for aiding attention and reducing stress and the like; it had no religious content or purpose. But this claim was successfully challenged by those who said its technique was based on a religion and that to make it mandatory in schools would violate the separation of church and state. Sure enough, all the specific mantras or sacred sounds that were its chosen meditation objects came from Hinduism. Transcendental Meditation was not religiously neutral, even if no one had to convert to Hinduism to practice it. Yet the ambiguous status of TM or of yoga or passage meditation or any of these remains, because the underlying issue is how much and which elements of a traditional practice can be residually continued in new settings and stripped of the original rationales.

Or, take the interesting example of yoga and its residually religious ambiguity. A course on yoga taught in the religion department cannot require students to perform the postures, for this would violate church-state separation binding on a public university. But yoga in the physical education department is a two-credit activity course, offered side by side with badminton and aerobics. It is not religious, not in violation of any constitutional prohibition. Meanwhile, young American Hindus (children of Indian immigrants) now run a program called Take Back Yoga, to reclaim it as an expression of a religious philosophy. I believe there is absolutely no point in trying to determine once and for all whether yoga is "really religious." But it does make a difference, because yoga as a two-credit class is a practice in a different sense than is yoga as an ancient wisdom technology. It is foolish to conflate them entirely and assume the benefits of the latter will automatically appear within the confines of the former.[16]

Yoga and passage meditation are at best loosely linked with recent definitions for spirituality. They might fit within Principe's definition— in fact, they certainly would—but he could not have imagined either as equivalent to badminton. He would have imagined yoga or concentrative meditation as equivalent to some of the prayer practices found in the middle rooms of *The Interior Castle*, part and parcel of someone's chosen religious ideal. From another point of view, the phys ed student who takes yoga over badminton may have made a decision based on beliefs about how difficult each will be or how much out-of-class time is required. Both yoga and badminton are practices in MacIntyre's sense, as phys ed skills. But the student's decision between the two is not based on willingness to commit to a chosen religious ideal.

In contemporary reflection and engagement with spirituality, we are long past Principe. The right question may be how these practices— developed to serve very well-articulated chosen ideals—serve to enhance spirituality when spirituality itself is defined so as to make it inescapable. If we practice passage meditation, yoga, or anything similar, the implicit promise is that these can help us to become the kind of spiritual persons Teresa or Patanjali, the father of yoga, hoped to form. But this may be a false hope, for we have seen how difficult it is to discover even whether the virtues endemic in practices are still present, carried over in the techniques described in *Spirit, Science and Health*. Passage meditation looks like an attenuated or residual version of divine reading, the receptive prayerful attention to the texts of Scriptures. But we cannot say that this qualifies it as a discipline of the spiritual life. Nor can we say that justice, honesty, humility, and courage are still important in learning it. Yes, something is still retained when yoga is learned in a phys ed class, but it is likely to be identical with what is learned in practicing how to take any college class (coming on time, paying attention, completing assignments properly). What differentiates recital of the Twenty-third Psalm as Teresa of Avila may have experienced it with her Carmelite sisters from the practice of passage meditation is harder to determine. I am inwardly convinced that some residual benefits remain in passage meditation, perhaps due to the presence of the divine Spirit in the words of these texts themselves. But the residual elements of a practice are hardly guaranteed to produce the original results.

One could learn to kayak in a large swimming pool. One could certainly learn the arm motions for different paddle strokes. But beyond this, to paddle in a swimming pool is an inadequate method. A swimming pool has no current, no rocks or hidden logs, and, if it is indoors, no wind. The analogy should be clear. We have a range of wonderful traditional practices. We have a vague, generic, and decontextualized understanding of spirituality. The well-intentioned contributors to contemporary spirituality wishing to adapt wisdom technologies may be paddling in a swimming pool.

CHAPTER THREE

Virtues and Values of Spirituality

The Debate over Values

So far, our discussion of learning to be spiritual and of the virtues embedded in the very concept of practice has been focused on individuals and their intentions. We have seen how certain virtues are built into the basics of a practice, even if these are rarely mentioned in discussions of spirituality. Unfortunately, the language of values is often oversimplified, as are the categories of religion versus spirituality. For some advocates of spirituality, it is religion that is filled with dos and don'ts, with rules and prohibitions. Religious values, then, have little to do with what is intrinsically natural and beneficial for people as individuals and a lot to do with impulse control and the power of an institution to restrict behavior. Spirituality, however, encourages us to follow our own inner wisdom and exhibit compassion and forgiveness. Spirituality's virtues are not rule based; they flow from our own deepest nature, which will provide sufficient ethical guidance to make religion's elaborate codes unnecessary. "Religion is about creeds, rituals and dogmas. Spirituality is more a state a being."[1] Those who oppose this kind of thinking equate the human potential movement, New Age, and spirituality with antinomianism, selfish narcissism, and an ethic that begins and ends with the Nike slogan, "Just do it!" This debate preceded the current flowering of spirituality—but not by much. And it has not by any means been settled. Even at a recent scholarly conference, accusations of "narcissism" versus "dogmatism" flew back and forth among participants, illuminating mean-mindedness more than anything else. The arguments and accusations flew, but little was accomplished. When conducted on these terms, this debate seems as unresolvable as that over the status of yoga. It is a challenge to get beyond the dreary exchange of charges and countercharges.

As we saw in chapter 1 when we looked at the language of inner human potentials and true self in the contemporary definitions of spirituality, we found the language of humanistic psychology, which bequeathed imagery of growth and the assumption of an invisible harmony of all individual goals. These together substitute for sustained ethical reasoning, according to Browning, and this limit continues to plague all who use this language uncritically. While they precede the flowering of spirituality as a separate category, the terms of the debate also continue, relatively unchanged. For the enormous effects of this vision of the self and its growth included pervasive adoption of expressive individualism as the primary language Americans use to reflect on their lives and choices. This is individualism guided not by external material goals or by commitment to a chosen external ideal but by the self's own feelings and desires.

The debate over values took its contemporary shape in a famous, widely discussed study by sociologist Robert Bellah and associates, *Habits of the Heart.*[2] By 1985 the middle-class, white Americans interviewed by Bellah used this "first language" of expressive individualism to explain themselves. A choice or decision was justified because it "felt right," it enhanced a sense of self, or it furthered personal "growth." No other reasons were offered or believed necessary by many of Bellah's interviewees. People made choices, held onto commitments, fulfilled obligations. We were not, in that sense, a nation of narcissists. But we could not explain even to ourselves why we did what we did, except that at the time it felt okay or "natural" or furthered our self-actualization. Those who emerged from Bellah's interviews were people who believed that their self-actualization drew them into certain situations and directions, and so, for now, that is where they headed. By next year, they would perhaps be drawn elsewhere, and they had no coherent way to defend or debate the grounds for anything. So, if one of Bellah's subjects had divorced and remarried, there was no particular guarantee that he or she would not, in the future, once again divorce or decide to return to the first spouse. Or live as a hermit in the woods or move back with his or her parents. "Self-actualization," expressive individualism, and "feelings" were the only moral vocabulary available. As Bellah comments on one of his subjects, "His choices are without any more solid foundation than his momentary desires. He lacks a language to explain what seem to be the real commitments of his life, and to that extent his commitments themselves are precarious."[3]

According to Bellah, this language was not nearly sufficient to anchor and honor our real and abiding commitments. To many readers, expressive individualism did boil down to narcissism, a kind of self-worship that left a trail of broken promises, betrayals, and abandonments in its wake. In contrast, the sociologists somewhat reluctantly admitted that the evangelical Christians interviewed for the same study did try to ground their lives in principles, not emotions, and were able to articulate a code of conduct that could endure over time. It was limited and privatized, but it included a second language of obligations beyond the self.[4]

This book prompted a huge amount of debate in 1985. Advocates and opponents of spirituality inherit this discussion. For instance, Robert Fuller in *Spiritual but Not Religious* tries to refute the charge of narcissism by offering a clinical reinterpretation of narcissism's meaning.[5] This is irrelevant to Bellah's original claim, which is about ethical reasoning rather than psychiatric diagnosis. Both the language of expressive individualism and the vague sense of its inadequacies are still a topic today. There is a felt need to show how those who are spiritual are indeed good, ethically engaged citizens, even if they do not rely on the teachings of a church or traditional community to tell them how to behave. An excellent example of this kind of anti-Bellah argument is the study by Elizabeth Tisdell of adult educators and activists, *Exploring Spirituality and Culture in Adult and Higher Education*.[6] These people were "spiritual" using a definition similar to those we examined in chapter 1, but Tisdell wants to show how they developed into persons with meaningful social and community commitments over time. They were not "expressive individualists" in Bellah's sense. It galls them and their champions such as Fuller and Tisdell to be told that only the religious have real "values" or to find themselves perceived as hedonists. So they protest, in a manner analogous to the New York City sign that read "Atheists are patriotic!" We do not know, however, whether they really have overcome an issue raised by Bellah, that their language and thought structure are inadequate to validate the actual commitments they have made. This, and not narcissism, was the challenge of his critique. To call these activists and educators spiritual does not by itself solve the underlying problem.

Still another group examined for spirituality, who could challenge Bellah's disrespect for expressive individualism, comprises the artists in Robert Wuthnow's interesting study *Creative Spirituality: The Way of the Artist.*[7] It is apparent that his subjects developed and formed their vocational identity as artists with relatively little direct help from any organized community or tradition. As individuals, they were expressive, but not exactly in the sense Bellah used this term. They were craftspersons; they practiced in the same fashion as do others who learn over time to do something difficult with excellence. Becoming an artist is a relatively lonely practice in America, yet they emerge from Wuthnow's interviews as persons who were intensely focused, hardworking, and able to articulate commitment to their craft. We could examine the case studies here for exemplars of honesty, courage, fairness, and perseverance, the classic practice virtues identified in the previous chapter. These artists did not appear to be narcissists. Probably difficult to live with, yes. While "follow your feelings" may have guided Bellah's interviewees, when one practices a craft (painting, poetry, dance, music), this clearly is not enough, which is decisively confirmed by a guidebook titled *The Artful Journal.*[8] When it comes to spirituality, these authors are definitely expressive individualists à la Bellah. They offer advice for a spiritual journal whose written component has no other rules or standards of excellence but to record feelings, emotions, intuitions of a core spiritual self with no attention to the craft of writing. Yet, when it comes to the visual art that accompanies their journaling, their advice is detailed, specific, and adamant about knowing brushes, paper, and inks. No amount of true self and growth images will teach one how to select the right kind of ink for specific textures of paper. There is a technical craft to be mastered, and, as do Wuthnow's artists, the *Artful Journal* authors take this very seriously. (Poets who craft language carefully might object that these authors treat writing as analogous to a child's finger painting.) The artful journal that results is a mix of expressive individualist prose and technically adept visual designs.

Here let us notice an interesting feature of both Tisdell's activists and Wuthnow's artists: almost every one of them was raised religious and was influenced by religious training, even though few continued to practice actively the religion in which they were raised. Their histories include some very tortured as well as some positive engagements with their religions of origin. By the time they were interviewed, in midlife, they had come to terms with this strand of their past and in the majority of cases would be considered among the spiritual but not religious. Tisdell and Wuthnow find that spirituality suffices to empower and motivate these persons; religion was no longer useful or necessary to provide a language or container for their deepest commitments. They believed that they had preserved a sense of values and virtues from it, linked to their adult chosen ideals.

But an alternative interpretation is possible. Perhaps what we called "residual religion" continues to work. Religion is much more than just a source of dos and don'ts, and both Tisdell and Wuthnow recognize its deeper power to organize a coherent set of symbols to portray the cosmos. Tisdell carefully explores how the activists' culture and upbringing shaped their current spirituality. The residual religion approach suggests that this may be a case of persons living off the past, just as a once-wealthy institution now depends upon its endowment for daily income. Some of their stated values, such as justice for the impoverished, seem to derive not from where they are now but from where they once were: in short, from religion and not directly from spirituality in and of itself, at least not as guided by its contemporary definitions. Residual is not nothing, but eventually it will wear off and be superseded by the environment and culture in which a new generation is actually raised. If these newbies (Gen Y? Millennials?) were raised by the persons in Bellah's study, for whom expressive individualist language sufficed for their ethical discourse, they will not have even what abandoned religion provided as their heritage. We are left wondering how powerful will residual religion remain and how long can spirituality secretly feed off it.

These studies of activists and artists do offer a challenge to those who equate spirituality with selfish flightiness pure and simple (narcissism in everyday speech). While both groups' engagement in life work that centered on practices in MacIntyre's sense may have resulted in gains in honesty (humility), courage, fairness, and perseverance, these are not the virtues being claimed by those who want to use artists or activists as models of spirituality. At times both groups do sound a bit more like Bellah's interviewees than their advocates, Tisdell and Wuthnow, want to admit.

Residual religion may prove a tricky category. If what remains after belief and communal worship and many of its specific rules and prohibitions are abandoned is a sense of other values, such as compassion for the homeless or a love of symbols, we do not know what else continues residually. We do not know whether different styles of "residual-ness" result from different religions of origin. Maybe residual Jewishness works very differently from the residual Catholicism in Tisdell's own history. There may also be residual political involvement, such as in the case of some members of my family who are descendants of dedicated (if unsuccessful) late-Victorian revolutionaries. This is, at least, a category that points us toward the biographies and legacies of individuals and their communities, while the definitions of spirituality ignore these in favor of an atemporal, universal human core. Just as a category of practice includes built-in virtues, residual religion includes some built-in assumptions about generations and their impact through time. But at least one knows more or less where to start looking for it. With spirituality, even after reading Tisdell and Wuthnow, we are never quite sure.

Compassion and Forgiveness
Spirituality's Intrinsic Virtues?

If we subtract the residual religion from spirituality, what remains? We need to inquire what values and virtues, if any, are embedded into spirituality in itself or can be claimed to belong to spirituality in the same way that fairness, honesty, and courage are embedded into practice or that humility was embedded in St. Teresa of Avila's version of the life of prayer. Possible candidates might be openness to new experiences (linked to a sense of connection, perhaps) or access to one's own inner states and feelings (since connectedness seems to be more about inward experience than actual bonds to external objects). Curiously, however, the two virtues repeatedly mentioned in conjunction with spirituality seem to have very little to do with these themes or to the practice dimension at all. These virtues are compassion and forgiveness. The Dalai Lama is cited as the authority for why these two are intrinsic to spirituality,[9] while values such as obedience to authority and dogma are supposedly intrinsic to religion. There is a certain irony when this world-class religious figure is cited as a champion of universal human spirituality ("which brings happiness to self and others") as opposed to oppressive and retrograde religion—although what he originally meant and the point of his remarks is lost in this use of his words. What matters is that compassion and forgiveness are spoken of, with the same admiring glow that surrounds spirituality. Compassion sounds Buddhist, forgiveness sounds Christian, but for those who wish to sever spirituality from religion, these associations are accidental or even misleading. I have found no good, coherent defense of the high place given to these virtues while other virtues are, by contrast, neglected, at least in conjunction with spirituality. It would take an even greater figure than the Dalai Lama to make a case for the importance of purity, chastity, and honor, for example, for contemporary spirituality.

Let us look at a serious attempt to define or discuss compassion and forgiveness in this context of spirituality's virtues and values. This close analysis will show up some of the problems both with selecting these virtues in isolation from others and with their expressive individualist definitions. According to Amy Wachholtz and Michele Pearce, compassion is "awareness of another's pain . . . a feeling of kindness . . . a desire to alleviate the suffering and doing what is within one's power and ability to allieviate the suffering."[10] Forgiveness is also defined using feeling language: "the replacement of negative emotions of unforgiveness by the positive, love-based emotions such as empathy, compassion, sympathy and affection for the offender."[11] These are about as detailed an account of these two outstanding spirituality virtues as can be found. And, to be blunt, they are utterly awful as definitions. They are all about feelings, desires, emotions. We feel compassion and we feel forgiving, and that is what these terms are all about. In the above definitions, however, there are some other terms, which have to be included as incidentals, almost. *Suffering* and *offender* seem to be unavoidable parts of what these concepts mean, but their relation to our feelings is truly obscure here. The authors of this essay assume that compassion is an intuitive, simple, and direct experience with an organic, neurological origin, not overlaid by any intellectual framing whatsoever.[12] They obviously try to do the same for forgiveness, which becomes a kind of cousin to compassion. This approach justifies their suppression of the intellectual content that these two virtues require in order to be understood.

Here we have the intrusive influence, like it or not, of the language Bellah labeled "expressive individualism," in which the central terms are our inner feelings and awareness and emotional states, now backed up by brain research. Bellah would cringe at these definitions, which sound just like the interviews with his 1985 psychotherapists ("feelings of unforgiveness," for example). Compassion and forgiveness, both profoundly transactional realities, require some language of relationships and simply cannot be understood solely with reference to one individual's inner feelings. Nor are they so intuitive-instinctive as to be precognitive and transcultural, as these authors want to maintain. Since spirituality for them is a universal human given, so too its central virtues must be primordial and universal.

If these feeling-based definitions are inadequate, a transactional definition offers the best contrast. Compassion—"feeling with"—assumes at least two parties. One, at least, is suffering. What is suffering? Suffering

may be a lack, a loss, a distorted experience of reality, or just plain physical pain. But it is something, and person A suffers. (Or sentient being
A, if one is Buddhist.) Person B comes along and is indeed aware of
person A's suffering. "I feel your pain," he says and walks on. No, true
compassion moves the observer, person B, to some vow or action, moving toward A and doing whatever is believed to help A. Those who hope
to evoke compassion know how to make the action simpler—click the
mouse, and your donation to earthquake relief will be made automatically—or to make the vivid in-your-face reality of person A's suffering
more apparent. For example, a close-up picture of a child with a hare-
lip in an ad for a charitable foundation assumes the viewer can both
imagine how the child is shunned and humiliated because of his or her
appearance and will not join in bullying and rejecting the child. (In
some cultures, this would not be the expected knee-jerk response, however. Persons may have been trained to shun or show disgust at the sight
of deformities.)

The expressive individualist definition of forgiveness is even more
woefully wrong. Forgiveness is a complex transaction and requires a
whole background that the authors who define it as "feeling" ignore
completely. First, there must be two parties. One offends the other. We
need to think about what *offend* means here; it could be insult or harm
or intentional harm. This choice depends upon a particular vision of the
human good, a particular standard, violated. The offender is then like
someone who has gone into debt: he or she owes the offended. Or, to use
another image, there is a balance in the world. The offender's action has
upset it, and the basic harmony of all beings has been damaged. To right
this imbalance, to repay the debt, is only just. We need a whole system
of what is right and just operating implicitly to guide our understanding
of what person A, the offender, does to person B. It is understood that
payback is required. Person A owes, person B demands what is owed.
This will restore the balance between them and in the world. But what
happens instead in forgiveness is that Person B decides to relinquish his/
her right to payback. Person B may realize that in the larger balance of
the world, he or she is also already indebted and in no position to grab
for repayment from A. And besides, in that larger vision of balance, it
may be less important to the restoration of harmony for B to get every
bit that is owed than for B and A to live together in peace. (See Matt
18:21-35 for the parable of the Unmerciful Servant, which makes this
point using this imagery of debt.) Or even if A will never experience this
peace (perhaps he or she has died already), some restoration of balance

and harmony is still a greater ideal than payback. And sometimes "70 times 7" signifies that keeping score over details of who was right and who was wrong diminishes everyone.

This is why there are rules about forgiveness as a transaction and disagreements over how to apply them. We are not speaking only of feelings that I feel. The cognitive complexity of forgiveness requires answers to questions such as "When and how can I forgive on behalf of another? Must A, the offender, seem just a little bit sorry before B the offended forgives?" and "Is some expiation—making up for the offense in a visible way—a necessary part of the transaction?" In the most obvious cases, "Does B's forgiveness relieve A of any obligation to return the stolen money?" These rules are real, and their violation may have grotesque and offensive results. I cannot forgive someone for an offense he/she never committed. I may, instead, need to seek forgiveness for my false and biased conviction that someone else was to blame for harming me. A definition by an expressive individualist, based on "feelings," misses these rules completely.

The history of the years since the end of World War II might be a history of how these rules of forgiveness have been hammered out and applied in very public ways. Issues of collective responsibility and collective guilt seem to call for some formal collective apology followed by a plea for forgiveness, if not for an offer of monetary reparations. The Japanese government should have offered an apology to the Chinese for atrocities committed against civilians in World War II. A personal apology—a request for forgiveness—from the Japanese prime minister as an individual fifty years later did not fulfill this obligation (although it was good of him to try). The transaction was not between one individual and another; it was between two nations and therefore required representatives of those nations to restore a sense of justice and balance. Nor did the Japanese expression he adopted, which translates into English as "we ponder deeply," work to convey a sense of debt. Pondering means thinking about, which is not the same as being sorry for. (This was explained to me by a professional translator who worked for Japanese TV and who was outraged by the inadequate wording.)

Or, take the following example of misguided collective guilt accompanied by a plea for forgiveness. A Euro-American woman at a conference came up to a Native American speaker and said, "Oh Mr. X., will you forgive me for the horrible things my ancestors did to your ancestors?" He shrugged her off, no doubt having heard something like this before. A more thoughtful person, hearing later about this request for forgiveness, commented, "It is wrong to act on behalf of ancestors who truly thought they were doing the right thing, and I do not want to betray them by attributing ideas to them which I know they did not hold." She explained how her ancestors had been kicked off their land in Scotland and sent to the west of North America to fight Indians. She was not going to deny this history in order to sound compassionate or apologetic. She clearly believed she owed her ancestors an obligation to understand their plight and point of view. It may be that the governments of the United States or Canada ought to apologize, ought to seek forgiveness—but that is different from a transaction between two sets of privately defined ancestors. This issue is complicated not because our feelings of unforgiveness need to be replaced, but because we need complex moral categories to sort it out at all.

If this sounds ultracritical about the treatment of compassion and forgiveness in the spirituality literature, it is not because these qualities or virtues are unimportant. It is because they cannot stand in isolation—they do not work when squeezed into the language of feelings, when they seem to float without references to the actual settings where spirituality ought to be manifested. Their rootedness in particular traditions and worldviews, including ethical conceptual frameworks, needs to be recovered from the obscurity in which enthusiastic advocates for spirituality and expressive individualist language shroud them. While neither term is as overtly narcissistic as the 1985 emphasis on self-actualization and growth favored by Bellah's study subjects, the way they are understood today is reductionist in the pattern of *Habits of the Heart*. Once again, this does not mean that the people who employ this language of feelings are selfish, immature, or negligent toward others. But the source of these positive character and behavioral attributes may not be spirituality; it may lie elsewhere—probably in the practice virtues of their crafts or in their residual religion.

Spirituality and Virtues' Opposites
Vices in Contemporary Spirituality

A complete discussion of virtues ought to include vices as well. The obvious opposites of compassion and forgiveness, cruelty and resentfulness, are conspicuously absent from discussions of spirituality's virtues. Instead, other vices are featured, which themselves reveal some of the underlying values of the authors better even than do the virtues of compassion and forgiveness.

We may note how spirituality in most of the definitions depends on a concern for inwardness, for one's own personal sense of meaning and connectedness. Some advocates of spirituality express this as care of "soul," language borrowed explicitly from the writings of Thomas Moore, a follower of Jungian archetypal psychology.[13] Soullessness would be the corresponding vice. Although it is rarely attended to in this direct a fashion, the quality of soullessness here would signify exclusive concern with appearances and externals, a character oblivious to the deeper purposes and meanings and humanity of others, and perhaps an obsession with material success at the expense of all else. These people would not necessarily be narcissists or sociopaths or cruel, at least not intentionally. But they would be tone-deaf to any of the concerns raised by advocates of spirituality. They would measure themselves and others by the brands of their clothes, cars, and electronic gear; they would value noise and speed over beauty and harmony. They would be T. S. Eliot's "hollow men." Or Tolstoy's Ivan Ilych, who in dying recognized that his entire life had been a lie.

But there actually is not much attention paid to them, not in the case studies and examples and personal narratives that constitute much of the spirituality literature. It is taken for granted that we all know persons like these. They are selfish and without any real inner self. Sometimes they appear ludicrous, as in the case of the man who regularly orders a $300 glass of wine but complains about it. They are not, however, the subject of diatribes or warnings or admonishments. Sometimes the attitude toward them is almost a vague pity. We should note that even some of Bellah's more blatant expressive individualists did not approach this level of soullessness.

No, the main attention to vices is to a different set of qualities. The most frequently mentioned negative qualities are intolerance, rigidity, self-righteousness, and authoritarianism. These negative characteristics are, no surprise, frequently associated with religion. Indeed, for authors such as Ian Mitroff and Elizabeth Denton, religion is in essence about these qualities and cannot grow beyond them.[14] But one may also say that these are the qualities that make for bad work colleagues and unpleasant neighbors and companions, and they are even linked to the personality of domestic abusers. They are attributed to persons with an enormous need for control, especially control over others, who therefore do not seem able to survive well in an environment of constant change and mutuality. Such people are inflexible, unable to tolerate differences and ambiguities, and ultradefensive in the face of any criticism. They invariably place the blame for their own destructive actions on others. For example, an anecdote about leadership focused on the way to cope with an employee who was "a very smart and competent woman who worked hard but also operated within very narrow boundaries. . . . There wasn't any reaching and stretching and flexibility, which . . . is important in working with other people. . . . Her approach was, 'It stops here and then it's your job.'"[15] Sometimes, behind the mask of an unvirtuous person at work, there is a story of how he or she got that way. So, a doctor who abused and tyrannized a nurse in the hospital eventually admitted that he "had grown up in poverty. . . . He admitted that growing up in the streets made him tough and angry and taught him to intimidate people. He was critical and tended to see a half-empty glass, an attitude that spilled over on the nurses."[16] Even more common as examples of the unvirtuous are those labeled "placeholders" by Judi Neal, persons who

> see boundaries instead of possibilities, who are focused on the past instead of the future, who use up resources instead of looking at renewal, and who value doing over dreaming. . . . Placeholders are a drag on organizational energy and are usually the ones who clog the organization's arteries with bureaucratic processes. . . . They will tell you why something cannot be done and will resist change because "we've always done it this way."[17]

We meet persons such as the narrowly focused woman, the abusive doctor, and these placeholders in the pages of writings on spirituality. They are the old-style managers whose corporate superiors cannot figure out how to replace or reassign them. They include the superreligious employees who insist on proselytizing during lunch hour. They are often persons who hold extremely old-fashioned ideas about gender roles and blame those who seem to blur or challenge them. The case histories of how to handle these people sometimes show great insight and compassion (as in the story of the doctor), recognizing that no one becomes this kind of rigid and difficult person overnight. But if there is an evil or negative example, a paradigm of vice, this is it. Often, the judgment is that such persons are fundamentally untransformable. They are who they are and cannot be fit into the newer, more open and flexible ethos of American workplaces or into the current health-care system's demand that patients bear some informed responsibility for their choices.

What characterizes such persons is not just rigidity and authoritarian style but their lack of awareness of themselves and their impact on others. In this they do resemble the soulless person described above, but it is not an innocent unawareness. *Selfish* is really the wrong term. It is not even that they are bigots, although some of them are. It is that they just do not get it, they do not know the current norms of diversity, tolerance, openness, and mutual respect of differences. They belong back in the 1950s, perhaps, when the expectations about work, gender, obedience, and so on seemed to fit their style. This may be a slur on the 1950s, when the concept of the authoritarian personality created by Theodor Adorno flourished—a concept developed to explain the appeal of totalitarian ideologies to otherwise normal persons. All of the above contemporary examples might qualify for Adorno's category. However, the 1950s was an era when norms about work and family seemed relatively set and when people expected that, once their identities were formed in young adulthood, that was the way they would remain. Today's rigid and controlling people might be nostalgic for such an era and try to pretend it can be perpetuated or believe that it ought to be. "We've always done it that way" is their mantra.

The pages of writings on spirituality introduce such characters, and most of us have met these persons too. They can be difficult to work with, worship with, or teach. Sometimes we refer to them as "control freaks," dismissively. But perhaps their real deficiency is their rough edges, their failure to fit in, or perhaps even their loyalty to a set of norms that did work for them earlier in life, as in the case of the abusive doctor. In short, their real vice is failure to conform to American postmodern norms, to what Adorno sixty years ago would have called "democratic values." These are the underlying norms that advocates of spirituality endorse, even when spirituality is introduced explicitly to restore soul and meaning and humanity to our lives and work. We will return to this question when we look at workplace spirituality in particular. One thing is certain: in all discussions of these negative examples of rigid, closed-minded, 1950s-style persons, it is not their lack of humility, their dishonesty, or their cowardice that is primarily criticized. Indeed, these flaws are unmentioned, and there is no reason to believe that these rigid closed-minded people we have described are any more untruthful or cowardly than their critics.

But clearly the person who resists change will be a problem, the square peg and the bane of a workforce constantly required to adapt to fast-paced, unstable situations. His or her opposite is the spiritual person with soul. Yes, maybe the latter is more compassionate and forgiving but also ironically the person who fits in best into a world of continuous adaptation to shifting norms. And although there is no way that bigotry and intimidation and closed-mindedness are desirable qualities in most North American settings today, it could also be that these "unvirtues," when interpreted differently, are a kind of resistance to exactly those soul-consuming features of contemporary life that the spirituality literature itself vigorously condemns.

We may ask, "How do I learn to be spiritual?" But a good answer requires this attention to context, to culture, to what people do (e.g., to what "work identity" means for occupational therapists). Spirituality as an innate universal human capacity does not by itself help to answer the question. We may move toward a practice focus, in which case we will find ourselves imperceptibly closer to a St. Teresa–Principe understanding of spirituality as a conscious effort toward a transcendent ideal. Or we may follow Bellah's interviewees in adopting the language of expressive individualism to venture into issues of virtues and values for which such language is inadequate. We have seen here some of the examples and consequences of that move. To move in positive directions with spirituality as a concept, we will eventually turn to three contexts in which it has gained influence and within which it is expected to fulfill specific, albeit different, hopes.

CHAPTER FOUR

The Intellectual Ecology of Spirituality
Psychology

Intellectual Ecology
Spirituality and Existing Fields of Knowledge

"If Elisabeth Kübler-Ross were working now, she would be doing spirituality, not psychology." And "If William James were working now, he would speak of the *Varieties of Spiritual Experience*, not of religion at all." These two remarks, made by academics at conferences, reveal how spirituality now appears to be the best, most fitting rubric for the work of leading thinkers from the past. Spirituality replaces psychology, and what James really wanted to write on was spirituality, had he but known the term we have today. We will eventually determine why both speakers were mistaken. But the remarks themselves bring home the reality that the boundaries float and flow among psychology, philosophy, and religion as fields of study that have never been clear and obvious. James himself switched fields, after all. Add spirituality to the mix, and this fluidity and porous boundary situation becomes even more complex.

Having looked at the history and some implications of the contemporary concept of spirituality in the first several chapters, we now will examine its emergence using another approach. In these chapters we will probe the fields and disciplines of study within and among which spirituality finds itself as an enterprise and object of study. A biologist can trace the evolutionary history of one species or can look at its ecological niche and its environment, at a configuration of interacting species. While our chapter on definitions did the former, what follows will be closer to the latter approach. Think of this as spirituality's "intellectual ecology." The landscape and environment of knowledge works as a system, and spirituality emerges with its own niches, to participate in this intellectual ecosystem. The current state of this intellectual ecology will show how a possible vacant place recently opened up for spirituality to slip into. It is not enough just to trace the existence of a concept; the ecology analogy reveals how a concept jostles and aligns itself within a complex system of other ideas.

To some, this may be an odd and excessively head-trippy question. Spirituality, like love, is a many-splendored thing, and we should study its variations. As we have already seen, spirituality is so hard to define that ninety-two definitions do not suffice. But now that we have spirituality as a term, we may ask where we put it, by which I mean something like, "Where would a department of spirituality belong in the modern university?" When spirituality was defined by Principe, the answer was clear: it belonged in the religious studies field, adjacent to theology but not within that discipline. But when spirituality is defined by the universal human capacity for meaning and purpose and sense of connection, there is no longer a clear answer. If it could be proposed as the core for occupational therapy as a profession, does that situate it within health sciences, along with physical therapy and nursing? But, if it also looks like psychology, philosophy, and religion, it belongs back in liberal arts, alongside English and classics. Maybe spirituality is a concept so intrinsically interdisciplinary that it "belongs" many places. Maybe the best parallel would be a field such as Asian studies, which draws on the methods and expertise of many departments (languages, history, literature, religion, etc.) because the "what" of the content is too complex to be fully understood by any one method or field.

In these chapters, we do not offer such a home nor propose such a new academic department as spirituality. What we do is look at three fields or disciplines that already shifted or changed in certain ways so as to make vacant territory and possible ecological niches for spirituality. These three are psychology, particularly personality theory and counseling; religion study as an academic discipline; and the sociology of religion. The changes within each field are specific to that field, arising out of its practitioners' responses to intellectual and cultural developments. There is no one process by which spirituality gained ground at the expense of everything else. There are, however, particular developments within psychology, religious studies, and sociology of religion as intellectual enterprises that have worked to enhance and expand possible roles for spirituality. To use our ecological image, a prolonged cold period kills off native flowers but allows for new growth better adapted to chillier weather. In response to long-term relative stability, insects gradually adapt their body shapes for optimum feeding on these new species, thus leaving new opportunities for other species to feed off their second-choice plants. The topic of our chapters is a challenging one, and this ecological image may help make it less abstract.

But does human knowledge really form a system of this kind? At any particular time in history, it looks that way. But this may be an illusion. What counts as a discipline, an academic area of study, has changed over the centuries—these days, over the decades. Medieval medical school education included astrology, considered necessary for an understanding of the workings of the human body influenced by the configurations of the stars. The modern university, with its many separate departments and division between undergraduate and graduate degrees, originated in Germany and spread in this country at around the beginning of the last century. While students today study and major in psychology, sociology, and criminal justice, these fields as disciplines carved out niches and territories all within the last 150 years. Newer fields within arts and sciences include computer sciences, cognitive neuroscience, and environmental studies, as well as area studies. It would be wonderful if we could claim that the current array of departments and disciplines somehow exactly mirrors reality in the natural and social worlds, but most academics recognize this realist conception as naïve. There are lots of alternative ways to slice the pie, and the news bureau of my university just released a story about the "emergent field" of crisis response management.

However, the whole curriculum does present itself as a system, a totality, in which each unit has its niche. Now, when Principe wrote "Toward Defining Spirituality" back in 1983, his proposal for level-three study of traditional guides and manuals for monastics could have been the mandate for an academic specialization in the study of Christian spirituality inserted into an existing religious studies program. Sure enough, something just like this was founded by Sandra Schneiders in the 1980s at the Graduate Theological Union (GTU) in Berkeley. It is grounded in a view of the subject very similar to Principe's 1983 definition. Bruce Lescher and Elizabeth Liebert's anthology, *Exploring Christian Spirituality*, written in Sandra Schneiders' honor, celebrates the achievement of a program in the academic study of Christian spirituality in a first-rate graduate theological institution.[1] This program, while it looks as traditional as Principe by contrast with other more recent perspectives on spirituality, was actually innovative in one respect. Theological education is divided into set areas, such as biblical studies, church history, and theology. The GTU program was not housed under theology but within history of religions, making it more historical/descriptive than philosophical/normative. At least according to the contributors to the Lescher and Liebert volume, this opened up the study of spirituality to methods from sociology, psychology, and other disciplines (which Principe advocated) while not excluding theology. Moreover, students are required to take some courses in non-Christian spiritualities as part of their program of study. This shows the intention of Dr. Schneiders and her colleagues to move spirituality study toward the study of world religious traditions and away from doctrinally defined Catholic theology. But, based on the current catalog, it is clear that Christian spirituality as an academic discipline at GTU is located in the field of religion graduate education. It is not within psychology or history or health professions. Indeed, Schneiders' GTU program serves as a clear example of an intellectual activity firmly niched among existing fields, precisely because, like Principe, Schneiders specified what it should include and where the students could look for materials to begin level-three study (using Principe's definition). The ecology of knowledge at any particular time has enough structure so that boundaries are possible, because there are real centers to each field of study.

Based on this view of intellectual ecology and the academic environment as a system, we may ask where any sustained examination of spirituality as meaning and connectedness belongs and what research methods and standards of excellence are needed to authorize its intellectual credibility and coherence. It would border some already-established fields or disciplines. Perhaps it should be in a humanities division, along with fields that primarily study and interpret texts using qualitative methods. Or maybe it lies closer to psychology, which claims to be the scientific study of behavior. Or maybe it belongs in health education, leadership studies, education, nursing . . . Do not even think that a thorough examination of "the world itself" can yield any answer to this. The question is about intellectual inquiry and methods, the lenses through which we systematically know.

Hufford provides an answer of a sort. That is, the whole literature on spirituality, in particular the spirituality and health focus, is too poorly grounded to be located at all. Hufford, writing for the Metanexus Institute, reviewed an immense amount of material and wondered to which community of scholars is this literature accountable. In spite of the enthusiasm over the topic, this work "has almost no scholarly infrastructure," and this in itself is a "serious weakness in the S/RH [spirituality/religion and health] field."[2] Contributors to this area have been too impatient to learn the relevant methods and theories of any field and so make do with naïve or discredited understandings of many basic ideas. We therefore cannot look for any well-grounded discussion of how spirituality intersects with better conceptual frameworks from adjacent fields or even for recognition of what constitutes adjacent. Hufford's critique does not make spirituality like the study of astrology in the medieval medical curriculum, for that did have some intelligible rationale within the knowledge of the time. Hufford makes spirituality as a current topic more like a possible course on astrology today cross-listed between astronomy and psychology: intellectually incoherent.

Hufford's answer is more negative than ours. There are some adjacent niches, and even if spirituality as a topic itself lacks "scholarly infrastructure," the nearby fields from which it has emerged to find adaptive niches can be specified and examined. Yet he has a point. If spirituality is celebrated as a "recent discovery," the links between it and psychology, religion study, and sociology will be missed or dismissed. Kübler-Ross and William James will be colonized or co-opted into its territory, regardless of what disciplinary identity they adopted at the time.

The Farther Reaches of Psychology

Psychology as the science of behavior is a creation of the twentieth century. Sigmund Freud's *The Interpretation of Dreams* was published in 1900, and Wilhelm Wundt opened his psychological laboratory in 1902. Both claimed the identity of scientist, and both models for the scientific study of the human psyche have had enormous influence. Although Freud was not a "psychologist," his work helped to form that branch of the emergent science known as personality theory and has served as a foundation for the professions of psychoanalyst, clinical psychologist, and counselors of all types. Meanwhile, Wundt's lab gave way to John B. Watson's behaviorism, then B. F. Skinner's version of this model, and experimental psychology became even more firmly lodged in academic departments across the United States. We do not have to review here how enormous this enterprise is, how many persons are involved in it, and how much time and money is spent on it. Psychology as a fixture of the current intellectual environment flourishes and will continue to do so for the foreseeable future. Intrinsic to its success has been its claim to be "science," as well as its connection to the applied professions of counselor, clinician, and so on. Other professionals, such as pastors, social workers, and educators, studied some psychology and used its models of human behavior in their work. In addition, psychology contributed to American society by creating standardized I.Q. tests, diagnostic instruments (such as the *DSM-IV,* etc.), and less formal methods, such as writing Advice to Mothers columns for magazines.

This success did not mean that the practitioners of psychology stopped fighting among themselves over who really was more scientific and which models of their discipline should triumph. Along with these intellectual debates went the fervor that this field was going to make a difference. Whether from the laboratory to the schoolroom or from the clinician's office to the home, psychology would provide understanding and guidance that would influence humans and society for the better. In the confident words of Perry London, writing in 1964, "Finding out what men are like will go a long way towards determining for us what we should try to make them be like."[3] The psychotherapist should be guided by "the dictates of his science," and this will lead to the betterment of all. When we know human nature scientifically, we will be able to determine what is possible, and this is an unshirkable obligation of psychologists. "The upshot is that as work progresses, we come closer and closer to an understanding of the nature of man, always assured that, as our propositions gain accuracy, they differ somewhat from their forerunners and will be revised yet again by later, better tests. . . . Even now, we might scientifically describe man as follows: . . ."[4] It does not matter what specifically follows or what London thought a scientific view of human nature was like. It is clear that for him psychology's role was to discover this, inform all of us, and provide guidance so as to shape our behavior. Psychologists who denied that they had such a moral obligation or claimed that there was no ethical imperative tied to their profession were shirking their valid role in society. Psychologists were to be the "Saving Guild"[5]—not because of personal wisdom or charisma or divine guidance, but because they were scientists.

London's words may have sounded like hubris even back in 1964, but they express the uncritical, unbounded optimism that now, and only now, do we all really have a chance to learn "what men are like." Accumulated ideas over the past thousands of years, when humans have pondered this question, simply do not count at all. They were not arrived at by scientific tests; they reflect biases and ignorance, not true knowledge. Knowledge is what psychology as a science alone can provide. From this view, it would confuse things to say that Aristotle or St. Teresa were "really" psychologists, because they did not study human nature scientifically. London ruled out of the "Saving Guild" anyone who lived before the twentieth century and who could not claim the legacy and intellectual niche of scientist. Maybe London did not speak for the entire profession, but he surely expressed a solid vision of psychology and psychotherapy as scientific and prescriptive, a vision very widely shared.

This is why such nonscientist types as pastors and social workers and teachers could all feel that the study of psychology was relevant and helpful for them in their own work. Seward Hiltner, a leader in the pastoral counseling movement of the 1940s and 1950s, championed psychologies and psychotherapy methods such as that of Carl Rogers in particular. Hiltner argued,

> What we want to suggest is that the kind of psychological understanding which is relevant to pastoral counseling is a social psychology of personality in movement, moving and being moved, motivated and being motivated, operating as a unit on a human social level. . . . We are simply distinguishing the kind of psychology that has something obviously to do with personality as we view it in the light of the pastor's counseling concerns.[6]

It was "obvious" to Hiltner that perspectives from personality theory, bolstered by science, could aid the pastor whose counseling was vital to his "shepherding" role. (In 1949, when this was written, the pastor was always "he.") Hiltner wrote with a great deal of integrity; his counseling pastor could never have been mistaken for a Rogerian therapist. Less attention to this distinction is shown by this quotation from a second-generation expert in pastoral counseling: "Pastoral counseling is the utilization, by a minister, of a one-to-one or small group relationship to help people handle their problems of living more adequately and grow toward fulfilling their potentialities. This is achieved by helping them reduce the inner blocks which prevent them from relating in need-satisfying ways."[7] The problems of parishioners or counselees used as both authors' examples are not religious and are best called "problems in living." They are not medical problems, although it is clear that pastors do not try to counsel persons with major psychiatric conditions. There is a discussion of referrals and community resources in Hiltner's book.[8] This kind of pastoral counseling was done by a clergyperson who could look to psychology, borrow its insights and methods, and share London's confidence that psychology offered real scientific information.

Since that era, there have been several relevant shifts, so that London's words today sound absurdly naïve and overblown. First, protests were voiced against the reductionist model of human nature that dominated both Freud and behaviorism, the two most popular alternatives midcentury. Both of these visions of who we are seemed inadequate; they seemed to eliminate freedom and higher capacities or to explain these away by invoking basic biological instincts. Frankl's meaning-based personality theory (attached to his logotherapy) is an instance of this approach. Surely something got left out in more conventional psychologies, something vital for understanding the fullness of human nature. These theorists all wanted to retain their identification with psychology as science, but with what Maslow called an "expanded science": "new developments in psychology are forcing a profound change in our philosophy of science, a change so extensive that we may be able to accept the basic religious questions as a proper part of the jurisdiction of science, once science is broadened and redefined."[9] Or, "man has a higher and transcendent nature, and this is part of his essence, i.e. his biological nature."[10] Maslow firmly believed that an expanded science could do justice to the existence of this higher nature and would open up the farther reaches of human nature for study.

But Maslow wants an expanded science, not a new and separate area of study detached from psychology's main identity as a science. This was the founding hope of the third force (his term) of humanistic psychology as a movement. This hope was not so clear in the fourth force of transpersonal psychology, proposed by Charles Tart. Here, as early as 1975, we find the claim that conventional psychology "fails to deal adequately with human experience in the realm we call the spiritual, that vast realm of human potential dealing with ultimate purposes, with higher entities, with God, with love, with compassion, with purpose."[11] Here we have all the language of contemporary spirituality. Tart gathered these terms together, as if in a package; today the package unwraps to constitute the various definitions of spirituality. But note how this collection was gathered up into an expanded psychology, a science that overcomes the limits of Western cultural assumptions about consciousness and normality.[12] To this end, however, Tart enlists the "mystical traditions" of the world and the disciplines they include and asks his contributors to "present their spiritual disciplines as psychologies."[13] What really stands out in Tart's volume is this claim that psychology did not start with Freud and Wundt; it can be "expanded" back to include *Visuddhimagga*, a traditional Buddhist text on meditation, and yoga. London would have been outraged, because scientific method no longer seems to count. To him it would appear that Tart "expanded" or simply jettisoned it in favor of prescientific, untested, and dogmatic systems of the sort psychology was expected to replace. By London's standard, the author of *Visuddhimagga* was no more a psychologist than was St. Teresa, and it is ridiculous to breach the boundary between science and religion in this fashion.

Tart tries to have his cake and eat it too. Psychology is still the category, but its contents and options are no longer bounded by Western cultural assumptions, and therefore any coherent theory of human nature that includes the spiritual realm can be entertained as a psychology as if it were placed alongside Freud or Skinner. It proved precarious for psychologists to stretch science this far. But this is still stretching an existing discipline.

Meanwhile, another thinker, James Hillman, wanted psychology to sever itself totally from science. Or rather Hillman wanted his own reinterpretation of Jungian personality theory and therapy to avoid assimilation into conventional theories, medical models, and any connection with London's style of progressive science. Hillman's *Re-Visioning Psychology*, which appeared just around the same time as Tart's anthology, kicks "archetypal psychology" (his term) right out of social and behavioral science and into something closer to classics, comparative literature, and religion.[14] This, in hindsight, proved unsustainable. Pastors and social workers, not to mention psychotherapists, need that tie with science if their psychologies are going to be credible at all. Otherwise, in spite of the Hiltner legacy, pastors might just as well return to traditional in-house Christian resources for counseling and forgo Rogers, Freud, or any other psychologists. And indeed, this return to Christian resources for counseling marked the 1970s and 1980s.[15]

However, these developments show discontent with mainstream models of psychology as the science of behavior and with mainstream personality theory because they left out the spiritual realm, the farther reaches of human nature. While all the efforts to rectify this that we have mentioned still ground themselves in psychology, the shape of that discipline was to be remolded. With changes in psychology came openings and vacancies that now can be filled by something no longer psychology, called spirituality. All the vocabulary now employed in defining spirituality ninety-two or more times was already available on the edges of Maslow's and Tart's expanded psychologies.

It awaited a newly available ecological niche. That is what happened next.

Remedicalized Psychology and Vacated Space

The kind of psychological help Hiltner gave certainly is still delivered by pastors. But psychotherapy and counseling itself has changed. Psychiatry "remedicalized" in the 1970s with the introduction of new drug therapies and has been more and more medicalized ever since. This has impacted on the work of all varieties of counselors. Many of the depressed parishioners seen by Hiltner would now be diagnosed as suffering from a medical problem, clinical depression, or bipolar disorder, and therefore would be referred to a medically trained specialist. Those who were addicted would also be referred, perhaps to a medical rehabilitation program, although perhaps also to AA. As psychiatry and psychology remedicalized, they also "rescientificalized." Meanwhile, spectacular new medical technologies of brain imaging helped draw psychologists and psychotherapists toward neurology (Freud's original medical specialty, somewhat ironically), whether they themselves were trained in medicine at all. Contemporary cognitive neuroscience is a branch of psychology that did not exist in Hiltner's, Maslow's, or Tart's day, and it has become the hottest subfield in my university's psychology program. Meanwhile, more cognitive models of behavior change reshaped the kind of behaviorism derided by Maslow and Tart.

Drug treatments and cognitive neuroscience and behavioral therapies all claim a scientific status to which Freud and Rogers aspired but never achieved. These new approaches could be assessed, positively or negatively, for their effectiveness (and their cost-effectiveness). They are tied to medical research, brain imaging, pharmacology, and the like. This is the prominent psychology model of today—and presumably of the future. Even if what counselors actually do does not always correspond to this, realigning with science and medicine has shifted the shape of psychology. The more this is highlighted, the further away it appears from what pastors who read Hiltner's book could really feel competent to master. Not only would they would now refer a good many of the persons whom Hiltner counseled; today's pastoral counselors are far more likely to be private-practice specialists, whose work situation and setting resemble those of a secular therapist. They will be influenced by exactly the trends, models, and scientific ideals that have revisioned psychology overall.

As psychiatry and psychology remedicalized, the practice of more traditional insight psychotherapy itself came under scrutiny for its claim to be both scientific and a source of moral insight (to be the "Saving Guild" in London's indecently arrogant phrase). For London, psychotherapies should or could be based on facts about human nature that could be discovered using scientific research methods. Maslow, as we saw, echoed this aim. Even when they wrote in the 1960s this was naïve, and by the next decade this bubble was pricked. The newer view held that psychology as therapy does not start out morally neutral, nor do its theories simply reflect scientifically discovered human nature. These theories depend on certain prior assumptions, values, and claims about the human good that are not directly falsifiable as scientific statements. The work of Don Browning, starting with *The Moral Context of Pastoral Care* and culminating in *Religious Thought and the Modern Psychologies*, demonstrates how psychologies such as Freud's and Rogers' are moral systems that rely on philosophical premises and assumptions psychologists have not clearly grasped or acknowledged. In short, therapies that had looked so scientific were in fact as much moral/philosophical systems as those of the pastors' own religious traditions. Browning's *The Moral Context of Pastoral Care* showed how the heavy reliance on psychologies had actually muted the voices of these traditions in "pastoring." His solution: "We need to rediscover the ancient context in which to place our non-moralistic attitudes. We need to learn that we can afford the luxury of not moralizing only when we have already developed a relatively firm moral outlook."[16]

Psychology needs this moral perspective but does not by itself adequately provide it. Religious traditions, including the sources used by Tart, are not psychologies in disguise; they are needed for some different role, a role that can put our psychotherapies in a firm and more self-aware ethical context.

The Browning critique was principally directed toward Rogerian and other post-Freudian insight therapies, such as those Hiltner advocated. It could and should also be applied to the claims and ideas of cognitive neuroscience, behavioral therapies, cognitive learning theories, and many pharmacological therapies. But as of today, all of these still appear better grounded in science, a claim that in the case of insight therapies appears less and less believable. And if future pastors want to learn an informed version of that "relatively firm moral outlook" they will need, then they had better study more traditional subjects in seminary—such as Principe's or Schneider's kind of spirituality—than focus on psychology.

And with the remedicalization of psychology and psychiatry, that claim of connection with science became even more necessary to psychologists. To be reimbursed by health insurers for treatment of clients and to be intellectually answerable to the community of psychologists matters. To have the proper credentials matters. London was correct that psychotherapists form a "guild," and this is still obviously true today. The space Tart and Maslow tried to open up for higher human nature and a spiritual realm still has an appeal for many persons, including many therapists. But it is not space annexable into the current, freshly scientific models of psychology. It lies vacant, unclaimed, when it is not claimed directly for religious traditions (whether Browning's Christianity or various forms of Buddhism or any others). It is dubious, contested space, and in the current intellectual ecology it has been filled by something called spirituality. The vocabulary was all there in Tart's 1975 *Transpersonal Psychologies*. What is missing now is the connection (however flawed) to science and to the community of psychologists as scientists.

From Psychology to Spirituality?

We began this chapter citing the remark: "If Elisabeth Kübler-Ross were working now, she would be doing spirituality, not psychology." By now we can see where this statement misses an important truth not just about the pioneer in death studies but about disciplinary boundaries and intellectual ecology. Kübler-Ross, when she wrote *On Death and Dying* in 1968, was clearly part of that community of psychotherapists London identified as the "Saving Guild." As a foreigner and a newcomer to the huge Billings Hospital, she may have been something of an outsider, but her professional identity was clear to her and to her readers. As a psychiatrist, she could use the theories and terminology of psychoanalysis with an insider's authority: her book is filled with discussions of "defense mechanisms," "the unconscious," "repression," and so forth.

She has a view of how "acceptance" of one's death is something like a return to "primary narcissism," an idea drawn directly from Freudian thought about infancy.[17] However engaging the case histories and however passionate the moral plea to attend to the experiences of the dying, the book is clearly intended to be an exploration by a psychologically trained expert on the psychology of dying hospital patients. There is, in this stage of her career, almost no attention to further reaches or extraordinary experiences, such as contact with the dead. Kübler-Ross, then, was "doing psychology," showing a solid, unequivocal commitment to psychology as the intellectual framework for the human experience of dying and to psychology as a discipline that had almost completely ignored this experience. Like London, she believed that a scientifically informed portrait of human nature guided her theories and practices.

This is why it does a kind of injustice to her work to say that Kübler-Ross would have opted for spirituality over psychology. At least for the Kübler-Ross of *On Death and Dying*, this is simply not the case. She wanted that community of fellow psychologists and psychiatrists to treat her as one of the guild. In time, she lost interest in this, but her case does, dramatically, reveal a feature of today's spirituality. It is not part of an expanded science, nor is it at home within even a very liberal form of religion. To no community of scholars or practitioners are those who do and study spirituality accountable. This was Hufford's complaint. Instead, it appears that those who follow in the footsteps of Hillman, Maslow, and Tart are now more likely to move beyond any claim to be scientists, to be doing psychology that in some way is answerable to the norms of a scientific discipline. Psychology as a whole has re-embraced science as its identity and therefore diminished the role of theories and practices that do not measure up to scientific standards. Nor has it been unhappy when those who focus on the farther reaches of human nature grab some of this turf for spirituality and opt out of presenting themselves as workers within the community of scientists. As psychology has moved back into closer proximity to medicine and natural science, it has been willing to cede the territory of insight therapies, the spiritual realm, and transpersonal wisdom to someone else. Call it spirituality—it may be a growth industry, but it is no longer psychology. The intellectual ecology has shifted not because of the discovery of spirituality, I believe, but because of factors and forces in psychology's own changing awareness of itself as an intellectual endeavor.

CHAPTER FIVE

The Intellectual Ecology of Spirituality
Religious Studies

Defining Religion

"If William James were working now, he would speak of the *Varieties of Spiritual Experience*, not of religion at all." Like the claim that Kübler-Ross would prefer spirituality to psychology, this one also seems on the surface to have some merit. James' book is filled with case histories and examples of personal experiences, deep, private, and passionate, with ultimate realities. It seems easy to forgo the category of religion altogether and equate what is in James' *Varieties* with what today is labeled spirituality.

Those who agree would be willing to define religion as "to be concerned with faith in the claims of salvation of one faith tradition or another . . . connected with this are religious teachings or dogma, ritual, prayer and so on."[1] Or they would believe that "religion has connotations of institution, ritual, articulation of doctrine, spirituality refers to something which is deeply personal."[2] More negatively, they would contend that "religion was largely viewed as formal and organized. It was also viewed as dogmatic, intolerant and dividing people."[3] Given these perceptions, anything personal and positive will be severed from religion from the start and linked instead to spirituality.

While these perceptions about religion may be based on real frustrations and disappointments, such definitions are very far from the ideas of those whose profession it is to study and reflect upon religion as a phenomenon. None of these definitions, focused on dogmas and organizations, covers the scope of what scholars and researchers would now consider religion. This is another clear case of the lack of scholarly infra-structure. The above definitions of religion simply bypass an extensive body of scholarship that guides the contemporary study of religions and challenges the conventional picture of religion as a formal and organized rigid moralistic system of dogma and rituals. In any study of spiritual-ity's intellectual ecology, this long-term effort by religionists needs to be included, in part because so many of today's spirituality writers are secretly and unconsciously indebted to it.

While the next chapter will deal with sociology focused on the practice of religion in today's society, this one looks at how religion is defined, studied, and interpreted by the academic scholars, including theologians, who consider this their field. What we find is that much of the vocabulary and themes of today's spirituality was actually first pro-posed as the core of religion's true meaning, and, like Tart's list of themes and topics left out of conventional psychology, these ideas form a bundle or package adopted and appropriated by advocates of spirituality. This is not a case of spirituality replacing religion; it is a case of remapping territory so that a perceived new ecological niche is created out of an older landscape. Where there was once one category, multidimensional, there now appear to be two, one positive and glowing, the other dismal, dogmatic, and divisive. But this is partly illusion. The story of spiritual-ity's intellectual ecology in relation to religion in some ways parallels the shifts within psychology that we just charted. The difference here is that today's spirituality drew from psychology what some critics such as Maslow and Tart believed psychology had left out. Here, religionists labored to define and include what spirituality advocates now want to claim as exclusively their own. The imagery of an intellectual ecology with jockeying competitive species can help us trace a rather surprising history, especially surprising to those who assume that spirituality as an entity is a recent discovery.

Enlightenment and Romantic Definitions of Religion's Essence

The discussion of religion's meanings and roles goes back a long way. It is best to begin with the Enlightenment, the eighteenth-century Euro-pean movement that created new models of both religion and the secular. The thinkers of that era lived under the shadow of the seventeenth cen-tury's wars of religion and knew that traditional religion could indeed be intolerant and destructive. The Enlightenment thinkers pondered the question of how to separate what was merely tradition and what was essential and "natural" to human beings, including our religiousness. Perhaps the entire structure of traditional Christian orthodoxy, Catholic or Protestant, was merely an edifice constructed by the superstitious, the ignorant, and the exploitative generations of the past. These thinkers hoped to separate universal, permanent truth from this mess of dogmas, doctrinal disputes, and power-hungry organizations. Not just religion but politics and government were given the same scrutiny.

In a radically Enlightenment manner of asking such questions about everything, the philosopher David Hume wondered: Suppose humans lived the life cycle of some social insects, whose parents die off before the new generation hatches. Each generation then could start afresh, creating from scratch its own forms of government or culture or faith. What would they decide to build?[4] However absurd this is from the standpoint of evolutionary biology, the ideal of a fresh start for each present generation without any image of the past is a powerful one; every teenager has probably grabbed onto something like Hume's fantasy insect-humans. Those insect-humans might end up by oppressing each other, but at least their parents' oppressive forms could never bother them. Meanwhile, the philosopher Immanuel Kant constructed his portrait of *Religion within the Limits of Reason Alone*, which shares Hume's ideal without the insect analogy.[5] A few—about three—basic beliefs such as God the ruler, a moral order, and personal immortality are enough, Kant believed, to re-vision what religion really ought to be. And it ought to stay within these limits if it knows what's good for it. It did not matter that no actual example of such minimalist allegedly natural religion was ever found, for it was the ideal of a clean slate, a tabula rasa, that mattered. In the case of religion, these speculations marked off and celebrated a gap of critical distance between revealed or positive religion (the actual religions people practiced) and an ideal of unoppressive, natural, and rational faith.

Proposals for reasonable and natural religion revitalized actual religion in interesting ways. Deism, the minimalist rationalism that postulated a benign but passive God whose actions ended with creation and who left humans free to become moral and rational beings, was one solution. This God had designed the universe as a watchmaker designs a watch; if done properly, the mechanism keeps going on its own with only an occasional winding. No need then for a lot of interfering miracles, and so there goes one of the conventional orthodox defenses of traditional, biblical religion. Deism looked pretty bare bones ("within the limits of reason alone"), but it could be advocated passionately, as it was by Thomas Jefferson.

These eighteenth-century speculations demonstrate that the quest for a better concept of religion than what lay conventionally in people's minds was already in progress several centuries ago. This quest for, and construction of, "natural religion" embodied the hope to refine, strip away dross, and promote a true and valuable core. This same hope could then be taken up by religion's own advocates and defenders, of whom the most famous was theologian Friedrich Schleiermacher. He tried to reply to those who thought religion was all tradition, dogma, and oppressive superstition. He did this not by paring it down to what could be defended by reason but by relocating the authority and power of religion more dramatically, in tune with German romanticism. In his *On Religion: Speeches to Its Cultured Despisers*, Schleiermacher argues that, beyond all the oppressive and superficial layers, there is a true and universal core for religion deep in the heart of all human beings, in the realm he called "feeling." Schleiermacher's "cultured despisers" are not just followers of Hume and Kant; they may be the intellectual ancestors of today's spiritual but not religious persons. That this book was first published in 1799 shows how long-standing the contention over religion's true essence has been.

Schleiermacher's own response to his intended readers is, somewhat ironically, the original version of what Kourie, Mitroff, and Denton and other spirituality advocates propose as an alternative to religion: "Every superstition shall be alike unholy," he declared, rejecting the traditional arguments, such as those from miracles, used to "prove" Christian doctrines.[6] According to his view, the true essence of religion is "a feeling of absolute dependence," not a set of beliefs or doctrines or ethical principles:

> The whole religious life consists of two elements, that man surrender himself to the Universe and allow himself to be influenced by the side of it that is turned towards him is one part, and that he transplant this contact which is one definite feeling, within, and take it up into the inner unity of his life and being, is the other.[7]

Real religion is the human awareness of and response to that which is ultimate and absolute, a sense of this Universe as a unity, which we intuitively know we depend on for our own finite and limited existence. This Universe need not correspond exactly to the personal anthropomorphic God of the Bible and Christian tradition, "for it is not necessary that the

Deity should be presented as also one distinct object."[8] From Schleier-macher's *Speeches*, one could postulate that a more pantheistic and non-personal divine reality was just as plausible. What should strike us now is how closely his definition resembles Van Ness' definition of spiritual-ity: it is two-poled, and it includes both the sense of the Universe as a coherent whole and our response to it as personal and integrative, mak-ing possible the "inner unity of life and being." Schleiermacher's point is, you only think you can get away from religion, but it is embedded in the deepest core of your being. Yes, you can get away from all those oppres-sive traditional doctrines and structures, but you will not want to throw out the baby with the bathwater.

Religion as feeling is also qualitatively different from what Kant and the Deists hoped for. It is very unlike philosophy. "Were I to com-pare religion . . . with anything it would be with music, which indeed is otherwise closely connected with it. Music is one great whole; it is a special, a self-contained revelation of the world."[9] Music is nonconcep-tual; it evokes emotions and a sense of mystery, beauty, and wonder. It is unifying, says Schleiermacher. Those are the characteristics he finds to belong essentially to religion. We do not ask whether music is conceptu-ally true. It does not exist "within the limits of reason alone."

Schleiermacher's audience was not only the cultured despisers of religion of his subtitle. The other group who must have been influenced by his *Speeches* would have been the orthodox of both Lutheran and Reformed Protestant communions (he later worked to effect a union of these two groups). For them, doctrines and confessions were the norm for what counted as religion. Any form, true or false, was founded on beliefs about God, creation, salvation, and the like. A vague feeling of dependence or of the universe would not do at all. But the Schleier-macher of the *Speeches* was telling them to liven up, to move beyond these rigid limits of understanding. He said in effect that those who iden-tify religion primarily with beliefs and organizations and rituals have already drowned the baby in the bathwater.

William James and Personal Religion

These debates over religion's core or essence did not get settled; they persisted through the nineteenth century. As Ann Taves tells the story in *Fits, Trances and Visions*, religion relocated deep in feelings or extraor-dinary altered states of consciousness was a destabilizing contested force whether in its elite forms (as with the transcendentalists) or its populist expressions (revivalism's huge camp meetings).[10] Taves' concluding figure, who wrote a little more than one hundred years after Schleiermacher, was William James, at work on the same issue. For James, in *The Varieties of Religious Experience*, there are also multiple meanings to religion: institutional, on the one side, and personal on the other.[11] He deliberately chose to focus on the latter, which is both more fascinating to him and more primary. So for James, religion "shall mean for us the feelings, acts, and experiences of individual men in their solitude, so far as they apprehend themselves to stand in relation to whatever they may consider the divine."[12] Feelings and experiences and solitude, not rationally defended beliefs, let alone organizations and rituals, are the core stuff about which people had already been arguing for many generations.

Like Schleiermacher, James has in mind two camps of readers. The first, whom we meet early on, are the skeptical rationalists, the "medical materialists," and those who think that religion is "really" about sex, brain disease, or some other human instinct gone awry.[13] He answers them by arguments that are still vivid and witty to read and philosophically astute. The tests of the value of religion, or of anything, are not about its origin but about its "immediate luminousness, philosophical reasonableness and moral helpfulness."

> St. Teresa might have had the nervous system of the placidest cow, and it would not now save her theology, if the trial of the theology by these other tests show it to be contemptible. And conversely if her theology can stand these other tests, it will make no difference how hysterical or nervously off her balance Saint Teresa may have been when she was with us here below.[14]

So much for medical materialism, which is still with us in new forms today.[15]

But James' other audience is his original Scottish one, which must have been filled with theologically orthodox scholars and clergy who distrusted philosophy and psychology, who distrusted a focus on experience (as did so many in Taves' book), and who probably distrusted Americans. Had they known that James was personally sympathetic to Spiritualism, they would have distrusted him even more. But it was an intrinsic part of his case to insist that real, "firsthand" religion was based on experience, was more individual than collective, and provided the most fascinating witness to the great power and influence of religion on human beings. The enormous collection of vivid cases in James' book testifies to his belief that this is where religion's worth and meaning reside. The choicest examples are the most extreme ones—but how else,

James argues, can one appreciate the power and passion of religion (or of anything)? James did not want to cede religion to the doctrinal theologians; he wanted to keep it fresh, personal, emotional, and firsthand. Indeed, as is well known, one of the weirdest and most unhappy of the case narratives, that of a "French sufferer," comes from James himself.[16]

It is for this reason that James would reject the substitution of *spirituality* for *religion* in the title of his book and the labeling of its contents. He had not yielded religion over to medical materialists, but, even more clearly, he did not want religion to be isolated from personal experience. Reductionists and doctrinalists might both want religion simplified into something easy to box in, defame, or defend. To distill spirituality out of religion would have left the whole enterprise of religion at the mercy of those whose narrow intellectualistic views of proper religion would have killed it off. Yes, James separated firsthand from derivative religion, but they were both religion, and the revitalization of religion would come by reuniting the two, not by leaving the category of religion altogether.

Rudolph Otto and the Holy

Even more central than James for the academic study of religion is Rudolph Otto. In 1911, his *The Idea of the Holy* appears as a kind of update of Schleiermacher's *Speeches* redefinition.[17] For Otto as for Schleiermacher, the temptation to reduce religion to belief and morality had to be countered by establishing some other more basic foundation or essence for it. This he locates in the experience of "the holy," or "numinous," a term now standard in debates over religious experience. The numinous is not a thing or object, yet "it" appears as "other," as frightening and awesome and fascinating. Otto uses Isaiah's temple vision of the Lord enthroned, surrounded by flying seraphs, to illustrate what he means. The seraphs cry:

Holy, holy, holy is the Lord Almighty,
The whole earth is full of his glory. (Isa 6:3)

And the prophet's response is to be overwhelmed by the power and glory and purity and majesty of it all (v. 5). This Otto calls the *tremendum*, and it lies behind the biblical expression "the fear of the Lord."[18] It is miles and miles beyond "the limits of reason alone." The English title of his book misleads if one thinks of the holy as an idea in the usual sense. What Otto offers is a concept of what religion is about, with which he intends to shake us out of our rationalism, our narrow focus on doctrines, and our small-scale vision of what we can expect from life. As for Schleiermacher, it need not be "the Lord Almighty" who evokes this wonder and terror. The sense of the holy is pervasive and universal across human cultures, even if not all individuals are capable of experiencing it in this way. Otto wrote with much more knowledge of Asian religions than Schleiermacher or James, and so he sought a core for religion that would look more adequate for religious forms that were unfamiliar to his Western readers. Like Maslow's farther reaches of human nature, Otto's holy or numinous calls us to go beyond what we find familiar. Unfortunately, current use of *awesome* has debased its meaning somewhat, but Otto truly wanted us to link religion's essence to what overwhelms, what is wonderful and mysterious and frightening and glorious, all at once.

Otto's contribution helps to ground the study of religion as a study about individuals' and groups' experiences of the holy and their reflections, responses, and elaborations of those experiences. There are criticisms of this as a method to understand religion, but it is—like Schleiermacher's—a reconceptualization that permits persons to gain distance from their conventional expectations and memories about what it means to be religious. For example, many people remember from their childhood numinous experiences like those Otto describes, even when they were never connected to whatever formal religious instruction and training the child was given.[19] Some of Wuthnow's artist-subjects shared vivid examples of such moments of childhood sacred awareness. Or this can happen as suddenly to adults as to Isaiah; a conventional Christian twentieth-century woman's most numinous and life-changing experience was a vision of a powerful sacred female figure called "the Companion," who consoled the woman after the death of her daughter.[20] Among the most numinous experiences I myself can recall was a visit to huge caves where prehistoric people came to paint mammoths and other now-extinct animals on the walls and ceiling. The prehistoric people themselves must have been drawn down to this place, deep below the surface, for Otto-like reasons. It was for them as well as for today's visitors a place of mystery, terror, and deep darkness, where they could visualize and paint the major animals of their world, right within the womb of the earth.

The strength of Otto's focus on the holy as the core concept of religion was that it could indeed be applied very widely to religious phenomena well outside Christianity and other Western monotheisms. It could be applied to tribal religions where no one had sacred written texts or lists of doctrines, and where there was little or no "organized" religion. Accounts of shaman's visions in such cultures make sense from Otto's perspective; we feel the wonder, threat, and transformation of their encounters with the spirit world, and Otto helps clarify how these have played an important role in world religions. Like Schleiermacher, Otto rescued religion not only from its contemptuous critics but from its dreary routine-numbed adherents.[21] The numinous, wherever it may be found, is exciting and disruptive. It is the opposite, just about, of formal and organized.

Paul Tillich and Ultimate Concern

Otto's relocation of religion onto the experience of the holy was not the last of the scholarly attempts to reconceptualize and broaden the meaning of religion. Possibly the most philosophical of the twentieth century's redefiners of religion was theologian Paul Tillich. He too was tired of those who mistook surface for substance, but he also wished to decompartmentalize religion for reasons Schleiermacher never faced so directly. Tillich wrote in the middle of the last century, a time dominated by competing political ideologies that exceeded conventional politics in the dreams they promoted, the hopes they inspired, and the destruction they unleashed. These movements demanded fanatical self-sacrifice, the submersion of personal identity into collectivities, and thus provided an overwhelming sense of meaning and purpose for at least some of their adherents. These movements claimed to be political or national, not religious. But Tillich could see that, in their ability to manipulate numinosity as well as humanity, they shared in many of the features of religions. The Nazi propaganda film *Triumph of the Will* is a vivid instance of how to manipulate numinosity so that even a contemporary audience responds with awe to the scene of Hitler's plane descending from the sky through the clouds, a new messiah coming to redeem his people.

Brilliantly, Tillich began with a redefinition of faith, the personal side of religion that is almost always confused with belief. In *Dynamics of Faith*, he claims that faith is the "ultimate concern." "The word 'concern' points to two sides of a relationship, the relation between the one who is concerned and his concern." And "ultimate concern is concern about what is experienced as ultimate."[22] This is as two-poled as Principe's definition of spirituality, but the big question, for Tillich, is that the concern, the objective pole, must be truly ultimate and not merely thought to be. The Nazis' thousand-year reich was a false ultimate for which millions of people died, and other evil pretend ultimates dominated Til-lich's era. These for him are the modern equivalent of ancient idolatry; the faith they evoke is idolatrous faith. Tillich's theory is much more prophetic here than Schleiermacher's or Otto's, for part of his purpose was to name and denounce the false ultimates that raged around him. Among these false ultimates are idolatrous instances of religion (con-ventionally understood). For some persons, the structures of the church or the text of the Bible or the forms of worship are their actual ultimate concern, and even their traditional and conventional God can be too small scale and petty to be a God infinite and altogether ultimate. As Tillich stated this, "God is a symbol for God," and sometimes our sym-bols no longer function to reveal true ultimacy.[23]

Once one allows for this gap between the "God beyond God" and all conventional symbolic representations or gods, the reconceptual-ization lies open to much wider possibilities than even Tillich seems to have envisioned. Moreover, Tillich's subtle discussion of idolatry and ultimacy should warn us against taking at face value all claims to mean-ing and connection and transcendence, such as those that dominate the contemporary spirituality definitions. We cannot assume that because something is a universal human capacity that it cannot go bad or that our sense of connectedness cannot be twisted if the objects to which we connect are flawed. As we will see in our concluding chapter, even the most enthusiastic and utopian proponents of spirituality must face up to this problem, although when they do their answers are far less adequate than Tillich's.

Contemporary Shifts in Intellectual Ecology

Schleiermacher, James, Otto, and Tillich all found exciting ways to relocate and redefine religion as a category. They theorized about reli-gion during an era stretching back more than two hundred years, when it was believed to need redefining. For none of these theorists was reli-gion the same thing as it is in conventional understandings, and their ideas enriched those involved with religion as practitioners. These four have had an impact on how religions have bounced back from dullness, habit, conflation with doctrines, and organizations.

It should not be lost on us how close these redefinitions are to many of the contemporary meanings of spirituality, in spite of the fact that the definers of the latter proclaim they have discovered something new. All four thinkers resisted the restriction of religion to institutions and doctrines, a view all found far too narrow. For religion scholars who have adopted Schleiermacher, James, Otto, and Tillich as their guides, it is clearly not necessary to create a whole new category. We just go back to these founding figures of our field and use their definitions, which seem to cover exactly the same dimensions of experience as do most of the definitions of spirituality collected by Unruh, Versnel, and Kerr. Probably this is the single major reason contemporary definitions of spirituality have made little headway among academic scholars of religion. Not because we are so committed to dogmas and organizations but because, within the history of our own academic field, our scholarly infrastructure equips us with very similar ideas long available and familiar.

Yet recent developments in the study of religion have redrawn the territory just enough to make plausible the introduction or intrusion of a new, separate term, one that seemingly ignores the innovations of the four thinkers' efforts. The extremely individualistic nature of Schleiermacher's, James', and Otto's vision of religion's core should not have escaped us, nor has it escaped their critics. Remember, "individual men in their solitude" was intrinsic to James' vision of religion's essence. In actuality, however, religion could not really be solely such a private, inner experience, for it is generally done in groups and handed on from generation to generation (since we are not Hume's insect-humans, this is always possible). Frankly, none of these theories nor many of the others that follow in their footsteps can actually account for these collective features of religions. So the persistence and ubiquity of groups and traditions could be a substantive and valid criticism of these theories of religion's real nature that isolate "men in their solitude" from culture and history.

But this criticism is not equally valid or relevant in all contexts. The individualism of James and Otto, as well as the potential of Tillich's theory of faith as ultimate concern to become just as idiosyncratic and individual, are embedded in the tradition of psychology of religion, practiced by psychologists but known and adopted by some religionists.[24] This is a subfield that, like Otto, studies religion and religious experience. The issues tackled, such as intrinsic versus extrinsic religion, the relation of personal religion to prejudice and authoritarianism, conversion, attachment and one's relationship to God, and religion and coping strategies: all rest on the study of individuals. For this reason, psychologists of religion have always studied what Schleiermacher,

James, and the rest defined as the focus of the field. An absolutely excellent example of this tradition is the essay "Advances in the Conceptualization and Measurement of Religion and Spirituality" by Peter Hill and Kenneth Pargament.[25] While they define spirituality as "the search for the sacred," they proceed with a review of all the traditional basic psychology of religion topics and call for a new set of measures that can be tradition specific and work for persons whose faiths and cultural heritages lie outside of Judaism and Christianity. Instead of claiming a universal core, they acknowledge that differing expressions of it exist and should be incorporated in psychological measurements. Once again, it seems pointless to argue here that they should have stuck only to spirituality and ignored religion or vice versa. Like James, they depend on a definition of religion that includes a personal, individual dimension as a necessary aspect; this makes a bifurcation between religion and spirituality unnecessary.

Not all religion scholars would be happy with this modified employment of the Otto and James approach, however. The theories reviewed in this chapter are all somewhat old-fashioned. They are not bad theories—they continue to be influential—but, in their individualism and hope for an account of religion centered on personal experience or ultimate concern, they seem to ignore the importance of religion in society, in public life, in global international developments. Tillich, as we saw, wanted to get at these issues, but much of the appropriation of his ideas went to making them closer to Schleiermacher and James. It is hard to leap from religion as a deep inner feeling of absolute dependence to an adequate understanding of Al Qaeda's Islam or to how Mitt Romney's Mormonism influences his politics. It is the re-emergence of religion as a factor in public, large-scale life that has marked both the news and religion study in the past few decades. Topics such as the new religious right, Islamic fundamentalism, and faith-based initiatives dominate news coverage of religion.[26] While this in itself does not make the Schleiermacher–James approach to religion irrelevant or obsolete, these theories do seem to have been overshadowed. Moreover, as scholars became increasingly aware of factors such as gender, race, and class (the "holy trinity" of the 1980s), thinking about religion without reference to them looks anachronistic and idealized. Recent discussions among religionists focus on the rise of the category of religion and its historically conditioned character, but without the implication that the category itself is not important now or that religion will cease to be newsworthy.[27] And yet, these recent inquiries into religion's rise as a topic could not be possible without the scholarly infrastructure we have reviewed. No one within that community of scholars begins from the kind of definitions for religion offered by the enthusiasts for spirituality. Those, as we already said, would be considered naïve and inadequate by all within the field.

We know that humans are not Hume's parentless insect-humans, and no theory of religion that pretends we are will be considered credible today. History, traditions, and cultures (not to mention gender, race, and class) are all important to any successful understanding of religion, even one inclusive of personal experience. Unfortunately, it is exactly this parentless, "men in their solitude" approach that so many of the definitions and treatments of spirituality do pretend to offer. To do so, they must implicitly sever spirituality from the realm of groups and traditions, and—as the occupational therapists Unruh, Versnel, and Kerr realized—from the world of work and social identity. As we have tried to show, this was far from the ideal of Schleiermacher, James, Otto, and Tillich, all of whom hoped to reinvigorate not just thinking about religion but religion as a living enterprise. Today's religion scholars continue to benefit from their creativity and insight but reject the path of disembodied, disconnected interiority, just as did Unruh, Versnel, and Kerr when they rejected spirituality as the core of their profession.

Spirituality claims a new place in a niche defined in terms of personal meaning and connection, a universal capacity for transcendence. Its language to identify this comes from the legacy of religious thinkers, none of whom would have accepted such a brand-new category that cut apart what they wanted to bring together. While Schleiermacher worried about those despisers of religion who threw the baby out with the bathwater, we may say that contemporary advocates for spirituality want a pure baby never submersed in the contaminating waters of religion. From this perspective, it would have been better to adopt Schleiermacher and company's approach and expand religion as a category so as to include all the expressions of faith that Tillich did than to create a brand-new category to muddy things further.

Meanwhile, sociologists of religion, working in another field, have done a better job to argue on behalf of a second term, *spirituality*, which will illuminate recent changes in how Americans are religious. Their arguments depend upon no eternal essence of spirituality, but upon particular historical and societal shifts. To this perspective we turn next.

CHAPTER SIX

The Intellectual Ecology of Spirituality

Sociology of Religion

Introducing Sociology of Religion

We have shown how recent changes in the intellectual territory occupied by psychology opened a new niche for a concept of spirituality. The ingredients of that concept—the exact vocabulary, in fact—were already available as the list, discussed in chapter 4, of what got left out of conventional psychology. Meanwhile, the study of religion generated its own surprisingly similar list, this time as the proposed central and authentic definition of religion. Those theories, in both cases, focused on individual experience and were essentialist: they dealt with timeless and universal human capacities, such as the feeling of absolute dependence. Presumably, the prehistoric artists who painted deep in caves shared these capacities, according to Tart, Schleiermacher, and the rest of the theorists.

But now we turn to a different sector of spirituality's intellectual ecology. Sociology of religion represents a coherent, continuous academic discipline that takes for its starting point the roles of religion in society. For this field, to locate religion primarily if not exclusively in individual experience is a major error. The sociology of religion may study individuals, but not as persons in their solitude. Individuals are interesting, even as case histories, because they typify possibilities of their society, class, or generation. Spirituality here may rest on some universal capacities, but what matters is that modern society has led to changes in the ways people are religious. History, economic shifts, and generational cohorts really matter when sociologists of religion talk about spirituality. The definitions they use have been developed for very specific purposes and entirely within an existing academic community's agenda: namely, to understand how religion works in today's industrial and postindustrial society. Therefore, it may well be that within this discipline's understanding, prehistoric or medieval people did not have spirituality. They did not need it, because they accessed and appropriated religion in different ways than we do.

But it is a mistake to think of this sociology of religion as a narrow, self-enclosed guild of scholars. Today, the work of Robert Bellah, Wade Clark Roof, and Robert Wuthnow, which has been made extraordinarily accessible and influential, exemplifies this approach. In public discussions of where contemporary American religion is heading, these are the thinkers whose work interprets data from polls most compellingly or whose ideas can be used to assess future directions of religious growth and decline. While a timeless universal definition of spirituality may or may not help occupational therapists understand their profession, it is of no use in exploring the effects of American immigration policy on religious pluralism and commitments during the past fifty years or how the dying off of "the Greatest Generation" (young adults during World War II) and their replacement by Baby Boomers (those born from 1946 to 1964) has reshaped religious and civic involvements.

We have already discussed some aspects of Bellah's influential *Habits of the Heart*. A twenty-year-anniversary appreciation of Bellah's work acknowledged this important public contribution and the legacy of his model of scholarship.[1] It is therefore no surprise that, when at the close of the last century church leaders and experts on religion in America wrote about the future of religion in the next century, they turned to these sociological resources. They wanted to imagine how personal meanings and experiences would be lived out under newer social, political, and economic conditions. In works such as *Vital Signs: The Promise of Mainstream Protestantism*, church leaders informed by scholarship on American religious trends chose sociological perspectives rather than opting for James' or Otto's or Tillich's contributions.[2] Only then could they start to think how institutions and organizations might respond to changing patterns of living. Here, then, we have a subfield of a major discipline with a relatively secure scholarly infrastructure, yet one within which the concept of spirituality would be defined in terms of existing frameworks and issues and understood by nonspecialists.

In the work of these sociologists, certain key factors become important that had been of no interest to Tillich, let alone to Maslow. Generational cohorts, they agreed, matter, not just for religion but for all engagements with family, work, and civic involvements. Age, ethnicity, income, education level, regional location, these factors shape us and cannot be brushed aside as so many thinkers we have discussed wished. While for the one-poled definers of spirituality such as Morgan it was inescapable to be spiritual, from the stance of Bellah, Roof, and Wuthnow, such claims are irrelevant and confusing. What they know we cannot escape is our location in history and society. Nor, for their work, does it make any moral sense to try for such an escape.

Durkheim and Weber
The Role of Religion in Modern Society

This sociological tradition is deeply indebted to the two giants of a hundred years ago, Emil Durkheim and Max Weber. Both struggled with how to chart the role of religion in their own era. Already, its influence in Europe was fading, as society seemed less and less controlled by the power of religious ideas and the authority of religious leaders. But perhaps religion operates with more subtlety and more pervasively, so that it would be hard to measure how secular (i.e., no longer religious) a group or an individual was. Weber's famous study of *The Protestant Ethic and the Spirit of Capitalism* showed how religious ideas and attitudes had shaped economic behavior over a period of several hundred years. Although ideas such as Calvin's predestination were no longer prominent in European society, their impact lingered and could be seen still as the productivity of Protestant workers remained higher than that of their Roman Catholic counterparts.[3] Weber's study makes the concept of residual religion completely plausible, even if he never used the exact term. An even more striking example of religion's social impact is Durkheim's *On Suicide*, where behavior that had always been interpreted in individual terms is examined as a function of membership (or lack of membership) in collectivities. Religions differ in the degree they create and maintain group belonging, and it is lack of belonging or changes in the rules for belonging that account for most suicides, Durkheim believed. He postulated that Catholics have a lower suicide rate than Protestants not because Protestants are "soft on suicide" but because Catholicism offers a sense of solidarity within a group that is the real protection against suicide, just as marriage protects by binding individuals into social units (not, in other words, because marriage makes individuals happier).[4] A species of religion entirely focused on Schleiermacher's core of inner feeling would make its adherents extremely vulnerable to suicide and other seemingly private troubles, according to this theory, precisely because such a form of religion has cut itself off from one of religion's major social functions. It is not the organization or the doctrines or the moral teachings that define religion for Durkheim but the way religion's collective representations create a sense of a community larger and more lasting than the individual. (While all of Weber's and Durkheim's claims here have been contested, the basic theme of religion as intrinsically social is hard to avoid or dispute.)

Durkheim and Weber wrote for and about their own Europe of 1900. They assumed that Europe was the leader of worldwide modernity, and so as went Europe so went the rest of the world. Individuals dropped out of religion, and religion faded from public life; these trends were well underway in Paris and Berlin even before Durkheim and Weber wrote. They assumed this would happen everywhere else, too. Therefore, they did not bother to write about all of Europe, even; those Romanian peasants whose great-grandchildren were to become Olympic gymnasts were left out of the picture. (Although Durkheim's suicide study includes statistics from southern Italy, which in his day would have been, like Romania, a premodern society.[5]) This Eurocentric vision has by now been noticed and sometimes corrected. The processes depicted by the two founders of sociology of religion cannot be applied automatically to the development of religion and society in North America, in Japan, and in Uganda. However, the theories suggest where to look for key differences and why secularity in any of these places is not necessarily identical with that of Paris or Berlin.

Sociology of Religion Takes on Sheila-ism and the 1960s

If Durkheim and Weber both struggled to understand secularization in their own day, over the past several decades, American sociology of religion has been preoccupied with understanding the impact of the 1960s on Americans. Its practitioners want to interpret and explain the changed perceptions of selves, communities, and commitments that can be traced back to that turbulent decade, now seen as a watershed in the American experience of not just religion but almost everything.

Secularization appeared too simplistic a term. The Baby Boomers and their religion, values, and commitments were the initial subjects, but subsequent generations have been studied for continuities and further developments. With a sociology of religion geared to these topics, it is hardly surprising how marginal approaches like James' appear, even when many Baby Boomers and younger cohorts will rely implicitly on James ("individuals in their solitude") to account for and interpret their own experiences. In short, from a sociological point of view, individuals who say, "I am in my solitude," are kidding themselves; they are part of a generation, a cultural pattern, and a language to describe identities that are anything but solitary. This is as true on a solo camping trip in the wilderness as it would be in school, work, or church.

Here we return to Bellah and associates' *Habits of the Heart*, already discussed when we looked at virtues and values linked to spirituality. Bellah used case histories to reveal the inroads expressive individualism had made on Americans' capacity to articulate commitments. This had severe consequences for religion, he believed, as well as for civic life. Religion reduced to what an expressive individualist could think and speak about was, for him, a travesty of what religion—as studied by Weber and Durkheim—ought to be. Expressive individualism reduces everything to individual feelings, preferences, and self-actualization. This was perhaps the ultimate outcome of Schleiermacher's redefinition, had Bellah and his associates explored historical antecedents.

Among the persons interviewed for *Habits of the Heart* was a woman whose pseudonym is Sheila Larsen. She was the extreme of all expressive individualists, for when it came to her religion, she replied that her own identity, self, and actualization *was* her religion. "My religion," she stated, "is Sheila-ism. Just my own little voice."[6] This was her ultimate concern, this was the way she spoke of "religion," and this was, to Bellah, the ultimate absurdity of expressive individualism. Sheila cultivated and practiced Sheila-ism and did not see anything wrong with a private religion focused exclusively on herself. Sheila was not the first such displayable example of personal religion, for more than ten years earlier, in a PBS series on religion in America, the last episode featured "Joe," whose personal religion seemed as restricted as hers. He was even less articulate about what it was and what it meant to him.[7] Joe and Sheila both would normally, in church-based surveys, have been labeled as "religious nones" and forgotten about. But by 1985 Sheila looked to Bellah like the dismal face of things to come.

For years after this interview, sociologists and others went desperately seeking Sheila, curious as to how many other Americans had reduced their religious involvement down to this very private absolutization of their own self-development.[8] Was Sheila Larsen typical or an oddity? Bruce Greer and Wade C. Roof used the term *religious privatism* and tried to measure it and correlate it with other determinants of interest to sociology, such as age and education level. But privatism did not exactly capture what made *Sheila-ism* stick as a label for the perceived new phenomenon. By now, in hindsight, she looks like the vanguard spokesperson for the "spiritual but not religious" 14 percent of the population. However, that is not how she described herself in 1985. She used *religion* and became a ludicrous figure as a result.

There were, however, attempts to rehabilitate Sheila. She was not self-centered in her actual life. It was noted that she had nursed terminally ill relatives and pondered the meaning of death; she was not a muffin-head in all respects. Fuller, in *Spiritual but Not Religious*, tries to defend her. "This young woman gradually accepted responsibility for owning her own set of beliefs. . . . Sheila learned to listen to her own inner voice and to be her own authority in spiritual matters."[9] The problems remained that (1) she had no way to talk about these experiences with care and suffering except through the language of expressive individualism, and (2) she identified her personal existential quest with religion, as if Sheila-ism were a direct competitor with Judaism or Buddhism or Christianity. While in retrospect Bellah's treatment of her looks mean-spirited and snobbish, the defense is not very successful.

Poor Sheila Larsen. For all we know, two years (or two minutes) after the Bellah study was completed, she may have joined an evangelical church, a Buddhist meditation society, or a hospice program as a staff member. That seems the footloose, never stationary pattern of so many of Bellah's interviewees and the subjects of subsequent sociological studies. Her limited "first language" of expressive individualism would have made it difficult for her to justify or rationalize any of these choices, and, had she then dropped out of such involvements, her reasoning would have been that her inner voice told her to leave. The little voice of self was the only criterion for her, as for so many of the *Habits* interviewees. The only thing that would have been consistent over time would have been this core of Sheila-ism, with every other involvement a means to the end of developing Sheila.

The pattern of Sheila-ism was given various names (e.g., privatism) by researchers such as Roof and Wuthnow. It is not really narcissism in the classic moral or psychiatric sense. It is labeled by the latter *seeking* in contrast to *dwelling*: "a traditional spirituality of inhabiting sacred places has given way to a new spirituality of seeking—that people have been losing faith in a metaphysic that can make them feel at home in the universe and that they increasingly negotiate among competing glimpses of the sacred, seeking partial knowledge and practical wisdom."[10] This formulation lacks Bellah's pejorative tone. Note especially that while *spirituality* is Wuthnow's term to describe both forms, it is defined by its relationship with worldviews, generational experiences, and social settings. Wuthnow intensifies the conceptual linkage of this contrast by reference to sociology of religion's two founders: "With Durkheim, a spirituality of dwelling pays considerable attention to ways of distinguishing sacred habitats from the profane world. . . . With Weber, a spirituality of seeking . . . concentrates on that mixture of spiritual and rational, ethical and soteriological, individual and collective activities whereby the person in modern societies seeks meaning in life and tries to be of service to others."[11] This use of the term *spirituality*, while it shares certain features with Principe's and Van Ness', is explicitly designed to identify the distinctive conditions under which persons in modern societies live their lives and appropriate their meanings. It is a use indeed in the traditions of both Durkheim and Weber, but not of James or Otto, let alone of the existentialists or humanistic psychologies from which most of the ninety-two current definitions of spirituality derived.

Consumerist Identity

Wuthnow seeks to be as positive as possible as a sociologist when it comes to a depiction of seeking. And yet this negotiated pathway of seeking can also be characterized as a consumerist mentality where every institution, organization, and tradition is transformed into a shopping mall or supermarket. These are filled with possible "resources" among which the individual consumer wanders footloose but eager to buy. He or she collects, discards, creates new combinations of items, just as Wuthnow outlines above, but with no interest at all in learning their original contexts and meanings. Take, for example, a catalog for women that purveyed the world's religions into jewelry and knickknacks, so that one could purchase an Egyptian ankh necklace, a Christian bracelet, Taoist earrings, and a menorah-shaped wall plaque, in any combination what-soever. This is a perfect symbol of what the spiritual marketplace at its lowest common denominator means. Baby Boomers, the generation of seekers of Roof's title, were the inventors, supposedly, of this style of appropriation (or colonization or co-optation) of religious traditions, both familiar and exotic.[12]

Baby Boomers did their seeking by moving in and out of groups and traditions—and sometimes back in again. The authors of such studies admit that the statistics on who joins and who disappears from the pews or meditation center are fluid: people of this cohort are on a journey and constitute a moving target for research that got its start by count-ing dwellers. Younger generations have intensified rather than reversed this pattern, as we will see. Sheila Larsen would definitely be counted as a seeker, of course. But her constant pole of reference would have remained herself and her growth, as well as her membership in a partic-ular generation that found seeking to be a better option than dwelling.

The pattern of the consumer model of identity as a social process precedes the prominence of Baby Boomers, for it was already noticed earlier, by 1967 in Thomas Luckmann's provocative study, *The Invisible Religion*. The youngest Baby Boomers would then have been entering kindergarten, not engaged as yet in religious seeking. Luckmann saw the consumerist identity as a pattern linked to the giant gulf between public and private spheres for contemporary life. Public sphere insti-tutions such as governments regulated some area of our lives but left enormous territory unregulated, relative to all traditional societies. And so we were forced to go shopping for what in previous generations had been handed down: "The individual is left to his own devices in choos-ing goods and services, friends, marriage partners, neighbors, hobbies and . . . even 'ultimate' meanings in a relatively autonomous fashion. In a manner of speaking, he is free to construct his own personal identity . . . a rich, heterogeneous assortment of possibilities which, in principle, are accessible to any individual consumer."[13] Today the list of what is shopped for includes gender identity, modifications of physical appear-ance such as hair color and plastic surgery, and other "consumables" that even Luckmann never imagined. This kind of seeking or shopping was, one might say, exactly the opposite of what Durkheim saw as the true belonging and community support that protected Catholics more than Protestants from suicide. Luckmann insisted that this process was a structural constant of contemporary society and not particularly linked to religion. Those who emigrate from traditional societies that lack this pattern must readjust to a society that leaves it up to individuals to pick for themselves what was, back in their home countries, picked out for them or simply assumed as an aspect of social belonging. For others, born into the new situation, the consumerist way seems "natural." A vivid illustration of this model of identity are funerals and memorial services for persons who have lived out this pattern in all its footlooseness and transiency. Family members from different marriages, spiritual advisors from different religions, and colleagues from different careers all speak about the deceased as they knew him or her, and it is not always clear to the rest of us that they knew the same person. (Typical comments might include "I didn't know she ever gave music lessons to children; when I knew her she worked for social services at the hospital." Or: "Who's that?" "It must be her sister-in-law from her first marriage.") To the deceased, as to Sheila Larsen, all these partial fragments of identity may be bound together, but what established continuity is the life pattern of seeking itself.[14]

The supermarket consumer model of religious identity is easy to sneer at. Too easy. The more careful and balanced sociological scholars note its liabilities but also how almost everything in contemporary life seems to intensify it. For example, we shop for brands that carry a glow for us, and marketers seek to enhance this magic glow of brands so that we do not just buy clothes, shoes, and cars; we buy pieces and traces of something numinous that can become in our imaginations pieces and traces of our selves.[15] L.L.Bean does not just sell clothes and outdoor gear; it sells mythic images of Maine and the outdoor life. What made the women's world religions jewelry catalog ludicrous is not the idea of religiously identifying earrings but the completely eclectic mix of religious sources in the same brochure (perhaps like having Bean and Neiman Marcus share the same catalog). The consumer model of identity sets the rules, and by those rules no fragments are completely incompatible with other fragments, for the private sphere of contemporary society is where individual freedom reigns.

When this situation is laid out as Luckmann describes it, and as Roof and Wuthnow explore it, religious affiliations take their place among the many identity fragments that can be taken on and cast off.[16] It is not only that persons affiliate and disaffiliate more freely than they ever did before; it is that the meaning and purposes of affiliation have been transformed. Take this example from an ex-student. She tried an experiment for Lent, a "secular Lenten fast," and posted her experiences on a blog (itself an invention that corresponds exactly to expressive individualism as an ideology). She had dropped out of traditional religion, taken some courses on world religions and Buddhism while in college, and was now of two minds about where to head next. So, for her Lenten experiment, she fasted from alcohol. Her father, a devout member of the Ukrainian Catholic Church, suggested that she should also try attending Mass now and then, if she were going to do a Lenten practice. "No," she replied, "That would be too radical." The whole thing was an experiment after all, not a wholehearted commitment to join or participate in anything.

The pattern itself was present before the 1960s; it simply becomes far more visible with the emergence of Baby Boomers into adulthood. With the next generations—Gen X, Gen Y (my student), Millennials—the pattern becomes more prevalent. My student's father was a holdover dweller from an earlier pattern, against which she consciously measured and distanced herself. The children of Sheila and the other *Habits* interviewees will have grown up in families and social environments accustomed to the reign of expressive individualist ideology, and they will lack actual present role models for alternatives. These children may no longer bother describing themselves as religious at all, no matter what the content of their parents' religion was. They will, if pressed, be happier to describe themselves as "spiritual but not religious."

Spiritual but Not Religious in Sociological Perspective

We have finally arrived at a specific, historically located context for the introduction of spirituality as a concept. In this sociological approach to religion, spiritual but not religious or no longer religious becomes a meaningful category within the framework of Luckmann's consumer model of identity and Wuthnow's seeking age cohort. Escapees from an older, institutionally based view of identity and belonging, many of these people are lapsed Catholics, secular Jews, jack Mormons, and (in the words of one such) "recovering Baptists." But these expressions (and I am sure there are more) do not capture what is most important to say positively about such persons. As we saw when we spoke of Wuthnow's study of artists, spirituality can work as an alternative to depict the experience of dedication, involvement, and expression of concerns no longer achieved through religious membership. It is not a generic, core, inescapable quality of universal human nature; it makes sense within particular social processes and generational sequences.

We now see the importance of the way of the artist, as Wuthnow's subtitle dubbed it. We met those people back in chapter 2 when we looked at practices. What now makes their lives of significance to Wuthnow and the sociology of religion is how they opted for a style of seeking that opened up a space for a more fluid, experimental style of life, work, and identity. *Creative Spirituality* did not omit the isolation and feeling of detachment experienced by many of these artists. But they had forged for themselves an identity that did not depend upon group joining, and their religious backgrounds had been retained as fragments and pieces rather than whole cloth. For them, *spirituality* seemed the appropriate term, because Wuthnow did not want to bend *religion* as Sheila did in Sheila-ism to cover their style of acommunal exploration. Wuthnow's version of spirituality here does include an intuitive, close-to-the-bone sense of transcendence or the sacred or reality, just as did many of the ninety-two definitions in chapter 1. The artists were sometimes able to connect this to a formal or public religious symbol, but not always. Their paintings, songs, and dances are expressions for them of this sense of mystery, although it is never clear whether the viewers and listeners share it. For example, one subject retells how she had as a child an inner sense of the supernatural that she could not connect to what she heard in church until a vivid touch of an ocean breeze brought her the awareness "God is a spirit."[17] Most of the artists experienced a similar disconnect between private and public but used their work to weave such connections as they could not discover otherwise. Not all use God as a symbol for this. For one poet, the key is that "some form of Truth or Reality is present in the universe, but this Truth or Reality is hidden from us by the language, symbols and material artifacts that make up our culture and influence our perceptions."[18] His poetry attempts to change our perceptions through the medium of words. In all the cases used by Wuthnow, spirituality is an elusive private stream that flows on, occasionally joining a public waterway, but continuously moving with a current of its own. The lives of these people appear to reflect the processes of identity formation under the conditions described by Luckmann. Wuthnow nowhere sneers at his artist-subjects, nor does he think of them as shoppers. They have worked hard, with originality and perseverance, to become craftspersons in their practices and to maintain a sense of spirituality defined above. The same might be said of Tisdell's activist-educators, whose complex relation to religion required a fresh concept of commitment, affiliation, and "spiraling" back to childhood to retrieve an interior sense of the sacred.[19]

We see now why these seemingly atypical persons are interesting for the sociologist of religion. For Wuthnow, "despite their distinctive talents and interests, these artists' search for spirituality resembles that of many Americans."[20] The struggle of these persons to create not only works of artistic merit but coherent and truthful selves over time is what newer patterns of commitment and identity and spiritual seeking are all about. From the perspective of Wuthnow, these artists are simply more adept at coping with a situation shared by all of us. Or, to put this even more simply, more and more Americans will be like the young woman who tried the secular Lenten fast experiment, and fewer will be like her father. We will all need to do better than Sheila-ism, but nonetheless our task will be to build lives that can cohere and connect to realms of meaning beyond ourselves. We will do this with, and increasingly without, the continuing influences of formal religion. For Roof and Wuthnow, the cup is half full, not half empty (as Bellah saw it); the personal stories of those who rely on spirituality—however elusive its definitions—are inspirational tales relevant to us all.

I am not so sure of this. The artists Wuthnow studied did not include rock musicians, persons who work in advertising, or commercial artists. He picked persons who are, so to speak, private-practice or entrepreneurial artists, separated from large-scale businesses and the world of bureaucracy. As we will understand better when we look at the spirituality in the workplace movement and the importance of spirituality for recreation, this fact may set them apart from the majority of us in significant ways. But Wuthnow would insist that, while it is possible my secular Lenten fast student may turn out to be an artist, the one thing that is certain is that she will not turn into her father. That pathway back to dweller from seeker is closed by virtue of her placement in history and cultural change. And she, like Sheila's intellectual descendants today, will endorse the identity of spiritual but not religious, avoiding the embarrassment of Sheila-ism as a religion while making a positive statement about meanings and her quest for some negotiated relationship with symbols of transcendence.

Conclusion
Intellectual Ecology's Importance for Spirituality

We see an interesting and complex story when we look beyond spirituality as an isolated concept and place it in a complicated intellectual ecology, a landscape in which several disciplines and areas of professional expertise claimed territory, vacated it, and revised what they said they did. The vocabulary of contemporary spirituality is very clearly derived from third force and transpersonal psychology, now liberated from the need to prove its scientific status. The other source of spirituality's language and ideas is the Schleiermachian tradition within religion study. Here, the major recent innovation of spirituality was to sever this tradition from intrinsic connection to religion, by creating a new and separate and seemingly more universal category. We stressed that in both these areas there was little attention to the theories and arguments of existing disciplines and communities of scholarship. It seemed unnecessary to spirituality advocates to track the discussions from the 1970s about models of the person in psychology, let alone debates from the 1790s about the possibility of natural religion. Nevertheless, these hidden histories helped us see where spirituality as a concept really comes from and what it is expected to do for us, in contrast to its explicit older usages traced by Principe, which are really irrelevant to modern meanings.

In the case of sociology of religion, we have a different contribution to the ecology. It is a discipline with an acknowledged history (Wuthnow's citation of Durkheim and Weber reminds us of this) and also an explicitly contemporary focus. Recent changes in religion's place and meanings in North America—of the 1960s and beyond—needed new concepts in order to be understood. Whether one labels this privatization, seeking, invisible religion, or consumer identity, new patterns of affiliation and commitments require a way to talk about persons as members of a society where things work differently than they did before. Within this particular historical milieu, spirituality as a concept makes sense for sociologists of religion to employ. Humans are humans everywhere, but spirituality as an inescapable human universal is not a useful sociological category.

The sociological perspective, however, does provide a kind of explanation for why such a category as spirituality would be so appealing to

North Americans. It works within the generational transitions understood as critical by Roof and Wuthnow. It dovetails into the process of modern identity formation already depicted by Luckmann in *The Invisible Religion*. It is a category that hovers between the grandiosity of Sheilaism and the pure secularity of scientific rationality London extolls as the source of answers to the question of the nature of man. It is also a category that includes a residual trace of religion—and sometimes much more than a trace.

But if we are not sociologists of religion, if we are instead healthcare professionals, businesspersons, or just plain human beings, do we need spirituality as a concept? Yes, say many persons. "Who Needs the Concept of Spirituality? Human Beings Seem To!" is the passionate title of one such defense.[21] Regardless of how murky our definitions are, the concept fills important niches, its glow lights up areas of our humanity, and its lack in our lives is the cause of our misery. Others disagree and do so vigorously. Current problems of life in today's society do not justify the use of a concept with ninety-two definitions, with all the problems that this entails. In the words of one such spirituality critic, Joseph Hoffman, who now regrets his previous tolerance of the term, "I argued that the term [spirituality] is just spacious enough—or fluffy enough—to accommodate all kinds of people who just cannot make up their minds about religion. Talk about wrong. Now I think that my defense of the word was a little like asking for a bigger ballroom for bad dancers."[22] We will see this better when we look at several specific contexts for spirituality and determine whether Hoffman and other critics have a point.

CHAPTER SEVEN

Niches for Spirituality
Health Care and R$_x$ Spirituality

Niches for Spirituality

The next three chapters examine three separate fields or areas of life in which the concept of spirituality has now found a home—or claims to have done so. Each of these areas has relative autonomy, has long-standing issues or problems of its own, and now includes those advocates who think that the introduction or injection of spirituality will help solve those problems. In a nutshell, we are going to agree that the problems are real, that the situations have created a sense of dis-ease and complaints, and that these conditions have lasted a long time. When we look at how spirituality is configured in each of these situations, we will find that somewhat different aspects of its multiple definitions have relevance to each area of life. Indeed, its exact meaning—if we can even speak about it having an exact meaning—varies considerably depending upon which of these areas we work within. What is not clear is that spirituality is the solution to any of these long-term problems or that the sudden introduction of this term will add clarity to an account of them. We know, or think we know, what is wrong with health care and work; we know, or think we know, what we crave from recreation. To add spirituality to these understandings may be a deceptive and needless complication. Or it may illuminate some aspects of our dis-ease but obscure important dimensions of the full situation.

I have chosen these three areas because within each a coherent body of writings already exists and it is easy to speak of a "spirituality and _____" movement within each. In other areas, such as education or law enforcement, there are those who want to interject spirituality into the discussion of the meaning or purpose of their field, so our three choices are not exclusive. I could also have chosen professional sports (a particular and peculiar example of "work") or social work or leadership studies or probably even more far-ranging fields and areas. All of these exhibit a pattern of enthusiasm for spirituality as the missing ingredient that will solve major problems in the area. The statement from the CAOT featured in chapter 1, claiming that spirituality lies at the core of their profession, is the model for this type of endorsement.

I have not chosen to examine religion as an area, however. The reasons for this are twofold. First, the turn to spirituality within religious communities is guided by definitions such as Principe's and is based on a model borrowed from what he called level two—that is, guidebooks such as St. Teresa's *The Interior Castle*. It would make an interesting but comparatively narrow discussion to see how such traditional resources have made their impact upon religious groups and individuals who never would have had any contact with Carmelite nuns prior to the last few decades.[1] But the appropriation of spirituality in this sense by religious persons now is not a very surprising story. The second reason for not focusing on religion is that the spread of spirituality into healthcare, business, and recreation *is* unexpected, new, and surprising. This is where the newer and vastly expanded definition, the umbrella quality of the concept, has been applied. It is here where the story becomes intriguing and where recent excitement surrounding the term is so novel and dramatic. And it is in these new contexts that spirituality has pushed its way into new niches, places where no one forty years ago would have expected to see anything like it.

Medicine and Human Meanings
A Long-Term Problem

The plight of hospitalized patients drew the attention of a doctor and a clergyman. They found that, in spite of an immense gain in prestige over the days when hospitals were where the poor went to die, the hospital remained an alien and terrifying environment. The scientific expertise on display in the modern hospital was awesome. But it was awesome in Otto's sense of numinous and overwhelming, too, an encounter with something not only mysterious but frightening. The specialized language, the environment with its own rules and regulations, the hierarchy of medical experts, all this made the experience of being sick dehumanizing. The problem was not just that the hospital was a "total institution," but that the very language used within it was foreign to any patient's normal way to tell his or her story and communicate with others. The hospital is the domain of narrowly focused experts, and the language of illness has given way to the language of medical jargon and of disease. Specialism is the result of narrow fields of medical expertise, and this worked to silence and demoralize patients further. Patients need specialists and the treatments they provide, but they also need an alternative to this language, something to "counteract the evils of specialism. . . . Doctors aim to banish, to curb or to prevent suffering. But the doctor has not always the skill to diagnose or to treat the mental part of illness . . . emotional starvation, occupational upset."[2] Therefore, patients need advocates; they need someone to care for them as fellow humans.[3] They need to be affirmed as persons with unique histories, not just as cases with symptoms. In the hospital environment, however, the opportunity to find meaning—personal, real, existential meaning—in suffering and pain is minimized. The opportunity to find a noble, dignified death is lost not because of cruelty or torture but because of the character of the very institution dedicated to saving lives. The tragedy and irony is that amid the celebration of medical science's achievements, the humanity of those being helped is sacrificed.

This picture of the hospital and its patients does not come from 2012. Nor from the work of Kübler-Ross in the late 1960s. No, it is taken directly from the pages of *The Art of Ministering to the Sick*, written by Richard Cabot and Russell Dicks and published in 1936. The technology we take for granted today was barely present, but all of the attitudes that accompany it and that we attribute to it were already in place. Being sick in this environment could be demoralizing. Being terminally ill meant that something or someone—the patient, the doctor, or the whole enterprise—had failed, and a war had been lost. The comfort of a traditional home deathbed was no longer available, and instead dying among one's family members, one died in the care of strangers. Already the authors could refer to the "old-fashioned country practitioner" as an almost "mythological being now extinct in many places," and they knew he would not return.[4] The world of Cabot and Dicks' book became the norm, the expected and anticipated way Americans deal with illness and dying. The hospital will be, for about 70–80 percent of us, the last place we will stay on earth.

Although the particular problems and issues surrounding something as important as health care change, there is a solid core of continuity between this picture from so long ago and the situation today. Even though new and mostly unforeseen topics have preoccupied biomedical ethics and public health-care debates for decades, the underlying theme of the 1936 volume remains central. We have an environment within which specialized, medicalized expertise reigns. Because of this, we have no other way to comprehend and cope with the human experiences of illness, suffering, and death. Within this realm, the knowledge that matters is unavailable to patients, is easily misunderstood by them (even if no one lies intentionally), and is impossible to translate into terms that ordinary persons normally use to make sense of choices and consequences.

The environment in *The Art of Ministering to the Sick* was the future, and doctors and other staff oriented toward the setting and rules of the hospital were the personnel with whom patients interacted. These people are strangers, not neighbors or old family friends. The hospital environment itself produces "strangers," possessors of expertise within the reign of "specialism." The environment itself defeats all attempts by individuals to overcome its power and influence.

Cabot and Dicks' solution was to suggest a new role for clergy, that of patient advocate. The hospital does not yet have a professional chaplain, but whoever comes to minister to the sick must discard the identity of religious specialist. There is already far too much emphasis on specialized expertise. Instead, he (this is 1936, remember) should try to offer another way to "minister," by being present and articulate, translating the language of the hospital back into the patients' tongue, and helping patients voice their own concerns in a style that the staff will respect and to which they can respond helpfully. This is not the traditional role of religious consolation, but it is the most urgent and necessary role, given the needs of patients. Yes, there will be time and opportunity to pray with patients, to do "religious" stuff for them, but these functions are subordinate to advocacy. Moreover, by 1936 there were many unchurched patients who had no regular clergy or religious community. These people needed advocates too, and so the minister who worked in the hospital found that his real congregation was potentially the entire patient population (and perhaps the overworked and stressed staff as well). This is how the two authors could find a new and wider meaning for *ministry* in this strange new environment.

One can see here the seeds of the future development of hospital chaplaincy as a specialized ministry. The clergy who work within the hospital realm will know its rules, procedures, and the personnel and their specialized roles. These clergy will fit in, up to a point, as trustworthy professionals who can communicate better with patients and their families than almost anyone else. Even as he or she works to undo the pernicious dehumanizing effects of too much specialized expertise, the chaplain becomes, inadvertently, one more specialist. In a recent essay on the role of the professional chaplain by Florence Gelo, the "local clergy" are perceived as ignorant intruders, whose bumbling attempts to make sense of the hospital environment will alienate the staff and not be helpful to the patients.[5] The professional chaplain, on the other hand, belongs there. It is sad that this triumph of specialization should have occurred, given Cabot and Dicks' analysis of the problem. But Gelo is probably accurate. Even when the local clergy has known the patient and the patient's family for decades, has baptized and married them and will surely funeralize them, the expertise relevant for hospital work is different. A local clergyperson cannot be an effective patient advocate within this setting, according to Gelo. We may dislike this conclusion, but it is probably true.

Cabot and Dicks wrote their book just before the advent of the high-tech medicine with which we are familiar but also shortly after a dramatic shift in the demographics of illness and death. In 1870, infants and young children were still—as they had always been—the most likely to die. Death was associated with the very young, and the specific diseases from which they died were so numerous and so poorly diagnosed that the medical causes were unknown and unimportant. Children died at home, mostly, although there are sad stories of small children who died in railway stations. By 1920 this reality had given way to the one we know today: death happens mostly to the elderly. The drop in infant and child mortality did not mean no children died. It did mean that childhood was no longer linked to mortality by that time, at least for mainstream North Americans. This meant that premature death could become a category, and a death that was premature could be any death up through late middle age. A premature death was also a potentially preventable death. Thus the real mission of the hospital became to battle against death itself. By 1936, when Cabot and Dicks wrote, the attitudes were in place to use warfare and military imagery to dramatize the role of the doctor, and the diseases themselves became enemies. One by one they would be defeated by science.

Of course, many of the patients to whom Cabot and Dicks minis-
tered had grown up with the older attitudes. They may have been ready
to die a "noble" or dignified death, even in the hospital.[6] But by 1936 their
perspectives and wisdom did not count in the hospital and did not matter to their treatment. None of their background or biographical details
mattered for their role as hospital patients, according to the official
language of medicine. And so we have a kind of transition generation,
many old enough to remember a different world of expectations, all of it
ignorable by staff and even by the minister who is trying to explain the
current environment rather than remember the past. As that generation
of pre-1870 patients died off, the only trace remaining was a nostalgic
yearning and vague knowledge that in some past era, things like illness,
suffering, and death were handled differently. They had once been part
of the wholeness of human life, and no longer was that the case.

Spirituality as Amelioration

To begin a discussion on spirituality and health care with this time
travel back to a past eighty-five years ago may seem odd. It would seem
more reasonable to begin with recent decades, when the whole interest
in spirituality and health blossomed. That is when the importance of
spirituality in the holistic care for hospital patients and others under
medical treatment became a major theme. But although the word *spirituality* is new, in the basic situation set forth by Cabot and Dicks we
find the same issues and basic problem for which spirituality is now
proposed as a solution.

The point of spirituality or any other proposed solution is not to
stage a revolution against the reign of the hospital and its medicalization of suffering and death, but to ameliorate the effects on patients that
Cabot and Dicks charted so well. There is no way to return health-
care to what it was before specialization, technology, and large-scale
institutions transformed care for the sick. No one seriously suggests the
equivalent to homeschooling for the treatment of major illnesses as a
general, large-scale public solution. There are indeed some niches for
alternatives, such as hospice care, but this niche has remained a small
one. Nursing homes may fill up with Baby Boomers, whose attitudes
may reshape end-of-life care just as they have reshaped religion. But
the need for hospitals to care for the sick and injured is unquestioned.
No matter how many treatments can be done on an outpatient basis, the
environment and vocabulary of the hospital and specialized medicine

will continue to dominate our society's vision of illness and dying for the foreseeable future.

Therefore, whatever can be proposed to alleviate this situation's negative side-effects and human consequences should be considered potentially helpful, or at least given a hearing. It may be the invitation to culturally specific healers to join the medical team (an extra outside specialist, or the new version of local clergy) or to counsel the families of patients whose cultural knowledge does not include the American health-care system. It may be to grant patients permission to include adjunctive therapies in their treatment, provided that these do not interfere or conflict with their mainstream Western scientific methods. Debates over how alternative or how mainstream any of these are continue, with acupuncture, for example, gaining acceptance for insurance reimbursement in the span of a generation. These therapies depend upon additional specialized experts, and so some of the underlying problem identified by Cabot and Dicks will remain even when the specialists received their training far from American medical schools.[7]

But within the hospital, someone must be there to help patients overcome the immense power of medical specialism. The professional chaplain fills the role Cabot and Dicks proposed. Patient advocate rather than religious specialist, the chaplain serves to bridge the communication divide and is a human presence at the times of greatest existential need. A chaplain is part of the hospital staff and as we have seen, identifies with this world, is able to move around within it. Neither outsider nor intruder, the chaplain offers an alternative language and vision of what illness means. Or, rather, the chaplain permits and encourages patients to voice their own visions, makes a space for the patients' personal experiences to be heard and valued. The chaplain does not come prepared to talk about religion but lets patients set the agenda, vent about the hospital restrictions, and eventually encounter their own mortality and frailty in a manner that fits their own life history and meanings. This is the core of what spirituality as it has come to be defined more than ninety-two times is about, and so it is obvious that spirituality and spiritual care are what the chaplain can deliver. And once this need is recognized for the patients, the hospital staff are also eventually included. They are bound by the hospital ethos and regulations; they must maintain a professional demeanor. Yet they deal unceasingly with suffering, and they may experience a series of deaths and losses with no opportunity to mourn. So, in this view, spiritual care for all in the hospital milieu is a necessity, a way

to alleviate the human stresses that the medical environment of specialized expertise still by and large ignores.

However, this approach raises the question of credentials and qualifications, which Gelo's discussion of the professional chaplain answers
in one fashion.[8] The chaplain may work in the hospital and be trained
in the hospital but is also an ordained clergy member of a particular
denomination or tradition. That is very clear, the religious bodies have
insisted on this, and it is their meaning of *professional*. Mainline Protestant
denominations have been, over the past decades, increasingly insistent
that ordination is the prerequisite for work as a professional chaplain.
There is no doubt or ambiguity about this. Roman Catholic hospital
chaplains also receive specialized educational training, although not all
are ordained priests. Very recently a program to train Muslim chaplains
was initiated at a major Protestant nondenominational divinity school,
an intriguing acknowledgment of specialism and a focus on credentials.
Religious groups within Christianity have traditionally granted ordination or withheld it based on criteria they themselves set, even when it is
known in advance that a particular candidate plans to work in a hospital
rather than a parish. This control over credentialing is understandable.
Clergy are representatives of a particular religious body, answerable to
it for their conduct; they are never freelancers.

Now, however, we come to a basic question about roles, duties, and
credentials. The role of minister to the sick as portrayed by Cabot and
Dicks has very little to do with specific, explicit religious training or
education at all. In fact, someone who identifies too exclusively with that
training could not do a good job ministering to a patient population that
includes atheists, Muslims, and neopagan Wiccans, for example. The
chaplain's human skills are what are really relevant, including the savvy
to deal successfully with the hospital bureaucracy on behalf of patients.
In short, the ministering could be done by someone whose training
is in counseling, social work, psychotherapy—or just a very humane,
experienced nonprofessional who could somehow miraculously gain
the respect of all the specialized experts. The exact title and training
may matter less than the credibility and skill of the individual. However
anachronistic this may sound, I am sure there are still examples where
the person who serves as chief "minister" has a position in the social services office, a bachelor's degree in art history, and a wonderful human
presence. Some of the founders of the first American hospice programs,
back in the 1960s and 1970s, had this kind of background and personal

qualifications, although by now they might not even be eligible to volunteer for such programs.

When the basic job is defined as above, we may well ask who is best qualified to deliver spiritual care. It is clear that religious care would be subject, for credentialing and certification, to the jurisdiction of the ordaining religious organization. But spiritual care, as we have seen, fits into a wider niche, yet one more specific to the hospital context. This is where turf wars and budget battles have raged for the past few decades. Given the actual tasks and role of the chaplain in the hospital, it seems foolish to pay someone whose specialized training is seemingly remote from what the job demands. When what he or she will do as patient advocate really does not require anything particularly Episcopal, Lutheran, or Baptist to do it well. Remember that the primary tasks defined as spiritual care or the fostering of spirituality fit the Cabot and Dicks model and the practical part of Gelo's just fine. It is the other part, the "religious specialist" that seems extraneous and therefore risks being cut from the hospital budget. Therefore, while everyone may agree that "spiritual care" is very important, it is up for debate whether a specialist-chaplain is really necessary in order to provide it.

From this perspective one theory about spirituality's use in health care is that it is a convenient term to decouple religion from the role of ministering to the sick. It will therefore cut out an ordained, traditional clergy style of chaplain altogether from the hospital budget. Social workers, nurses, and physical and occupational therapists are all involved in spirituality and can all share in providing spiritual care. The statement of the CAOT makes more sense in this environment, since the whole issue of who can provide spiritual care is so tied to hospital expertise, specializations, and professionalism. When we argue that spiritual care is everyone's business, even doctors are encouraged to speak with patients about the latter's beliefs and values and personal meanings, in other words, to step away from medicalized language and try to communicate on another basis with suffering patients. While this might seem a good thing and while many patients might want this, doctors have little time for this kind of conversation. They see too many patients, and their main responsibility is to learn the medical facts and communicate them to the patients. Specialism still trumps the quest for meaning and connectedness because of the demands intrinsic to the institution.

Other health-care professionals may recognize spirituality as a concern. But like the doctor their primary roles and tasks are defined by the hospital environment and its professional standards. These are mandatory. Within that framework, they can all also occasionally work to share the tasks Cabot and Dicks describe so vividly and therefore go beyond the limits of their specialized expertise, rehumanizing the hospital environment. Whether this is possible or fully realistic is doubtful; remember how the majority of the occupational therapists felt "unprepared" to deal with spirituality and confused over what their roles would be. But it does show how widespread concern for spirituality disperses the responsibility to attend to it and alleviates the need for one more specialist whose job is to overcome the tyranny of specialist knowledge.

The other argument in favor of spirituality in this context is the one that separates it from religion without necessarily turning the two into antagonists or opposites. Within this setting, it is not necessary to worry over "spiritual but not religious" in the sense that Wuthnow and Roof use the phrase, for it is far more important to rely on a generic category that can potentially apply to all patients and staff. Few of the conversations initiated by the chaplain are really religious in nature, not in Cabot and Dicks' day and not in ours. Today patients include the wide range of churched, unchurched, Hindus, Buddhists, Muslims, and so on. When a specifically Buddhist issue arises, the chaplain's role is to facilitate the visit from this brand of "local clergy" (as Gelo calls them) so that religion is not completely excluded. It may be invited into the world of the hospital, but, at least officially, it is subordinated to other, more generic needs. The very universal nature of spirituality, as it is now defined, is a way to make sure that the entire patient population is covered.

Moreover, there are times when religion can be intrusive and unwelcome. Gelo's stance toward the local clergy is less negative than the stance of many in the health-care world toward patients and their families whose religious beliefs seem to fly in the face of medical reality. Often in case histories, the family's religion appears to bolster their denial of inevitable death. They still pray for a miracle, or they are sure God will heal their dying, comatose, or vegetative member. They insist that to withdraw treatment, even the most futile treatment, is to disobey God's commandment against murder. In these situations, the chaplain is called upon in the role of religious authority to communicate to the family where the secular-scientific authorities have failed to do so. "Here's someone who can speak your language," the doctor might be saying to the religious family. "He'll be able to convince you of the medical facts, even when I cannot." In these unhappy situations, it is not the chaplain's religious knowledge but the authority that he or she brings, that may persuade.

These situations may not be that statistically common. And of course there are nonreligious families whose denial is just as prolonged and unrealistic. But these cases are memorable, make everyone unhappy, and are interpreted by the hospital staff as denial. Even when everyone feels sorry for the family, when as individual persons they are neither fanatical nor obnoxious, they obstruct and challenge the expertise and the functioning of the health-care professionals.[9] Worse, in many cases they prolong the suffering of the family member they wish to protect, whose dying becomes less peaceful and more painful than it could be. In these unhappy cases, the disputes are over the procedures, the lines of authority, and the limits of giving in to a family's unreasonable demands for endless medical treatment, as much as they are over religion itself.

Another example of the "intrusiveness" of religion is the case of someone on the staff—a nurse, say—insisting on "witnessing" to patients, trying to proselytize while on the job. Just as we will see when this situation arises in other workplaces, almost everyone writing on spirituality and healthcare condemns this as "inappropriate" and "unprofessional," even devout nurses who wish to depict their profession as a vocation.[10] This behavior oversteps the boundaries, taking advantage of vulnerable patients. It is especially obnoxious where patients from many different cultural and religious backgrounds need to know that their beliefs are respected (provided these do not challenge medical authority, as in the cases discussed above). Ironically, I recall a moving testimony by an ex-patient whose hospital nurse's aide did exactly this unprofessional and inappropriate "witnessing" right before the patient's surgery. The aide succeeded in converting the grateful patient whose strong faith was initiated by this encounter. Probably no one else in the hospital knew of this experience, and the overwhelming opinion among professionals— including those who favor spirituality—is that while the chaplain might raise such concerns, the rest of the staff should keep away from them. Just as they should not share secrets of their sex lives with patients, they should not intrusively introduce religion.

If this represents an antireligious bias, it is a subtle one. We should distinguish this norm of privatizing religion from the very different sharply antireligious attitudes voiced by individuals. Take, for example, the dialogue between a nurse in a British hospice unit and her patient's father. This comes from an autobiographical narrative of a young adult daughter's death, Victor and Rosemary Zorza's *A Way to Die*, which was written explicitly to recommend hospice. In spite of the origins of hospice philosophy in the personal faith of its founder Dame Cecily Saunders, the Zorzas are relieved that there is no trace of religion in the atmosphere of the hospice where their daughter died. The nurse and the patient's father carry on a conversation mocking religion, denigrating religious people as idiots (all religions share this, apparently), and the nurse assures him that religion is excluded entirely from the hospice unit.[11] I mention this example because it struck me as so anomalous, so atypical of the way religion, spirituality, and health care are normally placed in the hospital, let alone hospice, context. There is just no call to be so contemptuous of religion, one might say, in an institution where it is already marginalized and perceived as one specialized area, on which even the chaplain does not focus full time in the role of patient advocate. That style of antireligious bias is an anomaly, but the Cabot and Dicks portrayal of the hospital environment shows how the existential quest for meaning is unintentionally repressed and silenced.

Assessment and Research on Spirituality in Health Care

Spirituality as a concept works better in a clinical setting than as a research concept. The entire discussion of care in the hospital needs some ideal of rehumanization as a protest or protection against the dominant ethos and norms of the hospital. While religion can do this, the results can cause problems, because religion can take forms that jar or interfere with, rather than ameliorate, these norms, as in the above cases where religious patients or their families seem to obstruct proper medical decisions. Spirituality as a generic human capacity offers a reminder of what the hospital ethos lacks. But for spirituality to work as a concept today, it too needs to be incorporated into the specialized, scientific-technological model of knowledge. Hence, proposals for instruments or scales for universal spiritual assessment. The staff need to learn which patients, upon admission, suffer from spiritual distress and which exhibit spiritual well-being. For example, which patients already feel anxious, intimidated, depressed, or isolated and so will be especially in need of a spokesperson or a human presence to accompany them in their ordeal. Given that the chaplain too is overworked and cannot be equally available to everyone, these screening procedures make sense. Many of the items on such scales of spiritual well-being duplicate those for general mental well-being, so that correlations between spirituality and mental health based on these scales are fictitious, but for assessment purposes that may be irrelevant.[12] Some patients are suffering, whether emotionally or spiritually or both, and they need special attention.

However, even at this stage, a coherent and clear understanding of spirituality would help. Ideally, it ought to be possible to design a questionnaire that separates spiritual well-being from general mental health—but only if "spiritual" adds something distinctive to the wider category. But try to separate spiritual anxiety from normal psychological anxiety without reference to some more particular beliefs, such as "I feel myself unworthy and abandoned by God." The latter is surely what some hospital patients must experience, but to use such language on a form assumes a religious system in which God plays an important role and where the God referred to has a personal and moral concern for individuals. This may be a basic element of all Western theism, but it is exactly the kind of particularistic belief that the concept of spirituality is meant to bypass. So, instead of such language, a scale to measure spiritual distress might say, "I feel isolated and unworthy," or "I feel no one cares about me," or "I feel disconnected from everyone and everything." These phrasings evoke nothing explicitly religious, any more than does "I feel a sense of peace and well-being." A number of such instruments have been designed and tested by researchers. Their particular phrasings hover around the religious without being as specific as a form that measures religious beliefs and emotions would have to be. As clinical instruments designed to catch potentially troubled patients in advance, these questionnaires may work, but that they measure some entity called spirituality may be an illusion, needlessly complicating what the hospital staff really hopes to find out.

We can now see how, as a research concept, as an idea upon which to build hypotheses and test them, spirituality runs into many more difficulties. Suppose we want to learn how spiritual well-being affects health outcomes. We might review all the spirituality and health literature of the last two decades. The ostensible aim is to show either the existence of a relationship between spirituality and improved health or its absence; for example, whether spiritual well-being has an impact on physical health, recovery from surgery, or survival rates after heart attacks. The spirituality measures designed for assessment of incoming hospital patients are used as research instruments to ask these kinds of questions. Hufford, in 2006, tried to do a review of this literature,[13] as have others, such as Hill and Pargament in 2003.[14] In spite of the high hopes to connect spirituality with health, two revealing conclusions emerge from these reviews of the now-abundant research.

The first is that regular attendance at worship improves health outcomes and health generally by about 25 percent, which is pretty solid for this kind of research.[15] The initial health status of the subjects was controlled for, to eliminate the possibility that the very sick were just too sick to attend. Religion, in short, does not normally function to impede or intrude upon health; it may actually enhance and support it. Yet note that this is the most simplistic measure possible. It does not ask about inner connectedness, sense of peace, purpose, or meanings. It does not ask about any of the items that the spiritual well-being scales assess. Spirituality may be difficult to define and tough to measure, but the 25 percent finding is not based on the concept of spirituality at all. Nor is it based on Schleiermacher or James. It is based on frequent attendance at public worship.

Something must account for this positive association between public worship attendance and improved health outcomes. For all I know, it may reflect nothing more profound than "Half of life is showing up." But then, this itself may be more profound than the most deeply interior of the spirituality definitions, when it comes to staying healthy. Staying involved and participating in a group are both part of showing up. Moreover, the research reveals something more specific: it is not showing up for just any group activity held by a church, synagogue, or mosque. Apparently the 25 percent figure does not hold when people meet to discuss the budget or even to do group study. Social support may certainly play a part, but the additional benefit is due, apparently, to worship in itself. Worship is an intrinsically for-itself practiced activity. Few of us worship in order to stay healthy; we do so because we believe it to be innately worth doing, not a means toward some other goal. Curiously, worship may then work in the same way that the recreational activities to be discussed in chapter 9 do; it is not just a matter of showing up; it is showing up to engage in something deeply satisfying in and of itself.

The second conclusion from the reviews of the spirituality and health literature is that some research efforts are based upon flawed, mistaken analogies to other kinds of medical research. This is particularly true for attempts to test whether healing prayer works, a research topic that really ought to be discontinued.[16] After many studies that look as empirical as possible, the problems with these emerge as insurmountable. Two groups of patients, two groups of pray-ers, some patients receive prayer, some do not, every possible control set in place. . . . These studies look like double-blind tests of experimental drugs, testing for the placebo effect against the real effectiveness of the specific drug. Here, prayer is dealt with as a therapeutic intervention, a means to an end (a problem for some religious critics of these studies). Alas, there are always "unauthorized" pray-ers, dubbed by Kevin Masters as "out-of-protocol prayer," not part of the study, who are at work compromising the results. This is exactly the equivalent of the drug-study participants who receive a placebo from the doctors but who on their own take a similar drug bought on the street and so reap its benefits and confound the study results. Moreover, we do not know whether God listens to all prayer from all pray-ers equally. An out-of-protocol prayer by St. Teresa might be more effective than the prayers of ten experimental subjects who volunteered for the study. What Masters' good critique of all these studies really shows is that what starts out as a seemingly reasonable, medically relevant question cannot be dealt with as though it were medical research, pure and simple. The naïveté of the whole area is what Hufford's large-scale review documents and this example illustrates.

What has emerged from this research is not a clear and useful concept of spirituality, I believe, but a different understanding of how religion is present in sickness and in health. Religion may or may not be useful in aiding better health or health outcomes, but it is a force and factor in enough people's lives not to be dismissed. Meanwhile, the clinical use of spirituality is not the same as what the research covers. The need for some way to transcend the medicalization of suffering and dying, already documented by Cabot and Dicks, may or may not require a single concept such as spirituality. But the need itself is so real and the problems of the hospital from the patients' point of view so permanently part of the setting and institution itself that no doubt the niche for their alleviation will remain into the foreseeable future. Call it spirituality if you will, but, whatever its name, it is needed. Yet to label it this way gives the false impression of some thing or entity that is missing and that, once introduced, will solve the problem. R$_x$ spirituality, in other words, and we are back into the mind-set of medical specialism.

One final note: We have followed the standard critique of the Western high-tech hospital as the realm of specialization and expertise that Cabot and Dicks and many others have found so humanly defective. It might be that small community hospitals, where closer connections exist between the hospital and the world outside, could solve this problem. A friend who spent his last semester of medical school in a remote village in northern India worked at such a hospital. With no laundry or food service, the families of patients washed their sheets and took them food. The villagers loved their hospital, were very proud of it, and experienced little of the alienation and intimidation so often depicted afflicting for American hospital patients. The problem was that the standard of medical care in the Indian village was absolutely awful. It was low tech, and the standard of professionalism was dreadful. The one doctor scooted off leaving the medical students alone and in charge one day. They delivered a baby using their textbook as a guide. Do not wallow in nostalgia for the good old days, when it comes to health care.

CHAPTER EIGHT

Niches for Spirituality

Spirituality in the Workplace

Work in Western Religion

In this chapter, we examine the meanings and roles of spirituality in the workplace. That phrase, along with *spirituality in business*, might have seemed an oxymoron a generation ago. While illness, suffering, and death as universal human experiences do not seem foreign to whatever sense of the spiritual we hold, offices and boardrooms and business establishments do not enjoy this intuitive connection. Yet today, the idea flourishes, and experts, consultants, and inspirational speakers advocate the introduction of spirituality into places where Principe could never have imagined it. The contemporary concept of spirituality is flexible enough to make such a location at least plausible. The aim of workplace spirituality, as we shall see, is to stretch and relocate human core meanings and yearnings to include the world of work, surely a central area of our lives. Here, too, spirituality is proposed as the solution to problems of meaning and human fulfillment for contemporary persons. In this workplace context, however, the issues are substantially different from those posed by the hospital environment for patients. Therefore, the nuances of spirituality's meanings and functions will also be different. Yet, once again, the concept introduced as a solution cannot do justice to the many complex issues it is intended to solve.

We start from what seems obvious to many of us. As with health care, there is a real discrepancy between a major institution and the human meanings of those who experience it from within. The vast majority of adult Americans spend much more time at work than we do in the hospital. Even hospital staff are at work, not experiencing a health crisis. If there is one area of life that cries out for some connection to ultimate concerns, it must be the workplace. We are not speaking of traditional callings, professions such as doctor or scholar, which were vocations long before they became careers. Those are not the focus of the workplace spirituality movement. We speak here of jobs, especially of jobs in medium-sized and large-scale bureaucratic businesses or service organizations. People want to know how their time spent in the office, at their job, connects with who they really are and what they value. Why, at the end of my life, am I so unlikely to say, "I wish I'd spent more time at the office"? We seek a better relation between contemporary work and human meanings, the human core self. While workplace spirituality may not have a solution to this question, the problem itself is a major one.

To learn how we arrived at this dilemma, we need an historical perspective, for the history of religion and work is quite complex, to put it mildly. For the vast majority of human beings down until the twentieth century's end, work meant farming, and the simple answer to the question "Why do we work?" was "Because we need to eat." Farming, the most basic occupation since the agricultural revolution of about eight thousand years ago, has simply been there as the work people needed to do. However, the task of making things grow has been made ultimately meaningful by peoples everywhere who linked the fertility of fields and gardens with the fertility of the gods and human beings. Rites that promoted increase and abundance, fertility as a sign of cosmic life, included sexual acts performed in the fields. What humans did mirrored what the universe of the gods and goddesses of the crops did. In older English usage, *the farmer fucked his fields* meant that he ploughed and tended them, to make things grow.

The people of the Hebrew Bible were also pastoralists, herders of animals. Here, too, fertility and increase were not just good economically and practically; they were signs of God's blessing. Large human families and ever-larger herds of sheep went together in the stories of the patriarchs as specially blessed by God. The work put into pastoralism could be used analogically to express God's care for his people, as in "the LORD is my shepherd, I shall not want." And yet, in the Bible there is another strand of thought about work: it is toil, bitter and hard. In the story of the expulsion of Adam and Eve from the garden, work is punishment. Everything humans need will no longer be given freely, but it must be toiled for "by the sweat of your brow."

If we ask, "How did Jesus think about work?" the answer appears to be, "hardly at all." It is not in itself an important topic for him. The lilies of the field do not work at all. Work is something that people do, but by itself it does not seem to mean much. The rich fool, who prided himself on full barns and a successful harvest, was a fool because he would die that night, and accumulated wealth is useless and meaning-less (Luke 12:13-21). That, and not work per se, is a Jesus theme. Wealth and its accumulation is pointless and an obstacle. You cannot worship both God and money.

The kind of work used by Jesus for analogies and insights into the kingdom of God is servants' work. Since few of us today are or employ full-time servants, it is often hard for us to imagine this kind of life. Ser-vants did what the master commanded and did not need to be thanked for performing required duties. Only at the final end of time, at the con-summation of God's rule, would they hear, "Well done, thou good and faithful servant. Enter into your master's joy." However, some servants are entrusted with money and are given real responsibility in the house-hold's governance. These kinds of work are used by Jesus quite directly to guide those who wish to live in alignment with the ultimate will of God. God may be Father, but he is also Master and therefore Employer.

Elsewhere in the New Testament, we are told that any kind of work can and ought to be done "for the glory of God." In the Pauline writ-ings to members of the early church communities, even the toil and drudgery of slaves could implicitly glorify God if it were done in the right spirit, with the right attitude (Eph 6:5-8, for example). One can imagine ancient Christian slaves in Roman Empire households peeling vegetables for the glory of God. The problems arose when those who were unequal in status, wealth, and power all stood together in Chris-tian worship or sat down together for agape meals. Once again, though, work in and of itself is not a major topic or problem.

Work bound one to the world of production, family life, ordinary roles in society. When these were found to be problematic—"worldly"—then ordinary work was too. Those monks who lived in the desert, how-ever, still worked. Their primary "work" was prayer. Contemplatives everywhere, not just in Christianity, are seen as performing specialized, difficult, and very necessary work on behalf of everyone, not just for themselves. Those who devoted themselves to prayer and ascetic prac-tices were not just being indolent or hoping to avoid the life of a subsis-tence farmer. They toiled in their own fashion, as the biography of St. Anthony by Athanasius, the founder of desert monasticism, makes clear.

Eventually, the monastic tradition split Christians into two groups: those with religious vocations and the laypeople whose work helped to support them. The ideal of a special calling for a dedicated religious life was applied to only one group, sanctifying its work in a special way. That was the situation wherein the original meaning of spirituality arose, in Principe's review. The Reformation challenged this and changed it. In Luther's eyes, every Christian had a "calling," and therefore no special holiness could be claimed by the monk. Even the public executioner could be saved if "called" to his unsavory office.

This is where most treatments of the topic within the workplace spirituality movement begin. If they mention this history at all, it is to note how Calvin and the Puritans intensified this doctrine of the calling, so that the work that prospered became supposedly a sign of one's election by God for salvation. In Weber's *The Protestant Ethic and the Spirit of Capitalism*, this is one of the connections. With everyone called to work at his trade or business (farming was de-emphasized here), those who worked hard could secure their religious status. Thus, success was linked not just to generalized blessings but to a specific assurance of an ultimate matter within a religious system that did not offer many other reassurances. While success in business was not the primary Puritan goal, it was an expected by-product and so a sign of one's election for divine favor. However, Weber's book ends on a famously somber note:

> The Puritan wanted to work in a calling; we are forced to do so. For when asceticism was carried out of monastic cells into everyday life, and began to dominate worldly morality, it did its part in building the tremendous cosmos of the modern economic order. This order . . . today determine[s] the lives of all the individuals who are born into this mechanism . . . with irresistible force. Perhaps it will so determine them until the last ton of fossilized coal is burnt. In Baxter's view, the care for external goods should only lie on the shoulders of the "saint like a light cloak, which can be thrown aside at any moment." But fate decreed that the cloak should become an iron cage.[1]

Here we have the profound statement of the work world stripped of meaning, made into an "irresistible force" that is beyond our power to change. Short of ecological devastation so total as to make industrial society impossible, that is the way it will remain, Weber believed. And we experience this not as freedom from brute traditional toil but as "an iron cage" of the spirit.

One challenge to this offered in the 1950s and 1960s no longer appears credible. It was believed that the increasing mechanization of modern life (automation) would buy us all leisure, off-work time in which to do what we please. Robots and computers would free us to enjoy five-hour workdays and retirement at fifty. New interests such as travel, sports, or hobbies could flourish in the time freed from work. Everything that used to involve brute toil would be taken over by machines. No more "alienated labor" would mold us and repress our true possibilities for liberation.[2] It is hard to keep from laughing cynically at predictions so utterly and completely wrong about work, technology, and society. Leisure has not disappeared, but the projected ideal of a life where all the remaining human work is interesting, self-expressive, and creative is as bizarre as Weber could have predicted. Indeed, it is a widespread subjective perception that Americans work harder and harder and harder and under more anxiety.

But the kind of work we do has changed. Farming was out for Calvin as the preferred occupation because it depended too much on factors beyond our human control such as weather (also perhaps because his adopted hometown of Geneva was a trading city) and it is no longer what we or Weber mean by work. Then there is heavy industry, factory jobs that require muscle and stamina and ideally a sense of pride in making something useful. Construction work too depends on these qualities. This represented "real work" and to many persons still does. Workers needed strong arms and backs, physical toughness, and respect for their raw materials. But these too are no longer the jobs the workplace spirituality advocates have in mind. Many of those old-style blue-collar jobs are gone and are not going to return. People in China and other places far away now do that work, just as the garment industry has moved elsewhere. We need to focus on what kinds of work Weber and the workplace spirituality advocates have in mind.

The answer: business work, office jobs, managerial and administrative work, sales and banking, "information-age" work, none of it physically exhausting, none of it performed outdoors, yet it is work that is rarely experienced as easy. It is work that requires mental alertness and involvement. Moreover, and perhaps most importantly, it is work that is done where other people are the primary environment. What machinery there is may serve as a scapegoat or substitute for frustrations with people, as in the funny video "Bad Day at the Office," where angry workers attack their computers.[3] This kind of work is entirely part of the iron cage of the modern industrial order. Some of it draws on leadership skills and imagination and vision, but it is all directed toward ends set by the economic system of which the workers are inevitably part. There is no reason women or persons with some physical disabilities cannot perform it, but mental or emotional disabilities stand out as they never did before.

Does the Reformation idea of vocation or calling still apply to this kind of work? Yes, it can, if the office is part of an organization dedicated to a charitable ideal or where the joy and creativity of designing something beautiful inspires some employees. And, as for those ancient Christian slaves, any work at all can potentially be done for the glory of God. But, overwhelmingly, it is hard to reconcile this ideal with the qualities associated with contemporary office work. The latter remains an iron cage, as Weber diagnosed it. This is principally because while one's mind must be alert to perform it and one's "people skills" are intrinsic to success at it, so few of our deeper personal ideals, aspirations, and unique meanings are connected to the time spent at work. These ideals and meanings are what constitute who we believe we really are; this is why on our deathbeds we do not wish we had spent more time at the office.

Workplace Spirituality

The contemporary workplace spirituality movement begins with this situation and tries to connect the deepest core of the individual human beings at work with the organizations and human institutions for and within which they work.

> Spirituality in the workplace is about people seeing their work as a spiritual path, as an opportunity to grow personally and to contribute to society in a meaningful way. It is about learning to be more caring and compassionate with fellow employees, with bosses, with subordinates and customers. It is about integrity, being true to oneself, and telling the truth to others. Spirituality in the workplace can refer to an individual's attempt to live his or her values more fully in the workplace. Or it can refer to the ways in which organizations structure themselves to support the spiritual growth of employees.[4]

Note how themes of meaning and connection to others are central here. Mixed in with this language of spirituality is the language of values and virtues, especially compassion and integrity. The category of practice is not as relevant here as it might be; there is no focus on skill at using office machinery or chairing a meeting or delivering a sales presentation (the yoga one might do leading up to the presentation is spiritual practice, but not the work activity itself). What the above definition also lacks is any explicit reference to transcendence, the sacred, or higher power. For in this context these terms are "too religious" and put workplace spirituality over the boundary and into religion.

Another dimension of workplace spirituality is its commitment to holism and opposition to fragmentation. Lambert states:

> Many workers want to be recognized as holistic beings, and companies believe that the full potential and creativity of an employee requires holistic happiness as well as holistic dedication to corporate work. The corporate embrace of holism has now been classified as an expression of spirituality. Family-friendly policies and fitness rooms can thus be an expression of . . . the firm's openness to the spirituality of workers when this term is defined as harmony among all aspects of life.[5]

If *holism* is defined as "harmony among all aspects of life," then the alternation between work and not-work, so basic to most of our lives, would supposedly be mitigated or partially undermined. But there seems to be more behind this use of *holism*: a yearning to apprehend and connect with the cosmos as a whole, to echo Van Ness' language. When this ideal of holism and integration is stated in such a way and "religious" words are intentionally avoided, they nevertheless creep back into definitions and claims on behalf of spirituality. Spirituality, according to Mitroff and Denton, is "the basic desire to find ultimate meaning and purpose in one's life and to live an integrated life."[6] They then rely on the concept of soul as derived from Thomas Moore to explain this: "The soul is precisely the deepest essence of what is means to be human. The soul is that which ties together and integrates all of the separate and various parts of the person; it is the base material, the underlying platform, that makes a person a human being."[7] You could hardly find a clearer vision of a universal, inescapable spiritual core, unthinkable to leave behind or outside of anywhere we go. Spirituality is the extension of this "soul" and is inclusive, universal, and timeless.[8] It encompasses the sense that everything is interconnected, but immanently so, rather than connected through a reality beyond this world or realm.[9] So although no higher power is involved, one could argue that the word *soul* was deliberately chosen in the first place (over *psyche* or *self*) because of its deep, long-standing religious resonances.

From this perspective, it would be outrageous to ask workers or employees to become aspiritual, or soulless, beings while on the job. The authors in Jerry Biberman and Len Tischler's edited anthology, *Spirituality in Business*, cite Ken Wilbur rather than Moore but make the same plea for a generic, universal human core that ought to be given space and honor in our world of work.[10] Moore and Wilbur are thinkers who may have had much more "transcendent" goals in mind, but their work seems appropriate to back up a concept of spirituality in which meaning and human depths and universality are the key ingredients.

All of these wordings and definitions stress how important and humanizing it is when businesses make spirituality a priority. Advocates for workplace spirituality challenge the conventional assumption that profit and only profit is what business and work are all about. This is a false dichotomy. The hopeful assumption of the workplace spirituality movement is that profit—the ordinary business goal—and principles do not truly conflict. "Companies with a defined corporate commitment to ethical principles do better financially than companies that don't make ethics a key management component."[11] This message is repeated frequently, since it undercuts what seems to be accepted as common sense. "Many studies have shown that people-oriented management leads to improved results in *all* traditional measures of business success: return on investment, shareholder value, employee retention, for example."[12] Corinne McLaughlin and others who make this claim point out that an atmosphere of meaningful, self-actualizing values and respect will actually create higher morale and a better work environment for all. A workplace of terrified or demoralized persons who know they will be treated like dirt even if they work hard, on the other hand, will be a nasty environment with a high turnover. Once again, this applies to normal mid-American offices or businesses, not sweatshops or farms that employ illegal immigrant labor and could barely exist if they treated their employees as other than dirt.

The other just as explicit hope is that spirituality when properly understood will be compatible with American public-sphere norms and existing labor laws, such as equal opportunity regardless of race, gender, or national origin. This is why it is so important for those who offered the above definitions to avoid any identification of spirituality with religion. Religion in the workplace is not integrative or unifying; it is divisive and intrusive. When it comes to religion, Mitroff and Denton are adamant: "no expressions of religion are to be tolerated in the workplace."[13] The inevitable features of religion are intolerance, contentiousness, closed-mindedness, authoritarianism, and bigotry. The "zero tolerance" policy protects everyone on the job from the obnoxious, disruptive, and dysfunctional presence of religion. In their discussion of a religiously based business model, these same authors find the employers and their employees "primitive" and immature in their development and thinking, using Fowler's model of cognitive, emotional and faith development.[14] Nowhere in the American health and spirituality literature is there anything close to this undisguised hostility to religion in contrast to the glow that surrounds spirituality. The language of zero tolerance is normally applied to drugs around schools, and this analogy fits. Religion here appears as a dangerous force whose presence must be guarded against. There is, in short, no connection between religion when perceived in this light, and spirituality or soul, both of which constitute the core of our being.

The most obvious reason—if not the most accurate—for this hostility is that obnoxiously pushy expressions of religion disrupt the work environment. Employees who pressure other employees to convert, make moralistic judgments about their co-workers' lifestyles in the name of religion, or refuse to work side by side with members of other faiths would seem to be the justification of this zero tolerance policy. But what to Mitroff and Denton looks like reasonable zero tolerance may appear to some of the affected employees as discrimination on the basis of religion, which is as illegal as other kinds of discrimination. The actual cases that came to court were a bit different from what one might expect from reading through the harsh discussion of religion by advocates of spirituality in the workplace. There has indeed been a rise in court cases where religious discrimination is the ground for complaint. But on the whole, these involve very narrow, particular practices of specific religions.[15] The Muslim woman who insists on wearing her head scarf in the workplace or the pharmacist who refuses to fill orders for abortion pills are the complainants. In most situations, these workplace conflicts never come to court because everyone tries to accommodate. Another pharmacist handles all the orders for those pills, for example. The head scarf can stay on, but the employee is transferred to another department where the presence of a Muslim will not offend customers. The overall impression of the authors who reviewed these cases is that religious discrimination lawsuits are handled with far less acrimony than parallel lawsuits based on claims of race or gender discrimination.[16] Ironically, Mitroff and Denton and their colleagues in workplace spirituality would probably consider an employee who was transferred because her employer thought the public might be disturbed by an African American at the reception desk as a victim, while the company that caved in to this stereotyping would be condemned as cowardly and reactionary. When it comes to religious discrimination suits, however, these same authors obviously would not be the least sympathetic. Employers have every right, and even a duty, to enforce a zero tolerance policy, and if this feels discriminatory, it is justifiable for the good of the organization as a whole and for the protection of all.

Individuals and Organizations

Within an office or business that aspires to spirituality, it is not the specific tasks that become "spiritualized" or "enspirited" but the human relationships among those who perform them. As the earlier quotation defining the movement of workplace spirituality ("people seeing their work as a spiritual path") shows, spirituality is applicable to the atmosphere of a business, but it is a fundamental quality of the workers as human beings. One thing to determine is whether spirituality is applied primarily to the individual or to the organization as a whole. We have seen how individually based the language of spirituality is, even as it tries to include connectedness as one of its central themes. But as Lambert's elaboration regarding holism suggests, when workplace spirituality focuses on the individual as the subject, it begins to resemble a perk, like good family leave policies. Employees are offered a range of features that make working for this company a good deal. Along with a day-care center and a fitness center on the campus, there will be a place set aside for prayer or meditation and also a "spiritual counselor" or a "life coach."

Lambert's discussion of workplace chaplains, life coaches, and spiritual counselors in the workplace leaves it unclear whether they work for the company or on behalf of the individual workers who consult them.[17] It is not clear even in this statement from the International Coaching Federation: "Coaching is partnering with clients in a thought-provoking and creative process that inspires them to maximize their personal and professional potential. Professional coaches provide an ongoing partnership designed to . . . help people improve their performances and enhance the quality of their lives."[18] While it seems clear that such coaches or spiritual counselors are not religious authorities, they may have the status of full-time employee or contracted consultant for the company. They may be or sound appealing to counselees because (unlike psychological counselors) a visit to such an expert implies no defect or mental illness on the part of the employee. When there is a human relations problem in one office unit of the organization, the spiritual coach may be called in to resolve disagreements or to help persuade reluctant employees to accept changes in work practices, changes that would in the long run benefit everyone. One function of the spiritual counselor was illustrated back in our discussion of virtues and vices in chapter 3. Remember the cases of the uptight employee who "operated within very narrow boundaries," the abusive doctor, and the category of stodgy "placeholders" in work environments. These persons disrupt the smooth functioning and forward progress of an organization, even when they are not "bad" people, let alone truly mentally ill. The spiritual counselor's role is to mediate, to communicate to them in a supportive yet realistic manner just how their actions and attitudes affect other workers. As a model for what one writer calls "relational intelligence" in the workplace, the counselor aims at "creating mutual, not hierarchical relationships."[19] Thus spirituality is no longer solely an attribute of individuals; it is part of the organization's own functioning as a unit. And, like fitness programs, it can be abused to bully recalcitrant employees, although its stated values prohibit this. I am sure some of the "placeholders" whose motto was "We've always done things this way" see this kind of intervention as an attack on their own integrity, core selves, and deepest values, even when nothing of the kind was directly intended.

But a workplace that includes spirituality means more than this individualized application of themes drawn from Moore or Wilbur. It is not just the employees as individuals who are souls and have spirituality; it is the organization as an organization that may seek to become more spiritual. This goal is much trickier. It includes the expectation that basic operating principles will aim to enhance the humanity of the workers and customers and that the business or organization is explicit about its core values and principles. (Explicit no matter what they are, because, in an environment that operates with mutual rather than hierarchical relations, open communication among all participants is itself a value.) We should stress how this ideal definitely does not equate with a company that is overtly religiously grounded, although sometimes these faith-based businesses are mentioned for contrast purposes.

However, it might help here to give a portrait of such an enterprise, to see how a religiously based business functions. While Mitroff and Denton might consider this case primitive, it is at least an interesting and provocative example of what its owners call a "faith based" enterprise. In West Philadelphia, the Second Mile Center operates a thrift shop in four adjacent storefronts. The shop sells furniture, clothes, books, and household items to the diverse populations of a run-down neighborhood. The premises are funky and crowded and security is a problem, and yet the store performs a service in providing affordable, basic goods to low-income residents. However, this is not its only mission. Although not a church, it is deeply and explicitly committed to "recycling things to redeem people." It describes itself as a training program, hiring people coming out of prison or addictions. It offers them a "faith based structured and supportive environment."[20] The religious identity of this enterprise is explicit in its name, in the prayer and Bible study that are required of all employees, and in the music playing in the background. When it won a commendation for its literacy program from the city of Philadelphia, the head of the program remarked that their primary "textbook" was the Bible.[21]

Although this is very definitely not what workplace spirituality endorses as its model, some of the positive aspects of this example are relevant. The assumption is that everything done at work or at home is to be done for the glory of God, including humble or unskilled tasks. (For persons with little or no work history, this may be all they will ever be ready for.) Here "work as a spiritual path" is instantiated within a very explicit religious framework. Moreover, the company behaves toward its customers as if to serve them is to serve Christ himself. Everyone, no matter how bedraggled or down and out or weird, is given attention and respect. The business' founder and leader is a role model of Christian service. As in the Gospels' ideal for the church, those who wish to lead do so by serving the others. They will do whatever it takes to assist struggling employees and will never disrespect or humiliate them. When there is no other choice than to terminate them, it will be done with regret and with genuine assistance and concern for their future. In such a religiously based organization, all employees' work and welfare and souls are of value in the sight of God, and policies about pay, benefits, and everything else should never ignore this for expediency. In this case too, the business was responsible to the environment in the sense of explicitly serving the West Philadelphia community. As one reviewer for businesses in Philadelphia noted, "This is not your typical thrift store."[22]

Although this is a Christian example, no matter which particular religion is involved, it would seem that this kind of workplace is *not* the model for contemporary workplace spirituality. Far from it—and for some advocates and experts this approaches a nightmare distortion of what they hope to establish. The explicit reason for this is that such a religious business is restrictive about who can be hired as an employee and therefore seems potentially oppressive and discriminatory by today's standards. The Bible is the literacy textbook, not the Qur'an or the Tao Te Ching. To a critic, the company requires a closed mind when it comes to religious matters. One cannot question Christian principles, even if how they are applied is continually up for discussion. By this standard, one could argue that any definitive adherence to a formal religion creates a narrow and restrictive environment, if not an absolutely authoritarian one. This at least is the portrait painted by those who want an alternative workplace spirituality ideal, and they reject a model they fear will stultify the very human qualities they want spirituality to enhance.[23] Ironically, one person's authoritarian and restrictive workplace is someone else's "structured and supportive" environment. For those fresh from prison or drug rehab, I doubt that employment at the Second Mile Center poses these issues. But as a blueprint for a more ordinary business that employs more mainstream workers, this ideal is perceived, at least by some, as intolerable. The other reason an example such as this one never appears in the writings on workplace spirituality is that the Second Mile Center reaches out to those "on the margins of society."[24] Those who wish to argue that spirituality and normal business measures of success are entirely compatible might cringe at the funky, down-at-the-heels atmosphere that makes the Second Mile Center so credible to its West Philadelphia neighbors.

These considerations lead us from the individual employees to the organization's own goals, values, and principles as they are embedded into the larger networks and meanings of society as a whole. We cannot imagine that a Christian company such as the Second Mile Center's primary business should be high-end designer jewelry or aggressive debt collection from the neighborhood poor. A company founded on religious principles—no matter how "closed minded" these may appear to outsiders—would have a hard time if it catered so directly to personal vanity or contributed to victimizing the vulnerable. To raise this concern is to ask owners and employees to consider seriously the role of the company in the larger fabric of industrial high-tech society.

Spirituality and Profits?

This is where the workplace spirituality movement seems caught in a dilemma. To demonstrate its advantages to a world of business, it must stress that a spiritual company can also be a profitable one, that the cost in time and effort to nurture the work patterns and humanity of the employees will be worth it in dollars in the end. This claim reassures everyone that spirituality will not be disruptive, will in some ways leave the larger context of business alone. Therefore, the necessity of what the company does or produces is not really much discussed, and I am not sure how it could be without entering territory that spirituality as a concept would find foreign.

Take, for instance, one of the most frequently cited examples of a spiritual and socially responsible company: Ben & Jerry's.[25] Although premium ice cream adds to the enjoyment of life for many of us, one may ask whether, in the cosmic scheme of things, it is what people should put their time into manufacturing. Perhaps this is a bit like Luther's discussion of whether the public executioner can be saved; it is easy to moralize that other people's livelihoods are frivolous or morally suspect. Yes, if the Second Mile Center sold Ben & Jerry's ice cream instead of used clothes, it might rehabilitate just as many addicts, but it would have failed in its service mission to its neighbors, who need affordable clothes and furniture more than they need premium ice cream. Whether Ben & Jerry's truly lives up to its spiritual reputation is another question. Even if it does, the focus on each organization as a realm or culture unto itself, implicit in the workplace spirituality literature, makes this kind of question difficult to face. The consultants work to transform the human environment of the organization and may indeed succeed; but the organization itself is part of a larger, more complex environment over which the company may have little control. Yes, here spirituality goes beyond the individuals as a realm unto themselves. But while some of the definitions refer to workers' desire to make a contribution to society, the focus on organizations almost bypasses this in favor of showing how "creating mutual, not hierarchical relationships" and aligning gifts, purposes, and passion (one of the essay titles in *The Workplace and Spirituality*) can transform this organization's culture. The language of generic connectedness so important to spirituality's definitions is not specific enough about how individuals, organizations, and the large-scale society and economy all connect. That is one reason such questions are so elusive in this literature on workplace spirituality.

In keeping with this, we should mention a feature of many of the materials, in print and on the Web, that present these ideas. In many cases the advocates for workplace spirituality are themselves entrepreneurs. They are in business, promoting their own expertise and consulting services. Their own business websites have inspirational names such as the Center for Visionary Leadership or Institute for Global Entrepreneurship. The research they report—the success stories are anecdotes that have some persuasiveness—rarely includes controlled studies with normal research designs. The consultant/expert will not be a disinterested party, testing out the efficacy of someone else's product. Their reports, including those "many studies" that show spirituality and business success to be compatible, are closer to a drug company's testing of an experimental drug that it hopes to market quickly. Or, even, to a commercial for a drug that cites selected research findings as part of its ad campaign. Basically, a consultant develops a program, set of workshops, or planned interventions, then is invited by a company to apply them to improve the morale or functioning of its staff. These interventions and changes may work, they may even work for the reasons they are supposed to work, but that does not make them parallel to the best of the psychological studies of health and spirituality we discussed in the previous chapter.

We are tempted to protest this whole endeavor of workplace spirituality head-on, joining forces with others such as Lambert in his relatively evenhanded but critical *Spirituality, Inc.*, and even with Carrette and King in *Selling Spirituality*. The latter see the contemporary glow for spirituality as the evisceration of religion's real power to protest the same capitalist order about which Weber wrote. Religion, when it is really working as religion, ought to be subversive and prophetic, disruptive at least some of the time. It ought not to be confined to issues such as head scarves and pills; it ought to challenge the whole world order of global capitalism, they believe. Carrette and King seem to think that the problem today is not that you are expected to leave your soul outside the door of your office. It is that your office, or its owners, want your soul, every bit of it, and have secretly stolen it away. They would judge the workplace spirituality consultants, who are brought in by companies to help improve and maintain functioning and productivity by increasing attention to employees' spirituality, as tools of this project, although probably unaware of their real function, ignorant of whom they really serve. This comes close to a conspiracy theory. I suspect, from the point of view of workplace spirituality advocates, this critique represents the haughty disdain of professional humanities academics for anything that smacks of business.

Meanwhile, since the recession of 2008, we wonder how many of the spiritual counselors, life coaches, and other expert resources documented by Lambert are still part of the scene. If a business downsizes or regrettably lays off a portion of its workforce, the perks ought to disappear first. Spirituality understood as a perk is no longer affordable, even though it may be needed more desperately, as the remaining workers worry about their job futures. And, we wonder how the spiritual companies used as examples in the workplace spirituality literature actually manage themselves in bad times. We hope that they follow what one exemplary company did—cut the higher-paid employers' salaries so as to preserve the jobs of the low-level employees. We want to believe their leaders become role models for self-sacrifice and service in this situation. We wonder how much spirituality as defined in this field can be used as a force of resistance to ordinary, mainstream, taken-for-granted workplace practices or whether these latter will triumph and spirituality in the workplace will be pushed aside when the going gets tough. Carrette and King judge spirituality as a phony solution, a bigger ballroom for bad dancers. Instead, we ask whether spirituality, as a universal human core, really helps us to dissolve the bars of the iron cage.

CHAPTER NINE

Niches for Spirituality

Recreation to Escape the Iron Cage

Recreation and Religion

As we saw, the movement for workplace spirituality had to adapt itself to the niche permitted for it by the rules and norms of the modern industrial workplace, of the world that Weber called "an iron cage." Spirituality could serve as a perk or an amelioration, but as a concept it did not fulfill the hopes of its advocates. Another niche for spirituality, however, is as a label for what we do in our times of leisure, as a way to value and honor those times and spaces of nonwork that for many of us seem vital. Here we look at attempts to turn recreation into a "spiritual path." Here the interrelation between spirituality and practice that was irrelevant to both health care and the workplace organizes our coverage. Ordinarily in recreation spirituality is the concept stretched to cover practice as well.

At the close of the last chapter, we pondered the iron cage of the modern world of work. Weber's grim image symbolized the world most of us inhabit during daylight hours, whose limits we perceive as stifling to the soul. The workplace spirituality movement tries to soften the cage bars, to reconnect our deepest selves with the world of the office and to make work a place of human fulfillment, community, and service to others. Whether it succeeds in these goals, portrayal of the soulless world of work is a good jumping-off point for the whole area of recreation, sports, and leisure activities as these become the locus of spirituality for many persons. While no one regrets not spending more time at the office, many of us display bumper stickers that boast "I'd rather be fishing" (or hunting, playing golf, cycling, etc.). We may commute to work, but we would really rather be headed off to some natural environment where we can immerse ourselves in activities that are pleasurable for their own sake. These activities restore our souls; they are beyond the iron cage. To use the language of spirituality's definitions, the activities we would rather be doing enhance our sense of connectedness, linking us to an order and sense of beauty and peace beyond our normal selves. In some cases, Nature with a capital N may be the higher power and cosmic oneness with which we connect, a connection we yearn for as we sit in traffic on the way to work. But activities that are done on a special designated playing space, such as a tennis court or golf course, also share this "outside-the-cage" quality. They constitute a "second world," in the words of Andrew Cooper.[1] We will examine how this second world coincides with what some of the definitions of spirituality point toward or how it perhaps confuses two alternatives that have essential differences. These questions arise as soon as recreation is valued as more than distraction. If we are on a trail in the woods or in a boat on the lake or on the golf course, we want to believe that our souls have moved outside the iron cage.

This chapter looks first at recreation that gets us out into Nature, where the link to spirituality as already defined is more obvious. Then we will look at recreation activities that have been assimilated into practices and linked sometimes very explicitly and directly to Zen, yoga, and meditation for the purpose of perfecting (or improving) one's performance. But to highlight the importance of these topics today, a brief review of the sad lack of connection between recreation and religion in the West is needed, just as we needed a long-term perspective on work and religion.

While other cultures participated in sacred games (for example, Shinto shrines held archery and sumo contests), the Western pattern was to sever religion from anything that smacked of sports or games. Athletic contests, made noble and important by the Greeks, appeared to Hellenistic Jews as pagan and idolatrous exhibitions. Moreover, the nudity of the participants appeared shameful, not noble. To join in these organized games was taken as a sign of defection from *torah*, from Jewish life and community. The early Christians inherited this attitude. In addition, their martyrs were often the victims of brutal Roman entertainments. "Christians to the lions!" meant fun and entertainment for spectators, the bloodier the better. It was hard to overcome this heritage and establish any positive link between religion and organized sports. However, in all reviews of the historical relationship, the Puritans come in for the most blame, as they supposedly taught that pointless exertion and physical activity (especially on the Sabbath) was godless and a waste of time and therefore of money. There was no such thing, in Puritan eyes, as innocent recreation. This overstates the reality. Apparently John Calvin played bowls on Sunday with his friends. But the violent and unruly atmosphere of many sports, filled with drunken profanity, did make them seem antithetical to what proper Christian behavior required. Early ball games, the precursors to modern baseball, shared this atmosphere of masculine mayhem with now-defunct sports such as bear-baiting and ratting (betting how many rats a dog can kill in one minute).

This changed only in the nineteenth century, and then only in a very specialized, selective environment. Boys' boarding ("public") schools in England were the place where organized games such as rugby were designed to teach the values of gentlemen and to inculcate "muscular Christianity." Nick Watson and John White's review of this movement to link athletics with faith (in *Sports and Spirituality*) emphasizes how expectations about masculinity, rule-governed behavior, and "fair play" were all meshed with the belief that the playing field would prepare young middle- and upper-class men for "the game of life."[2] To what extent this idea still holds, and whether it is true, is still under debate.

While organized, often violent sports continued to be problematically related to religion, other recreational activities could be pursued in an atmosphere of peace, beauty, and leisure. The seventeenth-century classic *The Compleat Angler*, by Izaak Walton, promotes "the most honest, ingenuous, quiet and harmless art of angling," which "begats habits of peace and patience."[3] It appears that this marks the articulate introduction of a recreational practice or art pursued for its own sake, a second world set apart and "compleat" in itself. This kind of fishing is done by gentlemen, with intensity and fervor, but not because any major utilitarian practical outcome is at stake (the anglers sometimes give their catch away to pretty girls they meet on the road back to the inn). The fly-fishing father and sons of Norman Maclean's *A River Runs Through It* continue the tradition. They are Presbyterian, but their real religion is fly-fishing.[4]

By 1900 fishing was not the only such activity that could be pursued in this manner. Both boys and girls could pretend to be Indians, learn woodcraft (sometimes from real American Indians), and paddle. This was fitting for the era when national parks were established, when wilderness became for the American public something other than undeveloped resources and real estate. We shall soon see the consequences and meanings of this transition. But although the scouts and their crafts are an interesting chapter in how Euro-Americans co-opted American Indians and their culture, there was nothing taught as explicitly religious in these activities.[5] Whatever the other links between scouting and Christian formation, it was not because canoes and tents linked one with God. Just as gymnastics has nothing to do with Eastern Orthodox Christianity in Romania, so the roots of the connection between outdoor recreation and spirituality had to come from elsewhere.

One negative connection is suggested by Tillich's redefinition of *faith* as "ultimate concern." Suppose one pursued angling, or golf, as one's ultimate. Tillich really had no trouble dismissing this particular challenge to his thinking, since such pastimes did not rise to the level of menace of Nazism, which claimed to be the replacement for worn-out religions and political ideologies. Angling (or golf) was, as Walton assured us, intrinsically harmless. But golf or fishing could still be pursued *religiously*, with the kind of fanatical devotion and tunnel vision that bores nonparticipants and resembles an addiction more than a pastime. We all know persons who play unplayfully, who obsess about their game, and who keep elaborate statistics about their performance. They are popularly the butt of jokes, as in P. G. Wodehouse's story "Those in Peril on the Tee."[6]

But perhaps these examples are distortions of some more fundamental and valid quest to perfect a practice, to achieve an excellence in what we do, not for the sake of an external reward but just for doing an activity perceived as really excellent in itself. If so, then aid from the wisdom traditions' spiritual practices might make more sense, be more fitting. It is not that golf is someone's real religion but that it could be pursued with the same craft, care, devotion, and intrinsic values that any traditional practice teaches and with the same intrinsic virtues of courage, honesty, and fairness. In mastering the craft, the practitioner is somehow ennobled, stretched into becoming the best as a human being, not just an excellent player. Stretched toward the universe as a "maximally inclusive whole," to use Van Ness' definition of spirituality itself.

Nature Spirituality

"In wilderness is the salvation of the world," claimed John Muir, an early voice in the American environmentalist movement and an activist on behalf of the national parks. We may wonder where Muir got such an idea and whether it was indeed as potentially anti-Christian as it sounds. In his case, the answer to the latter question is yes. Muir's charming autobiography of his childhood, *The Story of My Boyhood and Youth*, tells of his superstrict Calvinist upbringing and harsh schooling in Scotland and his spontaneous discovery of wonder and joy in the observation of Nature.

> This sudden plash into pure wildness—baptism in Nature's warm heart—how utterly happy it made us! Nature streaming into us, wooingly teaches her wonderful glowing lessons, so unlike the dismal grammar ashes and cinders so long thrashed into us. Here without knowing it we still were at school; every wild lesson a love lesson, not whipped but charmed into us. Oh, that glorious Wisconsin wilderness![7]

He did not try to get away from God; he tried to get away from his father's tyrannical and oppressive God. He found an alternative ultimate concern in the outdoors, and he continued this quest that was never completely secular.

The contrast and conflict between Nature spirituality and organized oppressive religion is stark here. Advocates for the former contribute to the dichotomy's plausibility when they repeat in their own lives Muir's experiences. The dichotomy appears in the well-known poem by Mary Oliver, "Wild Geese," as the poet assures us that "you do not have to walk on your knees," repenting, but can listen to the wild geese whose cries announce your membership in "the family of things."[8] Nature offers us connection, not guilt and hellfire. Here we do seem to have a solid case where spirituality clashes with religion. Or, rather, it is not the inner universal human core of most of the ninety-two definitions but the spirituality of the older two-poled variety offered by Principe and Van Ness. Spirituality as used here depends on specific content: a vision of Nature with a capital N, motherly and charming. Nature is a whole, a cosmos, a numinous power even when seemingly peaceful and at rest. This is the Nature who "wooingly teaches" us. This is the Nature of the Hudson Valley school of landscape painters, of the transcendentalists. This is a Nature to be contemplated with awe, not the nature faced by the farmer who must remove rocks and tree stumps from the fields.

Roderick Nash's classic, *Wilderness and the American Mind*, tells the story of how this Nature was discovered as a sacred cosmos.[9] Before, nature as "wilderness" had been scary, chaotic, and at best waiting to be "tamed" by Europeans who could turn it into farmland. But Nature for its devotees (this is the right word) was different. It did not need humans to be completed. Actual human inhabitants, the American Indians, were assimilated into the landscape as part of Nature, one more form of wild-life. As "Nature's children," they had a place in it. At the same time, Europeans started to climb mountains not to get to the next valley but because the mountains were there. They especially loved the Swiss Alps or the mountains around the British Lake Country to give themselves the experience of contemplation, an encounter that awed, freed, and connected them to the cosmos in its sublime beauty. Mountains might remind the Deist of God the watchmaker, but nothing in this human response to them could remain "within the limits of reason alone."

The story of Nature as the locale for this sense of spirituality is most classically found in Henry David Thoreau's *Walden*. Walden Pond was not very "wild" geographically, but it was outside a settled place, and therefore it was as good a place as any for Thoreau to practice his experiment in alternative lifestyle. While for the wretched Irish family he displaced it had just been vacant land for squatters, for Thoreau it was the entrance to a vision of life outside social conventions. Thoreau (or, at least, the narrator of *Walden*) perceived the bars of the modern iron cage even as they were being forged, and he wanted a place to dwell outside it, at least for a while. This voluntary removal to the woods had to be solitary, so as to minimize distractions and reinforce the sense of self-reliance he cultivated. "I went to the woods because I wished to live deliberately," he tells us. "To front only the essential facts of life . . . I wanted to live deep and suck out all the marrow of life."[10] Those who emulate him do not necessarily stay the full two years. For some, fifty days of solitude is more than enough (as in Doris Grumbach's dismal narrative's title).[11]

Thoreau applied the ideals and metaphysics of New England tran-scendentalists, the "inventors of mysticism," to outdoor living. The rest-less souls of Leigh Schmidt's history were urban, educated persons in a long-settled area. But move out to Walden Pond, and themes such as pantheism, universal harmony, and Nature take on a fresh reality. To live a transcendentalist mystical life, without having to clutter up one's life with other concerns was Thoreau's aim. For Thoreau, the individual

activities of daily living took meaning from the total natural environment in which he did them. This tension persists in the many more recent
accounts of "wilderness spirituality." It is not climbing or paddling that
releases the participant from the iron cage of the modern social order
but immersing oneself in a special total environment outside the human
world. A woman who undertook a strenuous and dangerous solo kayak
trip around the shores of Lake Superior did so in order to achieve personal empowerment, but the majesty of this largest and fiercest body of
inland water in North America forms the setting for her self-explora-
tion.[12] Yes, there are artificial indoor rock walls, and one can learn to
kayak in a swimming pool, but it is the natural world, Nature with a
capital N, wilderness as the world's salvation, that is the ultimate chosen
ideal for the one on a spiritual quest.[13] Principe's and Van Ness' language
of dual-pole spirituality is needed to depict the outer or objective pole
with which a connection is made.

But if this is a quest *toward* something, it is also an attempt at escape
from. For the Lake Superior kayaker, it was clearly an escape from her
husband and the restrictive confines of an unsatisfactory marriage. But,
beneath this, it was escape from society's roles and regulations, the iron
cage again. Weber wrote in 1920, when he could point to the enormous
force of the modern industrial order as an overwhelming reality. Thoreau's mid-nineteenth-century New England was hardly brutalized by
this force, at least not yet. But he saw it coming. For early industrial
society, anything large, fast, and mechanized represented "progress,"
and nothing symbolized this more than railroads. Thoreau was disturbed by the glimpse and sound of a train, which disrupted his wilderness experience. "We do not ride on the railroad, it rides upon us."[14] As
Leo Marx's *The Machine in the Garden* shows, it was the intrusion of a
train's roar into the quiet contemplation of one's private outdoor space
that became the parable for how American transcendentalist sensibility,
that of the advocates of Nature spirituality, encountered the modern
industrializing world. Emerson wrote in his journal:

> I hear the whistle of the locomotive in the woods. Wherever that music comes
> it has its sequel. It is the voice of civility in the Nineteenth Century saying,
> "Here I am. . . . Whew! Whew! Whew! How is real estate here in the swamp
> and wilderness? Ho for Boston. I will plant a dozen houses on the pasture
> next moon, and a village anon."[15]

There was always for him a sense of loss and threat associated with
the brute mechanical power of the world of industry, of progress and

urban sprawl. The train rushing through swamp and wilderness was an emblem of intrusion, one world about to conquer another. Emerson, Thoreau, and their friends were right to be threatened by these noises: do not look now, but the rural landscape of North American will soon be transformed into Chicago, Detroit, and Pittsburgh. The stage is set for John Muir, who could promise salvation in connection with Nature, far away from what trains and industrial cities represented.

By 1900, when Muir wrote, there was still a lot of wilderness out West. There is still a lot of wilderness today in Pennsylvania, too. It is easy to get to, compared with travel in Thoreau's or Muir's day. But it is distant from Philadelphia in every other way. Today, there are actually fewer train noises to disturb the hiker or paddler, because the railroads have come and gone, and many tracks are now turned into bicycle trails. What is different from Thoreau's day is that such spaces are now enclaves, separated and set-aside places where urban and suburban dwellers can visit and "recreate," but where permanent inhabitants find it harder to make a living except off visitors. The Pennsylvania governor wanted "night sky" areas, recreation spaces distant from all traces of towns; the locals wanted jobs. One such enclave is the state park surrounded once by farmland but now by housing developments and shopping malls, an unhappy fulfillment of Emerson's train's desires. When this happens, the park's function is now a local version of Walden Pond, even if the sound of trucks on the highway is not that far off.

The connection between this wilderness enclave for recreation and spirituality should be clear. The outer pole in the two-poled model is the cosmos as a whole, symbolized and accessed via the landscape and its creatures. The inner pole is the individual's yearning for meaning and completeness through intentional participation in this environment, for a place in "the family of things." Joseph Price's chapter on naturalistic recreations in Van Ness' *Spirituality and the Secular Quest* uses the two-poled definition of this volume and reviews how prevalent and plausible Nature activities now seem as candidates to reveal this cosmos beyond the iron cage. The boy who shouts "Yes!" while swimming in a California river explained to his puzzled father: "This is what life is all about!"[16] Sometimes it is not the dramatic large-scale Nature but its small-scale particularity that evokes this response. Come upon a young mink diving for fish by a lake's shore. *This*, and not what society usually values, is what life is really all about.[17]

There are, however, problems with this expression of spirituality, even beyond the recognition that the Nature it sees as its "chosen ideal," to use Principe's language, is a creative human imaginative construction as much as it is a fact of the universe. As with all types of spirituality that fit the two-poled model, there are ways it can go wrong, idolatries, to use Tillich's label. Nature spirituality may disappoint, disillusion, and destroy just as Muir's father's Calvinism almost destroyed the boy on the farm.

One of these ways Nature spirituality can destroy is that its divinity is not always warmhearted or charming, in spite of Muir's words. It can be deadly, and for some who quest for its heart, the risk must be high. "Extreme" outdoor activities are dangerous, and that seems to be what draws those who practice them. White-water rafting led one participant to exclaim, "You are riding so far on The Edge . . . your fear turns into ecstasy."[18] For others, fear turns into death by drowning. There is a collection of harrowing tales told by those who fell off mountains and managed to survive and another even more somber volume of tales from the widows of those professional climbers who did not. People think of a death on a high mountainside as somehow glorious, writes one of these widows. But when her husband's body was recovered on the slope of K2 in the Himalayas several years later, it seemed he had died the most lonely, forsaken death a human could endure.[19] This is not connectedness with Nature so much as disconnection with all that is alive and valued.

Other problems with the spirituality of Nature and recreation may seem less serious, but they reveal cracks in the glowing picture Thoreau, Muir, and others painted. Any activity in the wilderness requires proper equipment, including proper food. By now, anyone wishing to do anything outdoors can hardly have escaped the bombardment of specialized products marketed for their needs. Wilderness has not escaped consumer culture; it has been annexed to it, like the train that turned swamp and woods into future real estate on its rush toward Boston. While some of the gear now sold to those who venture into Nature is helpful for safety, such as helmets and water-repellent clothing, a lot is needless clutter, which would cause Thoreau to turn in his grave. It is marketed to persons who either feel unprepared and inadequate to face actual outdoor challenges or to those whose major motive is to show off their gear.

Not all of this "gear" is as physical as wet suits and helmets. We think we want to escape the iron cage, at least temporarily. We go off road and find our wild enclave, only to discover that we have brought all our habits and clutter, material and mental, with us. We carry a huge amount of baggage, much of it invisible to us. It is easy to laugh at the people who wanted a training video before canoeing on the Mullica River, a narrow, twisty stream that runs through the New Jersey Pine Barrens, where major hazards are logs and drunken paddlers. But there is something sad about this too. Wilderness was supposed to free us from the pressures of the marketplace, of the world of work and consumption. The noise of the train may be rarer, but people bring their own equivalent intrusive noises with them.

Thoreau pointed out that it is harder to pare down the clutter of mental possessions than to abandon physical ones. There is no training video for the Mullica River, and expensive accessories can be left at home. But the habit of treating outdoor recreation as if it were work, the office in the woods, so to speak, is much more difficult to break. If we wish to escape the iron cage and seek spirituality in Nature and be "re-created," pure and free and connected to the cosmos as a whole, then the mental baggage must be examined and rejected unless it serves this goal. Spirituality in Nature leads us into the role of practices that promise, or can be revised to promise, help in achieving this deliverance from unwanted clutter.

Recreation as "Zen for the West"?

Sometime during the 1920s, a German philosophy professor named Eugen Herrigel went to Japan, where he wished to study Zen Buddhism. Now Zen is not the majority school of Buddhism in Japan, but it had already been publicized by D. T. Suzuki, whose writings on this paradoxical and "unreligious" branch of an Asian tradition had intrigued many Westerners already. Herrigel knew from Suzuki that "Zen is not a philosophy, Zen is not a religion."[20] Therefore, it cannot be learned the way a Western philosophy or religion is learned. It is learned by instruction and practice in the traditional Japanese crafts, and so Herrigel studied archery, while his wife learned flower arranging. To learn archery, Japanese Zen-style, is to learn how to attend to each and every motion, with the eventual goal of becoming the bow, the arrow, and the target. The subject-object dichotomy of Western (and ordinary Eastern) reality is undone, and one's own being and that of one's craft objects merge. To learn archery this way takes time, practice, and a ruthless master who can spot shortcuts that a pupil will use to bypass real learning. This instruction is nonverbal, in that what is learned is not thoughts, words, or propositional truths but something much more basic about reality (or Reality or, for Buddhists, Buddha-nature or Emptiness). Herrigel's classic and delightfully readable account of his training, *Zen in the Art of Archery*, became the blueprint for an eventual genre of works that focus on perfecting a practice using the methods of Zen.[21]

Shockingly, Herrigel's book is something of a sham. It is not what it pretends to be, an actual account of real experiences. He was never in Japan long enough to have had the kind of training he describes. His teacher was unconnected to Zen, and the pupil's Japanese was so poor that he probably misunderstood many of his instructor's words. Herrigel wrote a composite of what he actually may have done, what he wished he had done, and what an ideal Western student might have done in learning Zen.[22] Perhaps this exposure of the "myth" behind Herrigel's book suggests that Zen fills an empty niche in the minds of Western intellectuals, a niche that Suzuki and then Herrigel perceived and claimed. A niche of yearning for some knowledge that lies outside religion and philosophy and some "practical" means to achieve it. Zen in this sense is a way of being and knowing that resembles the experiences we have just examined as spirituality in Nature: "Yes! This is what life is really about!" The difference is that books in the genre of Zen in the art of _____ link the joy and spontaneity of recreation in Nature with the rigorous atmosphere of a practice. To achieve connectedness with the cosmos as a totality, one must first concentrate and focus on doing very particular actions, with an intense, uncluttered, and yet detached focus.

This link between spirituality, recreation, and practice is indigenous to traditional Japan, not just to Zen. The arts of calligraphy, flower arrangement, and playing instruments such as the koto are learned by many Japanese as they come of age, and many adults continue to practice them for much of their lives. Their mastery is a never-ending lifelong quest for perfection. They study with masters, or eventually on their own, but there is no point at which they stop, because there is always room for further perfection. These practices resemble St. Teresa's system of prayer in *The Interior Castle*; they are intrinsically worthy in themselves, and the student's effort and perseverance itself is considered one of their benefits. Although no one would study and practice hard for a decade to produce something ugly or forgettable, let alone something known to be harmful, these traditional arts are not, today at least, truly "useful" in daily life, whatever their origins in former times. No one now learns archery to fight for his samurai feudal lord.

The package of Zen in an art was exported to the West, where it could continue the ethos of "Zen" Herrigel's book expresses. Take, for example, *The Tassajara Bread Book*, a cookbook produced by the baker for a Zen monastery in California. Since bread is not a Japanese food, the connection with Zen cannot come from the product or the materials used to make it. But the author, whose very un-Japanese name is Ed Brown, manages to convey just the sense of serious effort, simplicity, and beauty—with a touch of humor. "The most delicious food is made by someone who really cares about what they're doing. If you have never made bread, your first batch is going to be better than nothing. After that, no comparison! Each batch is unique and full of your sincere effort. Offer it forth."[23] On this page is a Japanese-style drawing of a monk about to cross a bridge—a fine symbol for the first step in learning a new practice. The recipes take about three times as long to prepare as those in the *Fleishman's Yeast Cookbook*, look much less elegant, and do engage those who follow them properly in an activity that demands "your sincere effort." True to the Buddhist ethic of detachment, Brown announces to his readers at the end that he now no longer cooks but builds stone walls for the monastery.[24] However, those of us who want to bake but not switch to stonework still use his book, which also inspired a respect for whole grains and other "natural" ingredients much less fashionable when the book was first published in 1970 than now. Yes, there are faster and more efficient ways to bake bread, and anyone can buy loaves at a store, but that is not the point of a traditional practice.

This model of practice can be applied to recreational activities, not necessarily in Nature but anywhere we do what will "re-create" us. Play, sports, the activities covered in the previous section, all of these can become "Zen-ized." There is something that we wish to reach or experience that these activities can offer. They therefore fling down a challenge to the Puritan in us who says that kayaking, golf, or baking are a waste of valuable time that ought to be spent at work. When done with sincere effort and genuine care, these activities are meaningful and fulfilling, and they bring us joy as well as sore muscles and seem to set us just briefly outside Weber's infamous iron cage. Here is where the consumer passion for gear is transformed into genuine effort to prepare and make one's experience free from needless discomfort. Even Brown has a section on kitchen necessities and on utensils, although it is very low tech even by 1970 standards.[25] The Zen in the art genre teaches us to be concerned with equipment in the sense of respecting it, not necessarily accumulating more or it.

The model of a practice used here is clearly separated from Nature in the sense that Muir and Thoreau understood it. Baking is not learned in the wilderness, and the whole Thoreau mystique of immersion in the natural world may be missing entirely. Sports take place on playing fields, crafts are learned in designated spaces, and baking requires an oven. A few sports do use the natural world as their venue, such as long-distance running and cycling. Even so, in contests there is a planned-out route set aside and marked off for participants. Nature is not central to this form of recreation.

Nevertheless, there is something of Nature that does not get left out and that is intrinsic to the Zen in the art practice. That is the human body. Even as many of these guides stress mastering the mental game (the subtitle of Joseph Parent's *Zen Golf*), the original Herrigel model of learning not through words and concepts but through physical actions remains.[26] The "mental game" may be to move the mind out of the way temporarily so as to let the body do its thing—after the basic pattern of controlled, disciplined motion has been established. Parent divides the actions of golf into preparation, action, and response and then further subdivides these so that, at every minute place in a sequence, one is ruthlessly aware of one's thoughts, movements, expectations, and anxieties. As a Buddhist, he observes the flow of thoughts and feelings, analyzing them into moment-by-moment arisings and subsidings. To perfect the mental game is to calm the mind, focus attention, let go of distractions (especially rumination on past failures). He points out the many negative messages players send themselves, so that the mental game defeats the physical game on the course. In fact, much of the mental game of Parent's teaching is to try to undo the habits of mind that exhausted and depleted us at work, so that we would rather be out on the golf course. Zen golf, like Zen baking, is an exercise in controlled, efficient activity. Bodily knowledge of this kind comes from doing, from repeated tries and flubs and more tries. It does not come from just reading or thinking. Indeed, a book by Tiger Woods called *How I Play Golf* was declared by a sportscaster to be as useful as a book by Beethoven entitled *How I Write Symphonies*, not just because of the level of expertise assumed by the author but because this kind of practice knowledge is just not taught through a book. Parent's Zen instruction book may work because he is a

Buddhist practitioner and a golf instructor, used to the kind of training on both fronts that Herrigel describes.

Embodiment matters for these expressions of spirituality as practice. This theme incorporates the anti-Platonic thrust of contemporary spirituality literature and its holistic thinking about health and wellness generally. We missed these motifs in the two previous sections of this chapter, for they are tied more to practice than to the definitions of spirituality that stress meaning and connectedness. To attend to the body's own messages and heed them respectfully: this part of the ethic of recreational practice falls under honesty in our earlier chapter's discussion of virtues. Measure your powers, stamina, and strength. Do not lie to yourself about what you are physically capable of doing. On the golf course, this apparently means to admit that a shot is "unplayable," if not by Tiger then certainly by you. Even those who risk their lives to experience "on the edge" moments must have some awareness of when not to ski down each and every mountain.

Sports, or activities such as golf or kayaking, have been called "Zen for the West." We should debate this, even if we use the most open, umbrella-like definition of spirituality available. Andrew Cooper, who spent time in a Zen monastery and writes about sports, believes the answer is, no, these activities are not really the same as traditional meditative practices. Both sports and religious meditation promise a second world outside the world of ordinary reality—but they are not the same second world.[27] As he and a few of the other American Zen trainees snuck off to play basketball,

> we shared a recognition, intuitive and largely unspoken, that sport has a basis that is intrinsically its own and is distinct from that of a meditative path. Also unspoken, and, at least for me, unconscious was a sense that to sully the difference by approaching sport as a kind of yoga was to diminish sport by placing it in a context with which it has no organic relationship.[28]

The proper context for Zen practice is Buddhism as a tradition, with a community, an ethic, a way of life within which meditation, and even baking, may fit. Basketball as Americans play it is not the same; its second world is on a court, and it includes (as Cooper believes all sports do) the motif of a contest at its heart. To conflate the two is to miss the point of both. Although there is a kind of transcendent perfection possible within the world of sports (*Playing in the Zone* is Cooper's title), this is significantly and irrevocably different from the transcendence offered through Zen or indeed through the system of prayer in *The Interior Castle*.

Both may offer escape from the iron cage of work and modernity, but the escapes are different and produce different results. Cooper could have drawn on Principe's definition of spirituality as tied to one's "chosen ideal" and all the rest in Principe that draws attention to central life commitments and choices. Without these features, it is much more difficult to articulate Cooper's intuitive insight. Some things can be meaningful, but their meanings are not to be "sullied" by confusion with other also meaningful things.

Here, we should remember, we are talking of the practice model of Zen or golf or any recreational activity. This practice model does not grow directly out of any contemporary definitions of spirituality; it has become attached to them, but the relationship and connections are far from obvious. Cooper and others wonder whether golf is spiritual after all because it is a practice that can be "Zen-ized," as in Parent's book. Or maybe it is spiritual because it is played outdoors in some lovely surroundings, so that Nature is in the background, so to speak. (If so, then basketball is out!) Perhaps it is spiritual because, as in Scott Peck's *Golf and the Spirit*, one can learn lessons of honesty, humility, and perseverance (basically, the virtues of any practice) that can then be applied to life.[29] One thing seems clear: the answer to any of these questions cannot be found via the definitions of spirituality. They are both too innate to capture the practice model's focus on effort and intentions and too global and diffuse to discern differences and boundaries among the various second worlds themselves.

These questions about recreation and spirituality themselves point us back to one of the niches that spirituality as a concept is expected to fill. It is expected, in this area of recreation, to let us cross that bridge portrayed in the cookbook's Japanese-style drawing, to open for us the world outside the iron cage. In spite of attention to materials of particular crafts, it does not seem to matter much whether it is golf, archery, baking, or outdoor Nature activities: we want a bridge to something beyond the world of work. To get at the depth of the yearning for this, I believe that Principe with his two-poled and old-fashioned definition is more effective than contemporary one-poled understandings of spirituality.

The principle dilemma for those who seek in recreation any of the release promised is that the world within the iron cage is not so easily left behind. The monk in the drawing easily crosses the bridge—like the early Puritan who wore the world's cares like a light cloak. But, for us, things are different. The railroad's "Whew! Whew! Whew!" whistles in our minds, not just in the woods. This is what Parent, the Zen golf instructor, can help us identify and hopefully silence. When golf is played his way, it apparently is less "like work"; it is more freeing and less debilitating to the ego. The human environment of the workplace was totally people centered, while in Parent's golf manual the other players fade entirely. Their judgments about you as a player are unimportant; their power to demoralize you is eliminated. You play your game, not theirs (or Tiger's). When this happens, you have truly left the workplace, the iron cage. You may not have overcome the subject-object dichotomy and become one with the club, the ball, and the green, but you will have crossed the bridge, and you are not in the office any more.

We have not discovered whether sports build character or whether Parent's kind of golf make one a better person or just a better player. Nor have we affirmed with Muir that, yes, in wilderness and the spirituality of Nature, there is salvation. Beyond these hopes lies one more grandiose, utopian, and absolute. This is a promise that turns spirituality into the world's salvation. Maybe this lies beneath the surface of accounts such as *Deep Water Passage*, whose author kayaked her way around Lake Superior and into freedom and personal empowerment, just as for Muir the wilderness was the source of salvation. But we will look in our conclusion at the more direct and recent attempts to find in spirituality, however amorphously constructed, the fulfillment of global, total utopian possibilities of a cosmic Change.

Spirituality Brings the Change
A Critique

The Promise of Global Utopian Change

We have seen how the murky yet attractive concept of spirituality expanded from humble and restricted beginnings and found niches in today's intellectual ecology. The concept now presents itself as the missing ingredient for health care and business, the secret liberating joy of recreation. We have reviewed the arguments and evidence for why spirituality has seemed so quickly and for so many to be the solution to long-standing and severe problems in these important areas of our lives. Maybe the concept is nothing but "a bigger ballroom for bad dancers" or residual religion for those who have left the religion of their upbringing behind. Nevertheless, spirituality has found a place in our world. In fact, it has found many places, not all of which cohere or match the abstract multiple umbrella-like definitions of the term.

Yet behind all the specifics of definitions and contexts lies the intense glow of the concept, the hope that in spirituality is the world's salvation. This is what lies beyond any specific evidence that spirituality increases good health outcomes or makes businesses more successful. This is what links the concept to hopes for world peace, restoration of the planet's environment, and deep personal fulfillment. Therefore, in this concluding chapter, we look at some visions of spirituality in which such utopian claims are prominent, where they mobilize hopes that in a traditional Christian religious context would be called "eschatological." That term refers to "last things," to the consummation of history and inauguration of the total reign of God, who will create for us "a new heaven and a new earth." We use *utopian* instead, because our spirituality advocates do not emphasize "last" and do not see God as the agent. What they picture for us is a gigantic, glorious Change, worldwide and liberating. It is a comprehensive vision of a perfected human world, where no one must settle for mere amelioration of present conditions.

In 1906 H. G. Wells wrote a science fiction novel called *In the Days of the Comet*, which tells the story of "the Change."[1] In Wells' story, a comet seems to menace earth. Everyone who looks up in the sky can see it and fears the day of collision. But when that day comes, there is no collision. Instead, the comet releases a gas that increases human intelligence, virtue, and appreciation of beauty. All of the characters suddenly are filled with loving-kindness and realize how idiotic and selfish their quarrels and rivalries had been. They immediately all join together and get to work to rebuild their world, replacing the ugly with the beautiful and distributing goods and services absolutely fairly. In this story, the comet does what no human government, religion, or educational system can, instantly and effortlessly. Human beings, and so human society, are simply Changed. Wells may have criticized utopian fantasies elsewhere, but *In the Days of the Comet* is a classic case of a utopian transformation made almost convincing. Everyone suddenly just *knows* how obvious the answers to all problems are, and thus all humanity enters a new age.

What Wells did well, as an imaginative novelist, countless other have done before and after. His comet comes from outer space (as if to make up for his murderous Martians in *The War of the Worlds*), and its numinous power overwhelms and transforms the whole human race. In more classic religious visions of this total transformation, God steps in to end history, raise the dead, and begin the era of his total reign. Religious versions also include a last battle against evil—its final defeat—but the outcome of that battle is never in doubt. In monotheistic religions and in Buddhism (where the future Buddha Maitreya serves the same function), the consummation is a joyous fulfillment of all that these faiths can promise.

Meanwhile, the more secular-scientific version of this theme uses the concept of progressive evolution to frame the same hopes for total transformation. Although evolution in biology is not teleological, moving forward to some end or goal, evolution as a utopian concept reaches forward toward final perfection, a unification of all seeming contradictions, and away from the partial, the primitive, the undeveloped. While today biologists argue over whether evolution comes gradually or in fits and starts ("moments of speciation"), those who use this concept to prophesy about human society see humanity now on the brink of a sudden, dramatic Change, a moment of incredible historical transition. Evolution here comes as a power from within the system of life, although in biology it is always change in relation to an environment, rather than a postulated internal drive to evolve. When their environment does not change, successfully adapted species do not either (think of sharks, which have persisted as well-adapted creatures through many earthly eras). Evolution understood as a vehicle for a utopian ideal propels humanity toward a goal without reference to particular changes in the physical environment. Although *propels* and *drives* may give the impression it will happen inevitably, without our help, most advocates of the new era of spirituality as worldwide Change believe people's own efforts do contribute to this movement.

In these visions of a Change, sudden and ultimate, spirituality serves as a central core. Spirituality today is what anticipates the Change and will triumph as it replaces the leftover obsolete failed phenomena like religion. Spirituality will, like Wells' comet, be a force for good that will make solutions to today's intractable problems seem obvious. Spirituality's triumph will make world peace achievable, solve the environmental crisis, and bring about a just distribution of power and material goods for all the world's people. Like Wells' comet, it will not bring these wonderful results about by force or political manipulation, because these methods would preclude the very real human actualization and freedom that spirituality itself releases. Spirituality will work, or at least begin its work, by worldwide individual re-creation. We will be the persons we were all meant to be, only even better. And our time, from this perspective, stands on the brink of such a momentous transformation and opportunity; the signs of this Change are all around, for those with eyes to see. Spirituality is then a light that shines both within all of us now and from a future we can imagine, showing us the path ahead. When that Change comes, as in Wells' novel, it will be a time to burn or bury the old without any regret and usher in the new. Although not totally new—the characters in his Changed world revive the ancient British festival of Beltane in order to throw the debris of their ugly industrial urban society into giant bonfires.[2] The revival of ancient paganism, as symbol but no longer as literal worship of anything, is a wonderful Wells touch, applicable to today's vision of spirituality as the light that empowers the Change. When spirituality comes to replace old-style religion,

any archaic symbolism is recoverable, and we can celebrate our freedom, happiness, and hope by such a revival.

God, evolution, or Wells' comet never work piecemeal. According
to this hope, there is never anything less than a global, total, holistic
scope to the Change. Therefore, to say that spirituality will replace
religion is misleading. Spirituality, in a sense, replaces everything. It
will leave no corner of the future untransformed; there will be no back-
ward provinces where the comet's gas could not penetrate. Words such
as *global*, *universal*, and *holistic* are so essential to this hope that they too
glow when used by thinkers who prophesy this kind of future. It would
not be possible or permissible to announce a Change that took in the
Northern Hemisphere but left out Africa, South America, and Australia
or that affected everyone, but in drastically divergent ways depending
upon region, climate, or gross national product. The totalistic vision of
Change fueled by spirituality cannot let such factors matter. Spirituality
is too universal, too ultimate, to be limited by historical, cultural, geo-
graphical, linguistic, or any other divisions. Once again, Wells' comet
passes into the atmosphere of the entire earth; it is the best analogy for
these more recent hopes.

Nor are any of these visions dualistic in the older Platonic sense.
There is no spiritual realm so severed from this earthly realm that the
fate of the two could be dramatically different. If that were possible,
then we could imagine a dire alternative future of a Change. Let us suppose that humans have fought a total nuclear war, ruining the earth for
higher forms life except under desperately awful conditions (this was
the picture of "nuclear winter" from the 1980s). A few types of bacteria
might survive, under the depth of the ocean, perhaps, but the surface
would be depopulated and silent. However, Heaven is crowded; no one
who died in the war is really extinguished. The heavenly dwellers eter-
nally inhabit a realm no longer limited by death or sickness or old age.
From here they gaze down to view a poisoned planet that was once their
home. Perhaps they are indifferent, grateful to be free of all earthly,
physical ties. Or they might be crushed with remorse and grieve for
what they had destroyed, knowing it could never be restored.

No true utopian could imagine such a future, such a total dystopic
alternative. What this awful possibility does is highlight how the idea of
spirituality as the core of the marvelous Change is not a scientific, factu-
ally grounded actuality but an expression of Tillichian "ultimate concern." Faith in the Change, the New Age, the next evolutionary stage,

the spirituality or consciousness revolution has replaced the political ideologies of Tillich's day. Many persons apparently believe in something like this. Spirituality as the key to the whole planet's salvation is what illuminates and gives meaning and direction to their lives. More than the actual contents of the ninety-two-plus definitions, it is spirituality's link to the anticipated Change that makes the concept a magnet for so many different aspirations and dreams.

Those who attempt to prophesy a future that is Changed consistently try to discern signs of the times that support their hopes. For example, those 14 percent of Americans who describe themselves as "spiritual but not religious" become the first wave of the spirituality revolution, reflected in Australian spirituality advocate David Tacey's title, rather than dropouts from a major institution. If enough people see them—or see themselves—this way, the picture of the past and present is altered, not just our predictions of the future. Here, novelist H. G. Wells was at an advantage, since he introduced an entirely unpredictable, outside-the-solar-system comet to effect the Change. There could have been no possible anticipated signs, portents, or warnings to alert humanity to what was coming. Whereas, for us, the question of what counts as a sign or a foretaste of the future is always up for debate.

Spirituality and a Postmodern World

Key to the claim that a giant Change is just ahead is the thesis that the modern worldview is being replaced by a postmodern world order and way of thinking. This shift, well underway according to its advocates, affects all areas of thought and many kinds of professional activity, and it will soon revolutionize large-scale social institutions. While a term such as the *Age of Aquarius* harks back to astrology and is clearly intended as an imaginative-mythic image, *postmodern* as used here is proposed as a sound, philosophically grounded concept. The thesis is that the modern rational Newtonian and Cartesian way of understanding reality has already been proved inadequate and false. Inaugurated in the seventeenth century, this mechanistic and dualistic worldview had its day, but that is now over. Quantum physics, relativity theory, and the discovery of body/mind holism have shifted our paradigm for understanding reality. Modern society, once mechanistic and industrial, has also been transformed so that information is its main commodity. Mechanical models of functioning have been replaced by those focused on interactive feedback systems, ecological networks, and holistic views of persons, nature, and the world. This transition is so sweeping, so total, that it deserves the label *postmodern*. The phrase *paradigm shift*, which came from Thomas Kuhn's *The Structure of Scientific Revolutions* to cover specific changes in particular sciences, is used here in a much more wide-ranging and exuberant sense.[3] A paradigm shift requires that old-style thinking, reasoning, ideas, and images are now obsolete, and a new vision of reality already replaces them. As one can tell from the above description, particular discoveries in sciences and medicine are signs, evidence to support this portrait of a postmodern worldview. Whatever the meaning of Heisenberg's uncertainty principle or quantum theory for physicists, these examples are frequently cited as a sneak peak at a new worldview that goes far beyond what Kuhn saw as "scientific revolutions."[4] For example, David Griffin summarizes what "constructive post-modernism" includes: "Going beyond the modern world will involve transcending its individualism, anthropocentrism, patriarchy, mechanization, economism, consumerism, nationalism, and militarism. Constructive postmodern thought provides support for the ecology, peace, feminism and other emancipatory movements of our time, while stressing that the inclusive emancipation must be from modernity itself."[5] He adds that this new, emergent world will not be a return to the "pre-modern" but will involve a "creative synthesis of modern and pre-modern truths and values." Just as Wells' Changed protagonists reinvented Beltane, so Griffin's postmoderns will be free to synthesize premodern, modern, and contemporary truths. So, the particularity of disciplines, in which a paradigm shift sometimes is needed, gives way to a vision of a world transformed, Changed as thoroughly as by Wells' comet.

We chose Griffin's statement from 1988 as a sample because he was no lightweight thinker nor was he a spokesperson for what even then could be dismissed as "New Age fluff." He was a respected philosophical theologian and affiliated with a major educational institution. While Griffin and his contributors hoped to be "global," there is not much in their presentations that deals with specific situations, such as the impending breakup of the Soviet Union, the AIDS epidemic, or any other particularities. These were too grounded in history and locations. Maybe some developments meant the triumph of resurgent nationalisms or new recruits for the forces of consumerism. Maybe some emancipatory movements had a dark and dangerous side in addition to what Griffin saw. Bluntly, the vision of postmodern triumphant spirituality seems to be a claim about history, but it is really not. It is about a giant cosmic sweep heading toward the Change. In spite of Griffin's intentions in titling his anthology *Spirituality and Society*, that book is not designed to deal with what happens in Poland, in Syria, or in hospitals. Or even on the golf course.

Postmodern is intended to affect thought, to cover everything, and that includes what in modernity became identified as religion. By contrast with religion, postmodern spirituality will encompass thought, attitudes, and patterns of action, but not necessarily be institution based. There will be no "church of the postmodern" as a separate entity. But for Griffin what characterizes this new, emergent spirituality is its connectedness, its sense of relationships as constitutive of self.[6] We are no longer, as in modernity, isolated atomistic entities. The second quality, labeled "organicism" by Griffin, is better known as holistic, refusing an absolute separation of spirit from matter.[7] For Griffin, this means that postmodern spirituality "rejects both supernaturalism and atheism" in favor of a "naturalistic panentheism, according to which the world is present in deity and deity is present in the world."[8] These characteristics, particularly the last, reflect Griffin's own commitment to a Whiteheadian process thought metaphysics. But it is fair to say that they are not far off from the characteristics featured in many of the more recent or less philosophically sophisticated definitions. Organicism is clearly a continuous, by now familiar, feature; there is no interest in postulating separable "spirits" or in reinstating a flesh versus spirit understanding of persons. As for panentheism, none of the definitions surveyed by Unruh, Versnel, and Kerr used this technical theological term, and yet its basic theme of a divine being intimately connected to the human and the natural feels familiar, whether from John Muir or from the other sources that lie behind those definitions.

Postmodern spirituality has a unique sense of time and history as well as of the future.[9] It is willing to retrieve the traditions of the past, in a selective appreciation and appropriation of their positive features. However, in Griffin's portrayal, these characteristics do not define spirituality per se; they are qualities of a specifically postmodern spirituality. For Griffin, and for others who used the term this way, spirituality is still not quite a central core of the universal human; there are good and bad spiritualities. For instance, "patriarchal spirituality" is to be replaced by a "postpatriarchal vision."[10] This comes much closer to Principe's two-poled understanding than Griffin realizes. In both cases, there is a chosen ideal, and individuals orient themselves to it. Postmodern spirituality is a way to characterize that ideal, which can then be linked to potential changes in postmodern society. What is not yet clear in Griffin's 1988 work is that spirituality in and of itself will soon become the bearer of all those postmodern values, hopes, and emancipatory goals.

A more minor effort from the 1980s duplicates most of these features. *Bio-Spirituality*, by Peter Campbell and Edwin McMahon, begins with psychologist Eugene Gendlin's "focusing" technique of body awareness, which was developed as a tool for psychotherapy and turns it into a Cosmic Principle. Our bodies are the ground and source for wisdom and cooperation with the divine; any spirituality that neglects or ignores this is doomed, off the track of human evolution.[11] This is organicism, or holism, in a more naïve form than in Griffin. According to Campbell and McMahon, when we learn to rely on biospirituality, we will be able to prevent nuclear war and move into Maslow's farther reaches of human nature.[12] Biospirituality is more than a way to grow personally; it is a way to inaugurate the new, postmodern era of the kingdom of God. Here we have both panentheism and evolution as imagery, nicely paired. The divine understood panentheistically is no longer a Being outside the physical universe but one somehow intertwined and within it, pulsating its life and energy into humans and every corner of the earth. The author reacted against the lingering dualism between spiritual and material used for so long to distinguish monks from laity, as Principe documented. However, the way spirituality is used here still reflects a two-poled understanding, so we see the biospirituality advocated by the authors, measured against its inadequate and harmful alternative. Campbell and McMahon pushed for a revised religious ideal, one that expresses and depends upon the embodied totality of the person. They too believed the time is ripe for this, because the old Cartesian or Platonic dualist vision is now obsolete. What makes this book similar to Griffin's and others' utopian uses of spirituality is the global, total quality of its claims. Biospirituality will bring about not just a healthier, more aware person—perhaps one who can play golf more effectively too—but world peace.

In neither of these visions is *spirituality* a neutral term. It is filled with hope, endowed with the promise of a new era, a Change that glows already even as it lies in the near future. Yet the possibility of "bad spirituality" is always present. For these thinkers, the religious ideal of modernity, Descartes' or Calvin's God, is always back there as a bad memory. The more spirituality itself takes on its one-poled meanings, the more the problem of bad spirituality seems by virtue of definition to fade away—nothing so close to the core and heart of humanity can in essence be bad or deceptive—but it does not, not entirely. The problem and challenge of inadequate or trivial versions of their own ideals come back to haunt Griffin and his fellow postmodern advocates.

From Postmodern to New Age

In these accounts postmodern spirituality is given a specific content, as the core of the Change into fulfillment of the emergent postmodern age's promise. In this usage, the opportunity is there for a new spirituality that can be compared with premodern spiritualities or with modern spirituality, although modernity itself may suppress the holism or organicism that the very term *spirituality* includes. Some advocates of postmodern spirituality welcome the new and see the recent past—sometimes equated with formal, institutionalized religion—as vestigial. Griffin, as we saw, holds a more complex vision of the past, which he characterized as one more feature of the postmodern.[13] Irish author Diarmuid Ó Murchú in *Reclaiming Spirituality* echoes Griffin's themes of a new paradigm, the contribution of physics to undermining the modern worldview, the recovery of the feminine, and so forth.[14] Claiming that formal religion is a relatively recent development in human history—and apparently a pernicious one—he believes that "the ancient spiritual wisdom embraced our world in a holistic, organic way that mainstream religion does not seem capable of doing."[15] Thus, a new era of spirituality will once again restore wholeness to our existence, and formal religion will be an unnecessary and temporary episode in human history. The hope is to reject the recent modern past but to retrieve a wiser, more remote past selectively and no longer literalistically. Like Wells' post-Change inhabitants who revive Beltrane, they are now free from superstitious bondage to any one system of belief or symbols.

Therefore, the past revived will not necessarily be our own past or the past of our biological ancestors. It will not necessarily be the past of our nation's history, for remember that nationalism is one of the forces to be left behind in the Change. But it will be the past of everyone and all eras, the sum total of all traditions potentially available for any of us. In the words of Ken Wilbur, writing much more recently than Griffin,

> During the last 30 years, we have witnessed a historical first: all of the world's cultures are now available to us. . . . Today, not only are people geographically mobile, but we can study, and have studied, virtually every known culture on the planet. . . . Knowledge itself is now global. This means that, also for the first time, the sum total of human knowledge is available to us—the

knowledge, experience, wisdom, and reflection of all major human civiliza-
tions—premodern, modern, and postmodern—are open to study by anyone.
. . . We attempted, based on extensive cross-cultural study, to use all of the
world's great traditions to create a composite map . . . an all-inclusive or integral map that included the best elements from all of them.[16]

This point is made in order to show how unique the present moment is
and to bolster the claim that our current situation makes possible what
was never conceivable for the peoples of the past who were confined to
their local knowledge bases. Advocates of postmodern spirituality such
as Wilbur can claim to survey the past as well as the full array of the
world's wisdom, traditions, and experience. This totalistic, grandiose
possibility gives all of us living today a view of a gigantic, complete
landscape from a magnificent mountain summit, with great visibility
on all sides for many miles. I may live in urban Philadelphia, but I have
access to the wisdom and experiences and legacies of Siberian shamans,
West African tribal cultures, Buddhist monks, and even of extinct wisdom traditions such as that of pre-Christian Ireland. In Wilbur's and
Griffin's visions, we are now free to access anything from just about
anywhere humans have left traces. Probably for some of us, the better
image than the landscape seen from a mountain is that of the computer-
user, surfing and browsing through an Internet whose realm, cyberspace, has no particular location at all.

This dimension of postmodern spirituality is intrinsic to its hope
for world unity, for its sense of progress over what came before, and for
some of its sad omissions and major flaws. For while Griffin predicted
a vision that would undermine and eventually abolish consumerism and
economism (along with many other "isms" from the modern and premodern eras), the potential for re-energized versions of these accompanies Wilbur's presumption. The arrogance here resembles psychologist
Perry London's hope for a definitive understanding of human nature
based on scientific data, once and for all. For Wilbur, we and only we
can stand on the summit and therefore see more than anyone else before
us or those still on the flat ground. We in our wisdom will recognize and
appropriate "the best elements" from all of those cultures and traditions,
and as owners of "the sum total of human knowledge" we can share it,
package it, and (probably) post it on the Internet.

What Wilbur overlooked is what Luckmann could have told us back
in 1967. Consumer identity and its processes will be the social context
and the actual guiding force for all of our assimilation and appropriation
of the world's wisdom. This is why what actually came from Wilbur's

utopian vision of universal global knowledge resembles a bazaar in which bits and pieces of every one of "the world's great traditions" is up for sale. Pulled from their original contexts, these bits and pieces are reshaped to fit our particular ideas of what is "best in all of them." Use the landscape and summit image, and we have the mountaintop viewer pointing to this apple tree to the east, that river over to the west, a nice picnic spot further north . . . and then trying to yank them out of their places and pack them together to landscape his or her own back-yard. This poses a dilemma for those who, like Wilbur, seriously hope to integrate "the best elements from all of them." Far from overcoming consumerism, the appeal of this aspect of postmodern spirituality is its dependence on a consumer model of presenting and appropriating cultures' contents, ideas, symbols, and practices. Because an institutionalized multigenerational format for transmitting traditions is held to be part of religion rather than spirituality, it is rejected. Thus, the consumer process is allowed to fill in, to take over thoroughly when spirituality replaces religion. What comes to mind is that catalog of the world's religions transformed into knickknacks and jewelry, aimed at women who wished to buy identity fragments, and with items not necessarily made by representatives or members of the traditions. Their provenance and place of origin is as ostensibly irrelevant as the location of the computer through which the Internet surfer enters the realm of cyberspace.

Welcome to New Age, the movement that actually arrived to fulfill, or claim to fulfill, the goals and ideals of postmodern spirituality. *New Age* was its advocates' term, at least at first, and their message was that the anticipated Change is now already begun. We are free to practice, explore, expand our horizons and our psychic and spiritual powers. We are free to experiment with both old religious symbols and new, on-the-spot rituals. We are free to practice new, alternative forms of healing, as a demonstration that we no longer are bound by the Cartesian dualism of body versus mind. Yes, some of the things we do can seem risky and eccentric, but that is part of venturing into the new. Classic New Age advocates accepted in toto Griffin's diagnosis of the transition and most of his list of expectations. They believed themselves one of the "emancipatory movements" he celebrated, allied to other opponents of patriarchy, militarism, and mechanism. They said all the right things and were as eclectic, tolerant, and futuristic as Griffin could have desired.

Yet *New Age* quickly became a derogatory term. Not only by scathing sweeping critics such as Carrette and King, whose *Selling Spirituality* seems to blame the whole thing on Margaret Thatcher, Ronald Reagan, and neoliberal economics. Or by traditional defenders of the faith (any traditional faith) such as J. F. D. Pearce, in his *A Critique of Spirituality*.[17] Even articulate defenders of spirituality and postmodern Change have to back off from its New Age expressions. Tacey, in *The Spirituality Revolution*, applauds everything that Griffin advocates in terms of postmodern spirituality but notes "the poor symbols of the New Age": they are "regressive," fascinated with any and all archaisms. Characteristically for spirituality advocates, he interprets this impoverished result of their initial hope by blaming the continued failings of the "old age" institutions, not intrinsic flaws in their replacements. Tacey finds that the existing educational system and formal organized religion "fail to generate a sense of spiritual wonder and delight." Therefore, "our young people are attracted to these vulgar representations" of New Age goodies.[18] Although he explicitly advocates an "all-inclusive spirituality," some principle of quality control, taste, or aesthetics is at work to distinguish what is "vulgar" from what is authentic, what is "regressive" from what is liberating.[19] To balance this negative assessment, Tacey finds more to worry about from "old-style Christian fundamentalists" than from New Age enthusiasts.[20] The former are complete outsiders to Tacey's postmodern vision, and "all-inclusive" clearly does not include them.

Meanwhile, for Carrette and King the real source of New Age's tackiness lies elsewhere; they believe Griffin's hope that postmodern spirituality would overcome consumerism and economism is totally illusory, for the whole theme of spirituality rests exactly on these features of global capitalism. "Like the selling to private companies of public utilities and services in our modern neoliberal economies, such as gas, electricity, water, healthcare and transport systems, the material and cultural 'assets' of the various religious traditions are being plundered, 'downsized' and sold off as commodities."[21] Religious traditions are reduced to jewelry and knick-knacks, while the economic system thrives; they find that the spirituality revolution is thoroughly misnamed.

Perhaps what criticism of the vulgar or poor symbols surrounding New Age could have brought to light is that a spirituality such as Griffin's, Ó Murchú's, Wilbur's, or Tacey's is vulnerable precisely because it is so proudly deinstitutionalized, all-inclusively hostile to any force or principle that would try to regulate it. Because of this feature, touted repeatedly as a positive characteristic of the postmodern, the vacuum will be filled by other sources of regulation. In the case of New Age, it will be what the market will bear, what appeals to persons' "spiritual wonder and delight" but also their vanity, narrow vision, and greed. To raise this possibility dims some of the glow that shines forth from both postmodern and New Age utopian uses of this term.

And Now, for Dummies

Between Griffin writing in 1988, and Tacey, whose book is dated 2004, spirituality transitioned from a two-poled to a one-poled concept. For Griffin, as we saw, one could compare spiritualities, because he, like Principe, still thought in terms of particular contents. Modern and postmodern spiritualities could vie with one another. The inhabitants of Wells' comet novel changed their worldview and divided their lives into before and after the Change; Griffin tries to persuade us we are already in the process of doing so. While for Tacey and other more recent advocates of spirituality as a concept, it is intrinsically, universally, the bearer of certain virtues, such as compassion, and certain qualities, such as the sense of connectedness. As a core within the person, it is truly spirituality when it brings these forth. What Griffin might have termed "obsolete" or "defective" spiritualities are no longer spirituality at all but "religion" or "fundamentalism" or "scientism," or they are given negative psychological characteristics, such as "regressive." But true, authentic spirituality, the force that will illuminate and bring the Change, is always positive. It is positive because it is allegedly panhuman, absolutely universal, and it shows us the path toward the higher reaches of human nature. With this shift, the opposition between religion and spirituality plays a much greater role for more recent thinkers, since spirituality per se now is both universal and representative of a certain vision of the human, the social, and the divine. In a manner Principe could not have made sense of at all, religion is the perceived enemy of all that is truly spiritual. That is why Tacey's claim, that religion and the educational system are the ones truly to blame for New Age's flaws, makes sense to him, as he expresses his goal: "Breaking 'Religion' to Release Spirit."[22] Even though he has an interesting discussion of the suppressed positive role of religion in the lives of students who reject it, overall he assumes that spirituality will replace religion in the era of the coming Change, just as it has for so many of his college students.[23] Other advocates of this vision are much less nuanced than Tacey. What marks out Ó Murchú's exposition of the same basic ideas about postmodernity and the transition out of religion into spirituality is how exorbitantly angry he is at what he believes will soon become obsolete.

A final example of this genre that equates spirituality in and of itself with postmodern ideals and the promise of utopian Change, Sharon Janis' *Spirituality for Dummies*, takes its cue from Wilbur's global vision of our possible total knowledge.[24] In one readable volume, she, like Wilbur, wants to survey and select the best of the world's cultures and wisdom traditions, so she sprinkles her book with short quotes from them. Where this aptly titled work differs from Wilbur is that he at least claims that long-term serious cross-cultural study is a prerequisite to adequate or meaningful appropriation of others' wisdom. Janis, on the other hand, does not believe in this method. When in college, she writes,

> I was interested in learning more about this new cool theory called hologra-phy. But I discovered that first you had to take 2 semesters of the most boring and basic aspects of physics. . . . The same thing would happen if you decided to attend art school. First you'd have to take a semester-long class on how to draw straight lines, and if that didn't kill your creative spirit, you'd get to move on to some actual art courses. But that's not what you're going to get here. In this book, I give you the goods.[25]

Herrigel and all the Zen athletes would cringe at this, for indeed the essence of a practice is mastering the basics with honesty, courage, and plenty of patience. Indeed, one could use this passage to show how far spirituality, as Janis deals with it as the glowing promise of the global Change, can get from the essentials of practice. It was in conjunction with practices that we found some of the basic virtues and values that could anchor spirituality to models of human growth, to reasonable answers to the question "How do I become spiritual?" Janis' book is so aptly titled because the very wisdom traditions upon which she claims to draw would vehemently insist on long-term perseverance, acceptance of the master's teaching authority, and steadiness of purpose as pre-requisites for wisdom. "Dummies" cannot master this kind of wisdom. Only a true dummy would imagine one could.

Our underlying message is to highlight the appeal of the utopian Change, something that will accomplish what Wells' comet brought, without any of the step-by-step planning and effort normal changes usu-ally require. Just as Janis hoped to learn holography without bother-ing with basic physics, advocates of the Change rooted in spirituality understood as human universal core find the values they admire and advocate already in their possession, deep in human nature. They want to embrace the world and the divine in a holistic, organic way and they want a world of peace, beyond militarism and nationalism. They want a world in ecological balance and the energies and power of the genders also in balance. Neither religion nor politics nor science nor education nor any existing institution has been able to accomplish this, and in the postmodern era, when the Change has come to pass, none of these will remain as they are now. Some may no longer be needed at all. What will matter is that we, like the dwellers in the postcomet world of Wells' novel, will be renewed, fulfilled, and at peace with one another and the cosmos. Spirituality will be the key for this; its glow already leads us toward this Change ahead.

Conclusion

No one who actively accepts this vision of spirituality as the core of the Change would write about it as we have or would find the connections to social processes such as the consumer model of identity convincing. While those who work to infuse spirituality into health-care institutions or businesses find themselves constrained by the realities of those contexts and their imperatives—as those who kayak are constrained by the physical properties of wind and water—no equivalent restraints exist for those who hope for the Change. Spirituality as this total promise of transformation need not be limited to what hospitals or businesses can permit or tolerate.

Our focus has been on the concept itself, intrinsically both glowing and murky, both promising new areas of study and obscuring some of what we do already know about humans, religion, and meaning making. While it makes sense to use a theory-based concept such as Tillich's "faith as ultimate concern" or even spirituality as understood by sociologists of religion to isolate particular developments, we have seen how the overwhelming urge behind most of the ninety-two-plus definitions is to move past these uses into the territory of Griffin, Tacey, and Janis' *Dummies*. Or rather, it is as if the utopian vision of Change has infused more of the definitions, proposed meanings, and locations for spirituality than even some earlier advocates could have imagined. That was why, perhaps, it was so difficult for those Canadian occupational therapists to deny that spirituality was important, even as they confessed they hardly knew what exactly it was and they did not feel prepared to deal with it.

Meanwhile, the plethora of practices drawn from a wide range of wisdom traditions and adapted for baking and golf can continue to enrich our lives in intangible ways and offer a different and distinctive set of virtues from those explicitly espoused by advocates of spirituality today. These practices work in particular and narrow ways, especially if we do not emulate Janis' impatience with the rigorous gradual processes of learning them well. But whether they will carry along with them their traditional ultimates of salvation or enlightenment is unclear. It may not be possible to "take back yoga" entirely, to resituate all of these practices into the contexts from which they were borrowed. These practices, however, do not automatically cover the same conceptual territory as does spirituality. Not only is Zen meditation not the same as basketball, but, as two distinct practices, neither one is equivalent to spirituality as meaning making, connectedness, and holistic growth. The quick embrace of spirituality has obscured this important distinction not just for Janis and her dummies but for many of the rest of those who advocate both generic universal one-poled spirituality and specific practices. Our treatment of the concept of spirituality has, we hope, cleared up the confusions, conflations, and murkiness of these issues.

Our story of this concept's rise is not quite the tale of an illusion without a future, the bad dancers' ballroom. There is more to it than that. Certainly, the problems for which spirituality is proposed as the solution are extremely real and well documented. But spirituality as a concept is not a preview of Wells' comet in conceptual form, a force that will revolutionize our lives and our world, bringing with it postmodern illumination and wisdom. Today's spirituality is not a "solution" even to the particular problems we looked at in our chapters on health care, work, and recreation. "Spirituality" is a bundle of images, ideas, yearnings, and possibilities, drawn from a variety of sources and conflated by hopeful practitioners, professionals, and scholars to do triple or quadruple duty in multiple contexts. It is a fool's errand to expect of spirituality what its utopian visions promise. This is not stated as a prediction about the historical future. It is a statement about a problematic concept, whose current plethora of meanings does not seem destined to provide a scholarly infrastructure located anywhere in our intellectual ecology. The study of anything is over time filled with examples of concepts once believed wonderful but now discarded as inherently jumbled, misleading, based on faulty assumptions. Or on hopes as unfulfillable as Griffin's and Tacey's. We find that spirituality, unless it is much more carefully restricted in meanings and specified for particular contexts, stands a good chance to join these ranks for reasons of incoherence.

But then, should Wells' comet arrive and bring the Change, all such predictions would themselves become obsolete and happily forgotten.

Notes

Introduction

1   James Nelson, quoted by Kathryn McNichols and David Feldman, "Spirituality at the End of Life: Issues and Guidelines for Care," in Plante and Thoresen, *Spirit, Science and Health*, 192.

2   S. Kappen, "Spirituality in the New Age of Recolonization," in *Mysticism and the Institutional Crisis*, edited by C. Erricker and J. Erricker (London: SCM Press, 1994), 33. Quoted by Celia Kourie, "The 'Turn' to Spirituality," *Acta Theologica Supplementum* 8 (2006): 23.

3   Kenneth Doka, "Definition of Spirituality," Meeting of the International Working Group for Death, Dying and Bereavement Conference, Bergisch Gladbach, Germany, 2010.

4   Kourie, "'Turn' to Spirituality," 22.

5   Anita Unruh, Joan Versnel, and Natasha Kerr, "Spirituality Unplugged," review of *Commonalities and Contentions, and a Resolution, Canadian Journal of Occupational Therapy* 69, no. 1 (2002), 6.

Chapter 1

1   Walter Principe, "Toward Defining Spirituality," *Studies in Religion* 12 (1983): 133.

2   Principe, "Toward Defining Spirituality," 133.

3   Principe, "Toward Defining Spirituality," 135.

4   Principe, "Toward Defining Spirituality," 136.

5   Principe, "Toward Defining Spirituality," 136.

6   Principe, "Toward Defining Spirituality," 138.

7   Principe, "Toward Defining Spirituality," 138.

8   Kourie, "'Turn' to Spirituality," 22.

9   See Leigh Schmidt, *Restless Souls: The Making of American Spirituality from Emerson to Oprah* (Princeton, N.J.: Princeton University Press, 2005); and Courtney Bender,

The New Metaphysicals: Spirituality and the American Religious Imagination (Chicago: University of Chicago Press), 2010.

10   Peter Van Ness, ed., *Spirituality and the Secular Quest* (New York: Crossroad, 1996), 5.

11   Lucy Bregman, "Psychotherapies," in Van Ness, *Spirituality and the Secular Quest*, 250–76.

12   John Morgan, "The Existential Quest for Meaning," in Doka and Morgan, *Death and Spirituality*, 6.

13   Morgan, "Existential Quest for Meaning," 8.

14   Morgan, "Existential Quest for Meaning," 8.

15   Viktor Frankl, *Man's Search for Meaning* (New York: Pocket Books, 1963), 103–5.

16   A much more recent journal issue devoted to the concept includes several insightful (and sometimes sarcastic) contributions by Herman Westerlink, Pär Salander, and Peter La Cour, *Archive for the Psychology of Religion* 34, no. 1 (2012). See Herman Westerlink, "Spirituality in Psychology of Religion: A Concept in Search of Its Meaning," 3–15; Pär Salander, "The Emperor's New Clothes: Spirituality. A Concept Based on Questionable Ontology and Circular Findings," 17–32; and Peter La Cour, Nadja Ausker, and Niels Hvidt, "Six Understandings of the Word 'Spirituality' in a Secular Country," 63–81. These authors focus on the European rather than the North American context but raise many of the same concerns.

17   Unruh et al., "Spirituality Unplugged," 7.

18   Unruh et al., "Spirituality Unplugged," 7.

19   Salander, "The Emperor's New Clothes."

20   Unruh et al., "Spirituality Unplugged," 8.

21   Unruh et al., "Spirituality Unplugged," 8.

22   Unruh et al., "Spirituality Unplugged," 8.

23   Unruh et al., "Spirituality Unplugged," 9.

24   Unruh et al., "Spirituality Unplugged," 9.

25   Frankl, *Man's Search for Meaning*, 10.

26   Frankl, *Man's Search for Meaning*, 154.

27   Frankl, *Man's Search for Meaning*, 175.

28   Unruh et al., "Spirituality Unplugged," 9.

29   Unruh et al., "Spirituality Unplugged", 9.

30   D. Hufford, "An Analysis of the Field of Religion, Spirituality and Health." http://www.metanexus.net/archive/templetonadvancedresearchprogram/pdf/TARP-Hufford.pdf, 2006, 7.

31   Unruh et al., "Spirituality Unplugged," 12–13.

32   Abraham Maslow, *Religions, Values and Peak-Experiences* (New York: Viking Press, 1971), appendix B, 69–71.

33   Peggy Rosenthal, *Words and Values: Some Leading Words and Where They Lead Us* (New York: Oxford University Press, 1984), 81.

34   Don Browning, *Religious Thought and the Modern Psychologies* (Philadelphia: Fortress, 1987).

35   Browning, *Religious Thought*, 75.

36   Attentive readers will have wondered at the prominence of Canadians throughout this chapter. Principe, Morgan, the CAOT . . . is this an accident, or a meaningful pattern? Since the present writer is not Canadian, it is not due to nationalism or a

desire to patronize local resources. It may be that Canada offers a situation where religion is less strictly separated from government than in the United States, without a state-established church such as in many European countries. Thus, the touchy issue of religion and its possible relation to spirituality can be played out in Canada with slightly more ideological and legal flexibility than elsewhere. This is speculation, but I have no other explanation for the disproportionate presence of Canadians in the discussions we have covered.

Chapter 2

1   Doug Oman and Carl Thoresen, "How Does One Learn to Be Spiritual? The Neglected Role of Spiritual Modeling in Health," in Plante and Thoresen, *Spirit, Science and Health*, 39–54.

2   Oman and Thoresen, "How Does One Learn to Be Spiritual?" 41.

3   Teresa of Avila, *The Interior Castle*, Classics of Western Spirituality (New York: Paulist Press, 1979), 74.

4   Teresa of Avila, *Interior Castle*, 74.

5   Teresa of Avila, *Interior Castle*, 92.

6   Teresa of Avila, *Interior Castle*, 111.

7   Teresa of Avila, *Interior Castle*, 152.

8   Teresa of Avila, *Interior Castle*, 76.

9   Teresa of Avila, *Interior Castle*, 112–13.

10   Alasdair MacIntyre, *After Virtue: A Study of Moral Theory* (South Bend, Ind.: University of Notre Dame Press, 1981), 190.

11   Michael Novak, *The Joy of Sports* (Lanham, Md.: Hamilton Press, 1988), 263.

12   Tim Flinders, Doug Oman, and Carol Lee Flinders, "The Eight-Point Program of Passage Meditation: Health Effects of a Comprehensive Program," in Plante and Thoresen, *Spirit, Science and Health*, 74.

13   Flinders, Oman, and Flinders, "Eight-Point Program," 84.

14   Flinders, Oman, and Flinders, "Eight-Point Program," table 6.1, 74.

15   Flinders, Oman, and Flinders, "Eight-Point Program," 89.

16   In all fairness to the students, some who start with yoga for phys ed learn a little about the philosophy from their instructor and may out of curiosity enroll in a course on religions of India.

Chapter 3

1   Linda Ferguson, "Working Spiritually: Aligning Gifts, Purpose and Passion," in Marques, Dhiman, and King, *Workplace and Spirituality*, 24.

2   Robert Bellah, ed., *Habits of the Heart: Individualism and Commitment in American Life* (Berkeley: University of California Press, 1985).

3   Bellah, *Habits of the Heart*, 8.

4   Bellah, *Habits of the Heart*, 232. A pastor I knew commented that this was one of the first studies he had read where the evangelicals did not sound like idiots. Others noted how that role was taken over by psychotherapists, who appeared as uncritical champions of expressive individualism.

5   Robert Fuller, *Spiritual but Not Religious: Understanding Unchurched America* (New York: Oxford University Press, 2001), 162.

6   Elizabeth Tisdell, *Exploring Spirituality and Culture in Adult and Higher Education* (San Francisco: Jossey-Bass, 2003).

7   Robert Wuthnow, *Creative Spirituality: The Way of the Artist* (Berkeley: University of California Press, 2001).

8   Maureen Carey, Raymond Fox, and Jacqueline Penny, *The Artful Journal: A Spiritual Quest* (New York: Watson-Guptill, 2002).

9   Jerry Biberman and Len Tischler, eds., *Spirituality in Business: Theory, Practice and Future Directions* (New York: Palgrave Macmillan, 2008), 1–2.

10   Amy Wachholtz and Michele Pierce, "Compassion and Health," in Plante and Thoresen, *Spirit, Science and Health*, 116.

11   Wachholtz and Pierce, "Compassion and Health," 121.

12   Wachholtz and Pierce, "Compassion and Health," 116.

13   Ian Mitroff and Elizabeth Denton, *A Spiritual Audit of Corporate America: A Hard Look at Spirituality, Religion and Values in the Workplace* (San Francisco: Jossey-Bass, 1999), 3–6.

14   Mitroff and Denton, *Spiritual Audit of Corporate America*, 178.

15   Birute Regine, "Letting the Heart Fall Open," in Marques, Dhiman, and King, *Workplace and Spirituality*, 9–22,

16   Regine, "Letting the Heart Fall Open," 12–13.

17   Judi Neal, "Creating Edgewater Organizations: The Workplace of the Future," in Marques, Dhiman, and King, *Workplace and Spirituality*, 211.

Chapter 4

1   Bruce Lescher and Elizabeth Leibert, eds. *Exploring Christian Spirituality: Essays in Honor of Sandra M. Schneiders* (New York: Paulist Press, 2006).

2   Hufford, "Analysis of the Field," 7.

3   Perry London, *The Modes and Morals of Psychotherapy* (New York: Holt, Rinehart & Winston, 1964), 164.

4   London, *Modes and Morals*, 169.

5   London, *Modes and Morals*, part 3, 150–73.

6   Seward Hiltner, *Pastoral Counseling* (New York: Abingdon, 1949), 56–57.

7   Howard Clinebell, *Basic Types of Pastoral Care and Counseling* (New York: Abingdon, 1966), 20.

8   Hiltner, *Pastoral Care*, 111–14.

9   Maslow, *Religions, Values and Peak-Experiences*, 11.

10   Maslow, *Religions, Values and Peak-Experiences*, xvi.

11   Charles Tart, ed., *Transpersonal Psychologies* (New York: Harper & Row, 1975), 4.

12   Tart, *Transpersonal Psychologies*, see chap. 2, 59–112.

13   Tart, *Transpersonal Psychologies*, 6.

14   James Hillman, *Re-Visioning Psychology* (New York: Harper & Row, 1975).

15   For example, Thomas Oden's *Pastoral Theology: Essentials for Ministry* (San Francisco: Harper & Row, 1983) intentionally avoided all psychologically identified sources and relied only on what he saw as distinctively Christian resources.

16   Don Browning, *The Moral Context of Pastoral Care* (Philadelphia: Westminster, 1976).

17   Elisabeth Kübler-Ross, *On Death and Dying* (New York: Macmillan, 1968), 120.

Chapter 5

1   T. Jinpa, quoted in Kourie, "'Turn' to Spirituality," 24.

2   Kourie, "'Turn' to Spirituality," 26.

3   Mitroff and Denton, *Spiritual Audit of Corporate America*, xvi.

4   Cited indirectly by Karl Mannheim, "The Problem of Generations," *Essays in the Sociology of Knowledge* (London: Routledge & Kegan Paul, 1968), 277.

5   Immanuel Kant, *Religion within the Limits of Reason Alone* (New York: Harper & Brothers, 1960).

6   Friedrich Schleiermacher, *On Religion: Speeches to Its Cultured Despisers* (New York: Harper & Row, 1958), 62.

7   Schleiermacher, *Speeches*, 58.

8   Schleiermacher, *Speeches*, 50.

9   Schleiermacher, *Speeches*, 51.

10   Ann Taves, *Fits, Trances and Visions: Experiencing Religion and Explaining Experience from Wesley to James* (Princeton, N.J.: Princeton University Press, 1999).

11   William James, *The Varieties of Religious Experience*, Electronic Text Center, University of Virginia Library, http://etext.lib.virginia/edu/toc/modeng/public/JamVari .html (prepared from Random House 1929 edition, originally published 1902), 41.

12   James, *Varieties of Religious Experience*, 42.

13   James, *Varieties of Religious Experience*, 29.

14   James, *Varieties of Religious Experience*, 33.

15   It is hard to read popular accounts of today's cognitive neuroscience without thinking of James. "If it's in the brain, it must be real" or "If it's in the brain, the brain must cause it" are both vulnerable to his critique.

16   James, *Varieties of Religious Experience*, 138

17   Rudolph Otto, *The Idea of the Holy* (London: Oxford University Press, 1911; repr. 1958).

18   Otto, *Idea of the Holy*, 13–17.

19   Edward Robinson, *The Original Vision* (New York: Seabury Press, 1977), chaps. 3 and 8.

20   Mary Trauttman, *The Absence of the Dead Is Their Way of Appearing* (Pittsburgh, Pa.: Cleis Press, 1984).

21   In a recent conversation, a Philadelphian voiced anger and contempt at the Catholicism of his childhood. But then, suddenly, his eyes lit up as he asked me, "What do you think of shamanism?" Anything numinous or inviting now clung to the most far-off and exotic form of religion.

22   Paul Tillich, *Dynamics of Faith* (New York: Harper & Row, 1957), 9.

23   Tillich, *Dynamics of Faith*, 46.

24   For example, Lewis Rambo's *Understanding Religious Conversion* (New Haven, Conn.: Yale University Press, 1993) is in this genre.

25   Peter Hill, and Kenneth Pargament, "Advances in the Conceptualization and Measurement of Religion and Spirituality: Implications for Physical and Mental Health Research," *American Psychologist* 58 (2003): 64–74.

26   See Mark Silk's newsletter, *Religion in the News* (Hartford, Conn.: Leonard E. Greenberg Center for the Study of Religion in Public Life, Trinity College).

27   Mark Juergensmeyer, "2009 Presidential Address: Beyond Words and War; The Global Future of Religion," *Journal of the American Academy of Religion* 78 (2010): 882–95.

Chapter 6

1.   David Yamane, ed., "Symposium of the 20th Anniversary of *Habits of the Heart*," *Sociology of Religion* 68, no. 2 (2007): 179–87.
2   M. Coulter, J. Mulder, and L. Weeks. *Vital Signs: The Promise of Mainstream Protestantism* (Grand Rapids: Eerdmans, 1996).
3   Max Weber, *The Protestant Ethic and the Spirit of Capitalism* (New York: Scribner's, 1958), 38–39.
4   Emil Durkheim, *On Suicide* (London: Penguin, 2006; first published 1897), 156–70.
5   Durkheim, *On Suicide*, 171.
6   Bellah, *Habits of the Heart*, 221.
7   *Religion in America* produced by PBS. This thirteen-part documentary was shown in 1973, I believe. It is no longer available via PBS.org, having been replaced with more recent series with a more historical focus.
8   Bruce Greer and Wade C. Roof, "Desparately Seeking Sheila," *Journal for the Scientific Study of Religion* 31 (1992): 346–52.
9   Fuller, *Spiritual but Not Religious*, 159–62; quote on 162.
10   Robert Wuthnow, *After Heaven* (Berkeley: University of California Press, 1998), 3.
11   Wuthnow, *After Heaven*, 4–5.
12   Carrette and King complain even more ferociously about this pattern, writing from a British context where religion has no long history of "free market" activity. Jeremy Carrette and Richard King, *Selling Spirituality: The Silent Takeover of Religion* (London: Routledge, 2005).
13   Thomas Luckmann, *The Invisible Religion* (New York: Macmillan, 1967), 98.
14   For a look at the religious meanings of such funerals and memorials, see Lucy Bregman, *Preaching Death* (Waco, Tex.: Baylor University Press, 2011), 167–79.
15   On brandology, see Martin Lindstrom, *Brand Sense: Build Powerful Brands through Touch, Taste, Smell, Sight and Sound* (New York: Free Press, 2005).
16   Wade Clark Roof, *Spiritual Marketplace: Baby Boomers and the Remaking of American Religion* (Princeton, N.J.: Princeton University Press, 1999); and Wade Clark Roof, *A Generation of Seekers* (New York: HarperSanFrancisco, 1993).
17   Wuthnow, *Creative Spirituality*, 23–24.
18   Wuthnow, *Creative Spirituality*, 26.
19   Tisdell, *Exploring Spirituality and Culture*, 104.
20   Wuthnow, *Creative Spirituality*, 38.
21   William Breitbart, "Who Needs the Concept of Spirituality? Human Beings Seem To!" *Palliative and Supportive Care* 5 (2007): 105–6.
22   Joseph Hoffman. "Giving Up on Spirituality." http://rjosephhoffman.wordpress.com/2010/12/15/giving-up-on-spirituality.

Chapter 7

1   An early example of this impact, from the mid-1980s, was a course on Christian spirituality offered at Fuller Theological Seminary. Students liked the practices

they studied but balked at the theological vision underpinning many of them. Pseudo-Dionysius just could *not* be Christian, they agreed, even though most classical mystical writers, Teresa included, drew on him. Martin Luther, apparently, agreed with the students.

2 Richard Cabot and Russell Dicks, *The Art of Ministering to the Sick* (New York: Macmillan, 1936; repr. 1957), 3, 6.

3 Cabot and Dicks, *Art of Ministering to the Sick*, 22.

4 Cabot and Dicks, *Art of Ministering to the Sick*, 7.

5 Florence Gelo, "The Role of the Professional Hospital Chaplain," in Bregman, *Religion, Death and Dying*, 11–14.

6 Cabot and Dicks, *Art of Ministering to the Sick*, 299.

7 The appeal of adjunctive therapies is that they are selected by patients and thus restore more sense of control and knowledge for persons feeling victimized by medicalization as well as by their illnesses. The appeal at this level is exemplified by Lee Schreiber's account of her mother's cancer treatment in *Midstream*. The one specialist who seemed not only affordable but a fellow human was the Chinese acupuncturist. Schreiber arranged for her mother's visits to his office, and he charged her thirty-five dollars a session. The adult daughter loved him, especially since every other medical expert, including her physician-brother, lied to the family.

8 Gelo, "Professional Hospital Chaplain," 16–19.

9 Gelo, "Professional Hospital Chaplain," 21–22.

10 Judith Shelly and Arlene Miller, *Called to Care: A Christian Theology of Nursing* (Downers Grove, Ill.: InterVarsity, 1999), 229–34.

11 Victor Zorza and Rosemary Zorza, *A Way to Die* (New York: Knopf, 1980), 33, 163. This happened in England, where church and state are legally combined, but that is irrelevant to the conversation and attitudes expressed.

12 Peter Hill, Katie Kopp, and Richard Bollinger, "A Few Good Measures," in Plante and Thoresen, *Spirit, Science and Health*, 25–38; Salander, "Emperor's New Clothes," 25.

13 Hufford, "Analysis of the Field."

14 Hill and Pargament, "Conceptualization and Measurement."

15 Hill, Kopp, and Bollinger, "A Few Good Measures," 28.

16 Kevin Masters, "Prayer and Health," in Plante and Thoresen, *Spirit, Science and Health*, 10–24.

Chapter 8

1 Weber, *Protestant Ethic*, 181.

2 Herbert Marcuse, *Eros and Civilization* (New York: Vintage, 1955), 138.

3 "Bad Day at the Office" combined the song "So You've Had a Bad Day" with many clips of employees destroying office machinery.

4 Judith Neal, quoted by Lake Lambert III, *Spirituality, Inc.: Religion in the American Workplace* (New York: New York University Press, 2009), 38.

5 Lambert, *Spirituality, Inc.*, 39.

6 Mitroff and Denton, *Spiritual Audit of Corporate America*, xv.

7 Mitroff and Denton, *Spiritual Audit of Corporate America*, 5.

8 Mitroff and Denton, *Spiritual Audit of Corporate America*, 23.

9   Mitroff and Denton, *Spiritual Audit of Corporate America*, 22.

10   Biberman and Tischler, *Spirituality in Business*, introduction, 8–10.

11   Corinne McLaughlin, "Spirituality and Ethics in Business," *Center for Visionary Leadership*, www.visionarylead.org.

12   Regine, "Letting the Heart Fall Open"; and Marques, Dhiman, and King, *Workplace and Spirituality*, 11.

13   Mitroff and Denton, *Spiritual Audit of Corporate America*, 178.

14   Mitroff and Denton, *Spiritual Audit of Corporate America*, 74.

15   Kathy Lund Dean, Charles Fornaciari, and Scott Safranski, "The Ethics of Spiritual Inclusion," in Biberman and Tischler, *Spirituality in Business*, 189–203, esp. 193–96.

16   Dean, Fornaciari, and Safranski, "The Ethics of Spiritual Inclusion," 197.

17   Lambert, *Spirituality, Inc.*, chap. 6, 125–35.

18   Quoted in Margaret Benefiel and Kerry Hamilton, "Infinite Leadership: The Power of Spirit at Work," in Biberman and Tischler, *Spirituality in Business*, 148.

19   Regine, "Letting the Heart Fall Open," 11.

20   These descriptions are from postings by both merchants and consumers on http://www.merchantcircle.com and http://www.murltemple.blogspot.com.

21   Alas, its name is the same as that of the now notorious children's charity established by convicted child-abuser Jerry Sandusky. The two organizations have no connection.

22   Years ago, I was one of a group who substituted for the regular employees and ran this atypical thrift store when they went on retreat. It was a marvelous eye-opener. I still remember the Jamaican couple who were deaf-mute who bought a bed from us.

23   See Mitroff and Denton, *Spiritual Audit of Corporate America*; and also Lambert's chapter on "The Making of a Christian Company," in *Spirituality, Inc.*, 5–78.

24   Website self-description for the Second Mile Center, http://www.thesecondmilecenter.com.

25.   Lambert, *Spirituality, Inc.*, 42; Mitroff and Denton, *Spiritual Audit of Corporate America*, 138–41.

Chapter 9

1   Andrew Cooper, *Playing in the Zone: Exploring the Spiritual Dimensions of Sport* (Boston: Shambala, 1998), 48ff.

2   Nick Watson and John White, "Muscular Christianity in the Modern Age," in Parry, Robinson, Watson, and Nesti, *Sport and Spirituality*, 80–94.

3   Izaak Walton, *The Compleat Angler*, chap. 1, http://www.gutenberg.org/ebooks/683.

4   Norman Maclean, *A River Runs Through It* (Chicago: University of Chicago Press, 1978). The ban on women when men fish is part of the story and still seems powerful even today. Based on my observations, fishermen outnumber fisherwomen by a ratio of 100:1.

5   Philip Deloria, *Playing Indian* (New Haven: Yale University Press, 1998), chap. 4 has a fine discussion of this.

6   P. G. Wodehouse, "Those in Peril on the Tee," in *Mr. Mulliner Speaking* (London: Herbert Jenkins, 1929; repr. 1961), 97–114.

7   John Muir, *The Story of My Boyhood and Youth* (Boston: Houghton Mifflin, 1913), 63.

8   Mary Oliver, "Wild Geese," found on many websites. E.g., www.rjgeib/com/thoughts/geese/geese.html.

9   Roderick Nash, *Wilderness and the American Mind* (New Haven, Conn.: Yale University Press, 1967).

10   Henry David Thoreau, *Walden*, chap. 2, 16, http://Thoreau.eserver.org/walden00.html.

11   Doris Grumbach, *Fifty Days of Solitude* (Boston: Beacon Press, 1994).

12   Ann Linnea, *Deep Water Passage: A Spiritual Journey at Midlife* (New York: Pocket Books, 1997).

13   Having written this, I confess that I was awed by the completely artificial river where the London Olympics' kayak races were held. Of course, the water itself was real and behaved like water everywhere, but that was the only "natural" feature.

14   Thoreau, *Walden*, 17.

15   Quoted by Leo Marx, *The Machine in the Garden* (London: Oxford University Press, 1964), 17.

16   Joseph Price, "Naturalistic Recreations," in Van Ness, *Spirituality and the Secular Quest*, 414.

17   As should be obvious by now, I am myself a completely enthusiastic participant in this kind of Nature spirituality. I have paddled my kayak on a lake at dawn and also said, "Yes! This is what life is all about!" I do, however, believe that John Muir got things just a bit wrong; wilderness is not "salvation," spirituality here need not oppose religion, and I am happy to worship the same God through nature and through revelation (as did the author of Psalm 19).

18   Price, "Naturalistic Recreations," 430.

19   Maria Coffey, *Where the Mountain Casts Its Shadow: The Dark Side of Extreme Adventure* (New York: St. Martin's, 2003).

20   D. T. Suzuki, *An Introduction to Zen Buddhism* (New York: Grove Press, 1964), 39.

21   Eugen Herrigel, *Zen in the Art of Archery* (New York: Vintage Books, 1953; 2nd ed. 1989).

22   See Yamada Shoji, "The Myth of Zen in the Art of Archery," *Japanese Journal of Religious Studies* 28 (2001): 1–30.

23   Ed Brown, *The Tassajara Bread Book* (Berkeley, Calif.: Shambala, 1970), 43.

24   Brown, *Tassajara Bread Book*, 141.

25   Brown, *Tassajara Bread Book*, 12–13.

26   Joseph Parent, *Zen Golf: Mastering the Mental Game* (New York: Doubleday, 2002).

27   Cooper, *Playing in the Zone*, 48–75.

28   Cooper, *Playing in the Zone*, 96.

29   Scott Peck, *Golf and the Spirit* (New York: Harmony Books, 1999).

Conclusion

1   H. G. Wells, *In the Days of the Comet*, www.gutenberg.org/ebooks/3797.

2   Wells, *In the Days of the Comet*, book 3, chap. 3.

3   Thomas Kuhn, *The Structure of Scientific Revolutions*, vol. 2, no. 2 of *International Encyclopedia of Unified Science* (Chicago: University of Chicago Press, 1970).

4   A critique of this possible misuse of physics is found in Victor J. Stenger, "Quantum Metaphysics," in Brown, Barnard, and Hoffman, *Modern Spiritualities*, 243–53. Unfortunately, all contributors to this anthology assume that "spirituality" depends upon a dualist spirit/body split, which they uniformly reject. This is simply not congruent with the contemporary meanings of the term.

5   David R. Griffin, ed., *Spirituality and Society: Postmodern Visions* (Albany: State University of New York Press, 1988), xi.

6   Griffin, *Spirituality and Society*, 14.

7   Griffin, *Spirituality and Society*, 14–15.

8   Griffin, *Spirituality and Society*, 17.

9   Griffin, *Spirituality and Society*, 15.

10   Griffin, *Spirituality and Society*, 18.

11   Peter Campbell and Edwin McMahon, *Bio-Spirituality: Focusing as a Way to Grow* (Chicago: Loyola University Press, 1985), 56.

12   Campbell and McMahon, *Bio-Spirituality*, 22.

13   Griffin, *Spirituality and Society*, 15.

14   Diarmuid Ó Murchú, *Reclaiming Spirituality* (New York: Crossroad, 1998), chap. 7.

15   Ó Murchú, *Reclaiming Spirituality*, 78.

16   Ken Wilbur, *Integral Spirituality: A Startling New Role for Religion in the Modern and Postmodern World* (Boston: Integral Books, 2006), 1.

17   J. F. D. Pearce, *A Critique of Spirituality*. Latimer Studies 52 (Oxford: Latimer House, 1996).

18   David Tacey, *The Spirituality Revolution: The Emergence of Contemporary Spirituality* (New York: Brunner-Routledge, 2004).

19   Tacey, *Spirituality Revolution*, 38.

20   Tacey, *Spirituality Revolution*, 97.

21   Carrette and King, *Selling Spirituality*, 16.

22   Tacey, *Spirituality Revolution*, 86.

23   Tacey, *Spirituality Revolution*, 107–14.

24   Sharon Janis, *Spirituality for Dummies* (Hungry Minds, 2000).

25   Janis, *Spirituality for Dummies*, 1–2.

Bibliography

Bellah, Robert, ed. *Habits of the Heart: Individualism and Commitment in American Life.* Berkeley: University of California Press, 1985.

Bender, Courtney. *The New Metaphysicals: Spirituality and the American Religious Imagination.* Chicago: University of Chicago Press, 2010.

Benefiel, Margaret, and Kerry Hamilton. "Infinite Leadership: Authenticity and Spirit at Work." In Biberman and Tischler, *Spirituality in Business,* 141–59.

Biberman, Jerry, and Len Tischler, eds. *Spirituality in Business: Theory, Practice and Future Directions.* New York: Palgrave Macmillan, 2008.

Bregman, Lucy. *Preaching Death: The Transformation of Christian Funeral Sermons.* Waco, Tex.: Baylor University Press, 2011.

———. "Psychotherapies." in Van Ness, *Spirituality and the Secular Quest,* 250–76.

———, ed. *Religion, Death and Dying.* Westport, Conn.: Praeger, 2010.

Breitbart, William. "Who Needs the Concept of Spirituality? Human Beings Seem To!" *Palliative and Supportive Care* 5 (2007):105–6.

Brown, Edward. *The Tassajara Bread Book.* Berkeley, Calif.: Shambala, 1970.

Brown, Laurence, Bernard Farr, and Joseph Hoffman, eds. *Modern Spiritualities: An Inquiry.* Critical Studies in Religion. Westminster College-Oxford: Prometheus Books, 1997.

Browning, Don. *The Moral Context of Pastoral Care.* Philadelphia: Westminster, 1976.

———. *Religious Thought and the Modern Psychologies.* Philadelphia: Fortress, 1987.

Cabot, Richard, and Russell Dicks. *The Art of Ministering to the Sick*. New York: Macmillan, 1936; repr. 1957.

Campbell, Peter, and Edwin McMahon. *Bio-Spirituality: Focusing as a Way to Grow*. Chicago: Loyola University Press, 1985.

Carey, Maureen, Raymond Fox, and Jacqueline Penny. *The Artful Journal: A Spiritual Quest*. New York: Watson-Guptill, 2002.

Carrette, Jeremy, and Richard King. *Selling Spirituality: The Silent Takeover of Religion*. London: Routledge, 2005.

Clinebell, Howard. *Basic Types of Pastoral Care and Counseling*. New York: Abingdon, 1966.

Coffey, Maria. *Where the Mountain Casts Its Shadow: The Dark Side of Extreme Adventure*. New York: St. Martin's, 2003.

Cooper, Andrew. *Playing in the Zone: Exploring the Spiritual Dimension of Sports*. Boston: Shambala, 1998.

Coulter, M., J. Mulder, and L. Weeks. *Vital Signs: The Promise of Mainstream Protestantism*. Grand Rapids: Eerdmans, 1996.

Dean, Kathy Lund, Charles Fornaciari, and Scott Safranski. "The Ethics of Spiritual Inclusion." In Biberman and Tischler, *Spirituality in Business*, 188–202.

Doka, Kenneth. "Definition of Spirituality." Meeting of the International Working Group for Death, Dying and Bereavement, Bergisch Gladbach, Germany, 2010.

Doka, Kenneth, and John Morgan, eds. *Death and Spirituality*. Amityville, N.Y.: Baywood, 1993.

Deloria, Philip. *Playing Indian*. New Haven, Conn.: Yale University Press, 1998.

Durkheim, Emil. *On Suicide*. London: Penguin, 2006. First published in 1897.

Ferguson, Linda. "Working Spiritually: Aligning Gifts, Purpose and Passion." In Marques, Dhiman, and King, *Workplace and Spirituality*, 23–33.

Flinders, Tim, Doug Oman, and Carol Lee Flinders. "The Eight-Point Program of Passage Meditation: Health Effects of a Comprehensive Program." In Plante and Thoresen, *Spirit, Science and Health*, 72–93.

Frankl, Viktor. *Man's Search for Meaning*. New York: Pocket Books, 1963.

Fuller, Robert. *Spiritual but Not Religious: Understanding Unchurched America*. New York: Oxford University Press, 2001.

Gelo, Florence. "The Role of the Professional Hospital Chaplain." In Bregman, *Religion, Death and Dying*, 1:3–26.

Greer, Bruce, and Wade C. Roof. "Desperately Seeking Sheila." *Journal for the Scientific Study of Religion* 31 (1992): 346–52.

Griffin, David R., ed. *Spirituality and Society: Postmodern Visions*. Albany: State University of New York Press, 1988.

Grumbach, Doris. *Fifty Days of Solitude*. Boston: Beacon Press, 1994.

Herrigel, Eugen. *Zen in the Art of Archery*. New York: Vintage Books, 1953; 2nd ed. 1989.

Hill, Peter, and Kenneth Pargament. "Advances in the Conceptualization and Measurement of Religion and Spirituality: Implications for Physical and Mental Health Research." *American Psychologist* 58 (2003): 64–74.

Hill, Peter, Katie Kopp, and Richard Bollinger. "A Few Good Measures." In Plante and Thoresen, *Spirit, Science and Health*, 25–38.

Hillman, James. *Re-Visioning Psychology*. New York: Harper & Row, 1975.

Hiltner, Seward. *Pastoral Counseling*. New York: Abingdon, 1949.

Hoffman, Joseph. "Giving Up on Spirituality." http://rjosephhoffman .wordpress.com/2010/12/15/giving-up-on-spirituality.

Hufford, D. "An Analysis of the Field of Religion, Spirituality and Health." ttp://www.metanexus.net/archive/templetonadvancedresearchpro gram/pdf/TARP-Hufford.pdf. 72 pp.

James, William. *The Varieties of Religious Experience*. Electronic Text Center, University of Virginia Library. http://www.etext.lib.virginia.edu/toc/ modeng/public/JamVari.html. Prepared from Random House 1929 edition. Originally published 1902.

Janis, Sharon. *Spirituality for Dummies*. n.c.: Hungry Minds, 2000.

Juergensmeyer, Mark. "2009 Presidential Address: Beyond Words and War; the Global Future of Religion." *Journal of the American Academy of Religion* 78 (2010): 882–95.

Kant, Immanuel. *Religion within the Limits of Reason Alone*. New York: Harper, 1960.

Katz, Steven, ed. *Mysticism and Religious Traditions*. Oxford: Oxford University Press, 1983.

Kourie, C. "The 'Turn' to Spirituality." *Acta Theologica Supplementum* 8 (2006): 19–38.

Kübler-Ross, Elisabeth. *On Death and Dying*. New York: Macmillan, 1968.

Kuhn, Thomas. *The Structure of Scientific Revolutions*. Vol. 2, no. 2, of *International Encyclopedia of Unified Science*. Chicago: University of Chicago Press, 1970.

La Cour, Peter, Nadja Ausker, and Neils C. Hvidt. "What Is the Meaning of the Word 'Spirituality'?" Paper presented at Interdisciplinary Conference on Spirituality in the 21st Century: Theory, Praxis and Pedagogy. Prague, CR, March 2011.

Lambert, Lake, III. *Spirituality, Inc.: Religion in the American Workplace*. New York: New York University Press, 2009.

Lescher, Bruce, and Elizabeth Leibert, eds. *Exploring Christian Spirituality: Essays in Honor of Sandra M. Schneiders*. IHM, N.Y.: Paulist Press, 2006.

Lindstrom, Martin. *Brand Sense: Build Powerful Brands through Touch, Taste, Smell, Sight and Sound*. New York: Free Press, 2005.

Linnea, Ann. *Deep Water Passage: A Spiritual Journey at Midlife*. New York: Pocket Books, 1997.

London, Perry. *The Modes and Morals of Psychotherapy*. New York: Holt, Rhinhart & Winston, 1964.

Luckmann, Thomas. *The Invisible Religion*. New York: Macmillan, 1967.

MacIntyre, Alasdair. *After Virtue: A Study of Moral Theory*. South Bend, Ind.: University of Notre Dame Press, 1981.

Mahoney, Michael, and Gina Graci. "The Meanings and Correlates of Spirituality: Suggestions from an Exploratory Survey of Experts." *Death Studies* 23 (1999): 521–28.

Mannheim, Karl. "The Problem of Generations." *Essays in the Sociology of Knowledge*. London: Routledge & Kegan Paul, 1968.

Marcuse, Herbert. *Eros and Civilization*. New York: Vintage Books, 1955.

Marques, Joan, Satinder Dhiman, and Richard King, eds. *The Workplace and Spirituality: New Perspectives on Research and Practice*. Woodstock, Vt.: Skylight Paths, 2009.

Marx, Leo. *The Machine in the Garden*. London: Oxford University Press, 1964.

Maslow, Abraham. *The Farther Reaches of Human Nature*. New York: Viking Press, 1971.

———. *Religions, Values and Peak-Experiences*. New York: Viking Press, 1970.

Masters, Kevin. "Prayer and Health." In Plante and Thoresen, *Spirit, Science and Health*, 10–24.

McLaughlin, Corinne. "Spirituality and Ethics in Business." *Center for Visionary Leadership*. http://www.visionarylead.org.

McNichols, Kathryn, and David Feldman. "Spirituality at the End of Life: Issues and Guidelines for Care." In Plante and Thoresen, *Spirit, Science and Health*, 191–203.

Mitroff, Ian, and Elizabeth Denton. *A Spiritual Audit of Corporate America: A Hard Look at Spirituality, Religion, and Values in the Workplace*. San Francisco: Jossey-Bass, 1999.

Morgan, John. "The Existential Quest for Meaning." In Doka and Morgan, *Death and Spirituality*, 3–9.

Muir, John. *The Story of My Boyhood and Youth*. Boston: Houghton Mifflin, 1913.

Nash, Roderick. *Wilderness and the American Mind*. New Haven, Conn.: Yale University Press, 1967

Neal, Judi. "Creating Edgewalker Organizations: The Workplace of the Future." In Marques, Dhiman, and King, *Workplace and Spirituality*, 201–18.

Novak, Michael. *The Joy of Sports*. Lanham, Md.: Hamilton Press, 1988.

Oden, Thomas. *Pastoral Theology: Essentials for Ministry*. San Francisco: Harper & Row, 1983.

Oman, Doug, and Carl Thoresen. "How Does One Learn to Be Spiritual? The Neglected Role of Spiritual Modeling in Health." In Plante and Thoresen, *Spirit, Science and Health*, 39–54.

Ó Murchú, Diarmuid, *Reclaiming Spirituality*. New York: Crossroad, 1998.

Otto, Rudolph. *The Idea of the Holy*. London: Oxford University Press, 1911; repr. 1958.

Parent, Joseph. *Zen Golf: Mastering the Mental Game*. New York: Doubleday, 2002.

Parry, Jim, Simon Robinson, Nick Watson, and Mark Nesti, eds. *Sport and Spirituality: An Introduction*. London: Routledge, 2007.

Pearce, J. F. D. *A Critique of Spirituality*. Latimer Studies 52. Oxford: Latimer House, 1996.

Peck, Scott. *Golf and the Spirit*. New York: Harmony Books, 1999.

Plante, Thomas, and Carl Thoresen, eds. *Spirit, Science and Health: How the Spiritual Mind Fuels Physical Wellness*. Westport, Conn.: Praeger, 2007.

Prebish, Charles. *Religion and Sport: The Meeting of Sacred and Profane*. Westport, Conn.: Greenwood, 1993.

Price, Joseph. "Naturalistic Recreations." In Van Ness, *Spirituality and the Secular Quest*, 414–44.

Principe, Walter. "Toward Defining Spirituality." *Studies in Religion* 12 (1983): 127–41.

Rambo, Lewis. *Understanding Religious Conversion*. New Haven, Conn.: Yale University Press, 1993.

Regine, Birute. "Letting the Heart Fall Open." In Marques, Dhiman, and King, *Workplace and Spirituality*, 9–22.

Robinson, Edward. *The Original Vision*. New York: Seabury Press, 1977.

Roof, Wade Clark. *A Generation of Seekers*. New York: HarperSanFrancisco, 1993.

———. *Spiritual Marketplace: Baby Boomers and the Remaking of American Religion*. Princeton, N.J.: Princeton University Press, 1999.

Rosenthal, Peggy. *Words and Values: Some Leading Words and Where They Lead Us.* New York: Oxford University Press, 1984.

Salander, Pär. "The Emperor's New Clothes: Spirituality. A Concept Based on Questionable Ontology and Circular Findings." *Archive for the Psychology of Religion* 34 (2012): 17–32 .

―――. "Who Needs the Concept of Spirituality?" *Psycho-Oncology* 15 (2006): 647–49.

Schleiermacher, Friedrich. *On Religion: Speeches to Its Cultured Despisers.* New York: Harper & Row, 1958.

Schmidt, Leigh. "The Making of Modern 'Mysticism.'" *Journal of the American Academy of Religion* 71 (2003): 275–302.

―――. *Restless Souls: The Making of American Spirituality from Emerson to Oprah.* Princeton, N.J.: Princeton University Press, 2005.

Shelly, Judy, and Arlene Miller. *Called to Care: A Christian Theology of Nursing.* Downers Grove, Ill.: InterVarsity, 1999.

Shoji, Yamada. "The Myth of Zen in the Art of Archery." *Japanese Journal of Religious Studies* 28 (2001): 1–30.

Silk, Mark, ed. *Religion in the News.* Hartford, Conn.: Leonard E. Greenberg Center for the Study of Religion in Public Life, Trinity College.

Stenger, Victor J. "Quantum Metaphysics," in Brown, Farr, and Hoffman, *Modern Spiritualities,* 243–53.

Suzuki, D. T. *An Introduction to Zen Buddhism.* New York: Grove Press, 1964.

Tacey, David. *The Spirituality Revolution: The Emergence of Contemporary Spirituality.* New York: Brunner-Routledge, 2004.

Tart, Charles, ed. *Transpersonal Psychologies.* New York: Harper & Row, 1975.

Taves, Ann. *Fits, Trances and Visions: Experiencing Religion and Explaining Experience from Wesley to James.* Princeton, N.J.: Princeton University Press, 1999.

Teresa of Avila. *The Interior Castle.* Classics of Western Spirituality. New York: Paulist Press, 1979.

Thoreau, Henry David. *Walden.* http://www.Thoreau.eserver.org/walden00.html.

Tillich, Paul. *Dynamics of Faith.* New York: Harper & Row, 1957.

Tisdell, Elizabeth. *Exploring Spirituality and Culture in Adult and Higher Education.* San Francisco: Jossey-Bass, 2003.

Trauttman, Mary. *The Absence of the Dead Is Their Way of Appearing.* Pittsburgh, Pa.: Cleis Press, 1984.

Unruh, Anita, Joan Versnel, and Natasha Kerr. "Spirituality Unplugged," review of *Commonalities and Contentions, and a Resolution. Canadian Journal of Occupational Therapy* 69, no. 1 (2005), 5–19.

Van Ness, Peter, ed. *Spirituality and the Secular Quest*. New York: Crossroad, 1996.

Wachholtz, Amy, and Michele Pierce. "Compassion and Health." In Plante and Thoresen, *Spirit, Science and Health*, 115–28.

Walton, Izaak. *The Compleat Angler*. http://www.gutenberg.org/ebooks/683. Original publication 1653.

Watson, Nick, and John White. "Muscular Christianity in the Modern Age." In Parry, Robinson, Watson, and Nesti, *Sport and Spirituality*, 80–94.

Weber, Max. *The Protestant Ethic and the Spirit of Capitalism*. New York: Scribner's, 1958.

Wells, H. G. *In the Days of the Comet*. www.gutenberg.org/ebooks/3797. First published in 1906.

Westerlink, Herman, Pär Salander, and Peter La Cour, *Archive for the Psychology of Religion* 34, no. 1 (2012).

Wilbur, Ken. *Integral Spirituality: A Startling New Role for Religion in the Modern and Postmodern World*. Boston: Integral Books, 2006.

Wodehouse, P. G. "Those in Peril on the Tee." In *Mr. Mulliner Speaking*. London: Herbert Jenkins, 1929; repr. 1961, 97–114.

Wuthnow, Robert. *After Heaven*. Berkeley: University of California Press, 1998.

———. *Creative Spirituality: The Way of the Artist*. Berkeley: University of California Press, 2001.

Yamane, David, ed. "Symposium of the 20th Anniversary of *Habits of the Heart*," *Sociology of Religion* 68, no. 2 (2007): 179–87.

Zorza, Victor, and Rosemary Zorza. *A Way to Die*. New York: Knopf, 1980.

Index